QUIET FIRE

MEMOIRS OF OLDER GAY MEN

Keith Vacha

Edited by Cassie Damewood

WITHDRAWN

THE CROSSING PRESS, TRUMANSBURG, N.Y. 14886

Cover Design and illustration by Lewis McClellan
Cover drawing from a photograph by Kathy Cade
Typesetting by Martha J. Waters
The Crossing Press Gay Series
Printed in the USA
Copyright © 1985, Keith Vacha

Library of Congress Cataloging in Publication Data

Vacha, Keith.
    Quiet Fire.

    (The Crossing Press gay series)
      1. Homosexuals, Male--United States--Biography.
    2. Homosexuals, Male--United States--Interviews.
    3. Homosexuality--United States--History. I. Title.
    II. Series. III. Title: Older gay men.
    HQ75.7.V33 1985   306.7'662'0922   85-5699
    ISBN 0-89594-158-9
    ISBN 0-89594-157-0 (pbk.)

This book is a tribute to the survivors of an era beset by greater persecution than present. Its dedication, however, is reserved for the less fortunate men and women who took their own lives out of a feeling of desperation or who died at the hands of others, in particular, the men of the pink triangle.

But I, my life surveying, closing
With nothing to show to devise from its idle years,
Nor houses nor lands, nor tokens of gems or gold for my
friends,
Yet certain remembrances of the war for you, and after you,
And little souvenirs of camps and soldiers, with my life,
I bind together and bequeath in this bundle of songs.

Leaves of Grass
Walt Whitman

Acknowledgments

It is an impossible task to thank all those who have contributed in some manner to the research and publication of this book. Therefore, I will attempt to name those whose time, energy and encouragement were more exceptional than the rest—the die-hards. First there is Cassie Damewood who took on the role of special editor and assistant in the final stages of the project. Without her encouragement to resurrect the project when I had given up hope, these stories might have remained dusty tapes on the study wall. For their selfless hours spent in transcription, research or suggestion I want to especially thank Betty Merritt and Joe Schultz. Others who also contributed in that regard were Jinnie Connolly, Joe Muse, Jo Vanderham, Bj Bud and Arthur Thistlewood. For their votes of confidence and support I thank Dr. Don Clark, Dr. Eli Coleman, Marie Williams, Eleanor Metz, Ph.D., Phyllis LaVoie, Vincent You, Dr. Evalyn Gendel, Mildred Seltzer, Ph.D., Mark Taylor, Jordan Lee, the members of the G40+ Club, and my friends in the National Association for Lesbian and Gay Gerontology. For their professional advice and support I thank Jean-Pierre Nagy, Cossette Thompson, Terry Chris and my publisher, John Gill. Most importantly, I thank the many men, including those whose stories could not be used because of special limitations, for the generous disclosure of themselves.

Contents

Introduction by Don Clark   7

1   Don The Longshoreman   9

2   Todd Grison   23

3   Alan Williams   34

4   Bob Basker   43

5   Will Whiting   58

6   Richard Von Berg   73

7   George Morrison   86

8   Andrew Weiler   96

9   Raymond Friedman   111

10   Jonathan West   121

11   David Bowling   130

12   Al Hoskins   142

13   John Hall   155

14   Josh Holland   163

15   Greg Aarons   170

16   Jordan Lee   185

17   Tony Isaac   195

Summary by Keith Vacha   212

Introduction
Don Clark, Ph.D.

I have been involved actively with contemporary emerging gay society since the late nineteen-sixties. Repeatedly I have seen this wave of gay assertion shine its bright light in the dark corners of American society. We have forced the recognition of human sexual needs and their variety. We have forced awareness of needless harmful prejudices and bigotry that pits sibling against sibling and parent against child. We have forced the recognition of human vulnerability and mortality.

Gay invisibility has been a curse and a blessing. Seldom is a minority group able to watch and listen in the moments and places where its persecution is discussed and planned. We have witnessed family, presumed friends, neighbors, employers and rulers, insult and degrade us when they did not see us present. We understand all too well the needless negative aspects of human interaction.

We have been held captive as children, and longer, shamed and threatened into silent submission. We have suffered in all ways, yet our faith in the truth of our own identity has persisted in all times and all places. Perhaps it is that relentless faith in truth that frightens our persecutors so much that they would silence us.

And in our hurried emergence into visibility, we gay people, too, seem as guilty of damaging as those who do not see us. The revelation of visible gay people in the past fifteen years has shown the world the impressive beauty of physically fit youth, competing for recognition, determined as sexual champions. Yet, anyone who cares to look more closely sees the variety of the gay garden. We are all ages, all ethnic backgrounds, all shapes and sizes, and the full range of abilities and disabilities, needs and desires. But we are a raw, young, frontier society still, neglectful of the aging. America's frontier eyes have been stunned by the beauty of gay youth with its drive and vigor. Strong young bodies are prized on the frontier. Youth is equated with hope. *New* is synonymous with *better.*

However gay people are waking to another facet of our truth.

And as we do so, we shine our light in a dark corner of American society again. We are aware that we grow old. And as we grow, we shed some of the assets of youth as the assets of age take firm root. We gay people have worked hard to free ourselves in the formative years of childhood. We may never be free of the haunting shadows of some of those lies. But perhaps, once again, we can help others to see. There is no eternal youth.

Now we awake to our aging and search for our elders, our ancestors, living and dead. We want to hear their tales and touch their scars. We want to know the paths they followed. The beauty of youth and the beauty of age are ready to meet. We are drawn to one another. And what a meeting it is! A family, scattered and hidden from one another for centuries, is starting its treasure hunt. The treasure, of course, is union. And this treasure contains the appreciation of grace that comes with time.

This book presents the portraits of a few members of the family, living gay men who found their own way through the difficult night. They are the first to admit they might have found better ways and yet we can see that each did the best he could. Not only did they survive to tell the tales of elders, they tell the secrets of plain strength and endurance in an endless search for truth. They are mere people, flawed, sometimes mistaken, carrying the burden of regret with the comfort of satisfaction, guided by hope, trying to find a footing as they face the changing future. And they are more than mere people. Each has at some time transcended his apparent limits. This book presents a glimpse at beauty. It brings sadness and hope for us all.

The social focus is shifting. We begin. Here starts less concern for how to stay young. Here starts the hints of our lessons in maturation. Here starts the learning of how to grow beautiful while growing old. First the eye and ear must be trained to appreciate grace. Then we become able to touch the beauty of age. Then comes the softening of a raw frontier world, at last.

Of course some people, gay or not, will never learn. But this book is an offering for those who would.

1

Don the Longshoreman

This is the name Don goes by as a popular and frequent call-in guest on a local radio program. He lives in the ground floor apartment of his San Francisco home where he has created a warm, almost nautical atmosphere, complemented by a lush garden dotted by buddhas off the living room. Don has a full head of wavy white hair and his soft gravelly tones reveal a disdain for closed minds and an admiration for those who drink in the richness of each moment.

I THINK THAT RIGHT NOW IS A WONDERFUL TIME. I JUST HOPE I get another ten years or more of it, to find how things are going to come out. Imagine, within my lifetime—I was born in 1907—we've had telephones, electric lights, automobiles, radio, television, miracles of medicine like sulfa drugs, people have gone to the moon. . . . No time in history, I think, ever equalled my lifetime for such enormous accomplishments. It was a golden age, if there ever was one. But now I think it is running down; maybe, as Spengler said, it is "the decline of the west." I feel that society is incapable right now of solving some of the great social problems.

I always want to be open-minded. I keep thinking—if I want to hear more, I have to discard more. I think I've discarded a lot. To meet a young person who continues with the same religion as his parents, who belongs to the same political party, who votes the same political ticket, who has gone to the same college, or who has professionally followed his mother or father—I don't think I would have much time for such a person. To me, he wouldn't be a very probing person. We have been fed so much garbage by the people we love, our own parents. We have to reexamine the fundamental things and say, "A lot of it I don't accept anymore, put it in the social garbage can. Put a lid on it that's riveted tight."

It's not that many years ago that the great authorities of the American Psychiatric Association believed that a homosexual was a mentally ill person. I never believed it as a child, nor as a man. Now I see them reversing themselves, and I say, "Just chalk one up for us." I have seen it in religion too. When I was admonished as a Catholic child for eating meat on Friday because I would go to hell if I were to die in that state of mortal sin, I believed it. Who would have thought someone would come along and say, "Now you can"? Everyone who is in hell for having eaten meat on Friday is going to stay there? It seemed crazy when I was a kid.

I loved it when my father, who was a doctor, took me to call on the cardinal or the archbishop. My father would say, "I don't understand how someone so high in the Catholic Church can be so frightened of death. He is calling me very late; I tell others to wait until morning. It didn't seem as if the symptoms were that urgent. Now I've got to rush to the archbishop." And that drew me to him because I thought he was talking like a kid. He seemed to be thinking, to be questioning. He was not taking it hook, line and sinker. When he was an older man—he died at the age of ninety-four—we got close. I told him I loved him. I had never before articulated that love, nor he to me. He said to me, "I was putting up this front of being so devout in our church, when in fact I was climbing the ladder to be the head of staff at the biggest hospital in Milwaukee. I spent little time with you to make sure you were educated. You left with no education, and I wanted you to have a lovely home and saddle horses. I looked forward to your leaving home and having a big family. I was selfish." But that was humble pie. As a younger man he was a very structured disciplinarian. Some of it rubbed off on me. How lucky I was to have him live so long, so that I could go back to him and say, "My life is very different from yours. I have found happiness and I got a lot from you. I am as comfortable with a longshoreman as I am at the table of a judge in his home, or with a congressman who has achieved those things that are honored."

I think the most basic thing young people should know is that they ought to take care of themselves and their bodies. No one can enjoy life who is suffering pain of any kind. To avoid pain, you don't wait for a toothache, you go and have a check-up. It was mandatory in my home that I and the other siblings go and have a check-up with the dentist every six months. Yet I tell young people now what to do when I didn't do those things myself. I think youth is a time of cocksure ignorance. And to ask a question like, "What would you advise?" is the beginning of wisdom and comes much later in life.

I loved working on my grandmother's farm during summer holidays. While my brothers and sisters went to the small lake where my family had a summer home, I lived during those summers in a house that belonged to the manager, and I begged my grandmother to let me live in the bunkhouse where the other men lived. I had just learned to masturbate and discovered that it was more fun to do it with others. The bunkhouse, where five of us were in a dormitory, offered the possibility of these simple, uneducated, wonderful men. I have all my life gravitated to people with little schooling—foremen, seamen, manual laborers. It was a quirk maybe, in my personality, to go with them rather than with better educated people. Maybe it's because I felt that what I lacked in brawn I could make up in brains to outsmart them.

Soon I was going for walks at night with a young man from the bunkhouse whom I admired. He was strong, healthy, and handsome. We would walk through the woods at night, especially when the moon was full and things were so lovely. We bathed in a pond. When we came out, we hadn't taken a towel along—taking one would have attracted attention. But we were cold and wet, so we would embrace. To keep warm, we said. But the embrace was a sensing of our youth and the loveliness of our bodies. An erection soon followed, and other things, and I realized that it was not cows, not young girls, but boys that interested me.

But we were in the closet. As I grew older and became politically active, quite a radical in trade unionism, I was very moved by a quotation of Lenin's. I applied it in my youth and I am sure that other people who were gay did too. Lenin said, "You must meet trickery with trickery and deceit with deceit." Today people don't have to be so dishonest anymore. But when people were setting their patterns for us, I could say to myself, "Awww, fuck 'em, I'll throw up smoke if that is what they want, before I'll adopt the model they are setting for me."

I remember the pain of being different. My mother was having tea with a friend of hers, and I was slumped low in a sofa, reading, so my mother couldn't see me. My friends would come to the door to ask me to play ball. I did play ball, but I never excelled. The cook let in a young boy who was my mother's friend's son. He had a bat and ball and glove. He asked for me and my mother said, "I don't know where he is. Maybe he is upstairs reading a book." Then she looked from the boy to her friend, and she said, "My, but your son is a real boy." That crushed me. I figured then they didn't know me. I wanted to be myself but I couldn't except by trickery and deception.

I dropped out of college after my second year at the University of Wisconsin. I wanted to get away from people who knew my family, my uncles, my aunts, and my wonderful grandmother. I went to New York City, where I could get lost. That was a joy, to be among strangers! But I didn't know then that the stock market was in trouble. I arrived in May and the market crashed in November. My father had given me $500 — a lot of money in those days. He said, "If you can make it on this, I'll never have any reason to complain." I hadn't been in New York but a week when I sent him a note telling him I was doing very well and that he could have his money back, even though it was a gift. Later, when he was ninety-four and sometimes in the fog of his dotage, he would say to me, "Do you know what pleased me most when you were a youth?" Though I knew the answer, I would always say "No" because it pleased him. And he would say, "When you sent that $500 back to me. Then I knew you had the message to be independent and to make it on your own."

I had saved a little money from the days that I worked for my grandmother. I always believed that a penny saved was a penny earned. But everywhere I went people said, "You're uneducated, you're inexperienced, all you have going for you is youth, and New York is filled with talent. Here the opportunities are only for the most brilliant. What can you give?" I began to panhandle. I asked a black woman who was at the bus stop. She looked at me from head to foot, opened her bag, and gave me a nickel. She grumbled a bit about "young white men who couldn't get a job." The next day she was at the same spot—I didn't know it was the same woman—and she said, "Oh, you, you came up to me yesterday, and I gave you a nickel. I'm not giving you any more money. I haven't got it. I'm supporting five children, scrubbing floors, and you've got a hell of a lot of nerve to ask. How old are you?" I think I was nineteen or twenty. She said, "I have no more time to talk to you now, but be here tomorrow morning and I'll speak to you." And so I was there at the bus stop the next day. She took waxed paper and a piece of white bread out of her bag. She said, "You see all those people there? They have all got a coin in their hands and are getting on the next bus. Now when they are gone and nobody is around, you go up to that garbage can and you put that piece of bread on top of the garbage with the waxed paper under it. Don't talk to anybody. Just break off morsels of bread and eat at the garbage can." Even now it seems crazy, but it worked!

What is more remarkable still was that in a week or two I got a wonderful job. I worked for people who ran a New York office of architecture and interior design. They needed somebody who would go about collecting samples. They were very busy and were doing San Simeon Castle for Mr. Hearst. I'm forever grateful to these people for their love of beautiful things and the chance to learn something of their business.

You know, when you are young, invitations come without much trouble. Someone put me on a debutante's list in New York those first five years. They wanted at least five young men for every debutante coming out. All you had to have was a dinner jacket, nice manners, and clothes. So there were parties and invitations. But more fun than going to a debutante party was going to a party given by people like the son of the man who owned a large auto corporation. He was gay. I met a famous actor at one of his parties. He was a great actor. When Rudolph Valentino died, they needed a replacement, a man with almond eyes, nice swarthy skin, and black hair. So he was chosen. He played opposite Greta Garbo—usually standing on a telephone book to come up to her height. They were great pictures. He was born in Mexico, a Latin with a high temperament. When I met him he said there was a showing of "Ben Hur" in Spanish Harlem in New York. He said I could go with him if I liked and he had invited Richard Halliburton, too, who later became a very good friend of mine. I lost track of my actor friend though he gave parties and things. He had a butler who was a strong-arm for him, who would fight off people who would hurt him if they had a bad reaction after sex or went after him because of his money. He was murdered in Hollywood a few years ago.

Halliburton wrote many books about his travels. He was a great romantic who joined the French Foreign Legion, served in Africa, swam the Hellespont, and climbed the Liebfrau and the Matterhorn so he could spit a mile over the top. He told me of going to India and climbing the garden wall of the Taj Mahal to swim in the reflecting pool with one of the guides. Unwritten, of course, were the wonderful sexual experiences. His books sold well and he made a lot of money. He lectured at Vassar and Harvard and wherever women's clubs met. They would give him roses. He loved all that fanfare.

He had a fantastic ability to observe and listen. We would go to the Bowery together and dress down, trying to pass for what we weren't. We would try to pass for carnival or circus hands or racehorse people—the kind of people you would find in the Bowery. Sometimes I would shine shoes at South Ferry. But once a man told me, "You haven't fooled me. You're not a bootblack. Who are you kidding? I'm the District Attorney for San Francisco. I know a lot about people. What's your racket?" Well, that crushed me. I told Halliburton and he thought it was amusing.

After all he told me, he had me all fired up—I wanted to go to sea.

I worked as a sailor for several years but gravitated towards culinary work in the stewards' department because I found it to be more creative. When I worked as Chief Steward it seemed to me the morale of the ship was in my hands. Out to sea for months and months, we would run short of vegetables and you'd have to eat canned food or salted fish. With the crew complaining and bitching, you could still save the sprout on the potato and use it for a garnish on Sunday dinner. It made them think they were getting something better than they were getting during the week. I once went on a freighter that was at sea so long nothing but staples were left, dehydrated eggs and powdered milk, things like that. But I had bought thirty cases of Coca Cola out of my own funds and had them stored in my quarters. I had my own stateroom when I was Chief Steward. When they started complaining that they couldn't continue working if I couldn't serve them better food, I would tell them to wait until Sunday. Then I would break out a bottle of Coke for each one. I would try all kinds of tricks. I would get spices in foreign ports to jack up some food we were serving and make it taste different. I had the ability to satisfy the men. That was the role of a woman — or the role of a man! I don't know . . . maybe without a label.

In my travels I wanted to visit the pyramids and see the King Tut treasures in the Cairo Museum. They had been discovered in 1922, and I was there only a few years later. You could touch them; they weren't considered as precious as they are now. But neither were they shown as beautifully: the lights were amber-colored and there was dust on everything. I also wanted to climb the Great Pyramid at Gaza. I had met an exciting dragoman, one of the guides who wore a long burnoose, a kind of nightgown down to the ankles. And he had a fez. He came to the ship looking for me, and we planned a day when I would be free so we could climb the Great Pyramid. It's forty-four stories high or a little more.

Anyway, I made a date to climb the pyramid with this fellow. Tourists do climb up two or three floors because the risers are small. But as you go higher and higher the steps become greater and greater until it's a real feat to continue. He would go ahead and pull me up. The nosing of the stones would crumble and I tried not to look down. I never liked to go high, even as a sailor when I had to go aloft to tighten something or take care of a shackle. But here we were. We went up and up for hours and hours and my clothes were ragged from being torn on the stones. But when we got up there the sight was so rewarding. You could see the Nile and the fertile areas where it overflows its banks for fifteen miles on each side. There were great vultures reeling around, and on the floor of the desert was the dust of Cleopatra. And best of all, as I climbed I could look up that man's beautiful Arabian garment and see his penis and testicles. In the heat of pulling me after him, I got more excited and I never thought of the descent which later became the most frightening thing in my life, even worse than a shipwreck I suffered in later years. But up there on that apex where no others would go unless they were young, you could look down and see nobody else coming. We had sex up there. I couldn't wait to tell Halliburton about it. I told

15

him, "You have swum the Taj Mahal, done the Alps by elephant like Hannibal . . . but you never had a homosexual affair on top of Cheops, the Second Pyramid of Gaza." Topping his feats gave me a lot of personal satisfaction. So I think though we were living in deceit, we did have sex and an outlet.

I never wanted to hurt anybody and I never pushed too hard for what I wanted. I was at the Cafe La Fête in New Orleans when a man said to me, "It's your biological right to ask for what you want. If it's that beautiful young woman, let her know you like her. Or if it's that young man over there and you want him, let him know. It's your right to ask for what you want and to hear their answer. You might urge a little, but don't be too persistent." I took that as good advice and tried to apply it.

I've had a lot of wonderful sexual experiences. I've lived with men too, but I was of a more promiscuous nature. I wanted what was called in our vernacular "rough trade." And sometimes these people return; even now, at 76, they will phone me and want to come back — longshoremen, a truck driver here and there. And we still have pleasant sexual experiences. But I never cared to go to bed with another homosexual. I'm sure I was deceived. Now, I never catalogue anymore. I've gone to bed with men who have done the most onerous work on the waterfront, who were in prison too, who'd beat the shit out of anyone who said that they were a homosexual or that I was. They'd fight and yet I could fuck them in the ass or they'd go down on me. I was always interested in having anal sex when I could, and I did. And I do. But I was quite versatile, I do other things too.

I lived with some marvelous people. I lived with a man who was art editor with a wrestling and boxing magazine. We would go to all the wrestling exhibitions and boxing tournaments. I met a lot of people. I went to bed with a world champion, the fighter of his day, who was gay, but very much *macho* as all those people were. There were many boxers who were gay. One with whom I had delightful experiences came to the top of Madison Square Garden in the Golden Gloves contests. He was an Irish Catholic. He would sing "Mother Machree" or something before he would fight. An exceptional kind of a person, with a beautiful voice. After he was through fighting he was exhausted but so physically beautiful that I would go home with him and sleep at his home. His mother might have killed me if she knew that we were having sex in his big feather bed. But we had it. I went with him many times when he lost, and most of the time when he won. It seemed as though a lot of contact sport athletes, especially boxers, were gay.

I lived with the art editor in a love relationship for maybe one and a half years. It ended when he discovered I was playing with others. I would meet him socially at parties later. I would have loved to have another fling with him but he wouldn't consider it. The time was like that. If you had an affair and couldn't be loyal, you were through. Oh, I suppose there was every kind of homosexual then as there is now. Masters and Johnson said that of all the minorities — racial, sexual, national — the most varied is the homosexual. I like to use the analogy of the common cemetery ivy. I know of no plant that has so many leaves different from one another. Some are heart-shaped, some have two lobes, three lobes, others are like a shield. Yet for all the differences of leaves, like the differences of homosexuals, they all have the same artery supporting them. They have in common this great thing. Unlike other vines that are deciduously defoliating in winter, the ivy is forever green. It's turned on all the time, as I think gay people are.

I had friends employed in Washington as secretaries to senators — and there were a lot of gay senators, but they were all in the closet. There were only men secretaries and many were gay. But when the McCarthy era came along it was thought that gay people were mentally ill and that they were security risks. Nobody for any reason, if he were a true patriot, would employ a homosexual or a male stenographer. They fired all those men who were so valuable and began to have women for secretaries.

I was catapulted to union leadership, at least on ships, during the time of the McCarthy period. I was always afraid to take office ashore for fear that someone competing with me would find out that I was going to bed with men. I talked about things that were maybe sympathetic to socialism and I was branded a communist though I never was. I felt the communists had no understanding of homosexuals and never would have accepted me. I didn't want to be a communist any more than I wanted to be a Catholic. I wanted to be me, and to know a lot of people with different political and religious views. I had spent fifteen years on ships working as a sailor, dishwasher, cook and baker. One time after serving as Chief Steward, I sailed as a dishwasher. We were trying to teach in our union that a good craftsman could do anything. He didn't need to be apologetic about the most menial work if he did it well. And a good worker was a good union man. I went to hearings in Washington. You couldn't produce any witness but the committees had dossiers of information. I was accused of pulling a flag down from the stern of the ship and throwing it into the sea. How could anyone so despicable, so un-American ever be granted papers again? I said, "That's a goddamn lie. I was chairman of the ship's committee. One of the men took a little flag from the captain's table and put it on the bulletin board crisscrossing it with scotch tape. Next to it was an editorial from the *Hearst Examiner* saying that we were a nest of communists and that our union effort was prompted from Moscow, financed with rubles. I had made a statement at the union meeting that it was no way to hang the American flag and I removed it." But the story came out that I threw Old Glory over the side of the ship. It took six years of litigation to reverse the charges against me and about 2,000 others. We were reinstated but it was printed on my papers, "This steward is to be treated as if he had never been a security risk." Hell, that in itself was just like branding you. I was afraid to go to sea again, there were a lot of people after my hide.

I went back to college and took a course in horticulture and floriculture. I worked for a nursery and later for the longshoremen to landscape a magnificent new union hall down at Fisherman's Wharf. It was tremendous. They wanted to show that culture came from the common people—that Michelangelo was a man uneducated, gay, a working man, who created great cultural beauty. I had three men working with me. It was a thing of beauty. Today, I dislike any association with it; it's like a ghetto. People are not keeping it clean. The vines are not pruned. The beauty is lost. I spent fifteen years as a gardener and then retired.

I'd like to speak of my happiness as a retired man of 76 and my sentimental trips around the city. I like to go back to those places I knew during the time I was working. It doesn't mean I'm looking back all the time. I get pleasure from it, like playing a song that you've enjoyed. I go back to the waterfront along Aquatic Park, around the longshoremen's hall where I planted trees and I see these trees as friends of mine. I've shaped them, I've fed them, I've loved them. I go back to see the great beauty that's been produced. It's especially enjoyable when I see some of them that didn't seem to be making it and they've turned out to be great trees while other, better specimens fell by the wayside because a car ran into them or they couldn't find the soil they needed. I fantasize on these trips. I think that as I see them there's communication. When the fog comes in the Golden Gate and brings with it that wind that rattles the leaves, I sometimes think they're saying, "Look at us now in our great beauty," and "They're looking for you down here, Don." When the tourists first came through and asked what kind of trees they were I told them that they'd bear fruit, and when they did that I'd treat them to a martini. The trees seem to say, "We're bearing olives now and they're looking for you."

I took another such trip back to the Haight-Ashbury district a month or two ago. I had such pleasure there in the late sixties, observing the scene and sometimes even feeling a part of it. It was beautiful at the beginning, but then it got nasty and ugly. People were getting burnt. Those who wanted good hash were getting catnip and were out to kill the people who sold it. Those who wanted heavier things like cocaine or heroin were getting sugar. And I was back there looking at the buildings. A tree or a house or a street sign, "Haight-Ashbury," can be the catalyst to refresh that memory.

It was 1966 or 1967 when the flower children were in bloom. A man came along, a youth, and he said to me, looking at me from top to bottom, "Ya know what I think of you?" And I said, "No, it might be very interesting to hear. After all, my friends are very dishonest when asked an opinion. I think you don't know me, I'd like to hear it." He said, "I think you are a fat, ugly, old toad." Ooo, it was a shock! There was a little girl there, barely eight years old perhaps, and she had heard the conversation. She was dressed in a delightful manner. Everyone in those days, if you remember, seemed to be in a costume of some kind, fantastic clothes. She was wearing a long dress of her mother's, probably the child of hippies, and her feet were bare. Her head had a crown made of cardboard. In the points of the crown there were fresh flowers. She was a little princess with long hair flowing down her shoulders and she had a wand with a star stapled to the end of it. She listened to that man and she asked me, "Would you like to be a hippie?" I said, "I would, I would, but it's too late for me and too early for you. You know they turn it off at thirty, and I'm more than twice thirty. I couldn't be a hippie." And she said, "Never mind," and she put her wand up to my shoulder. I felt for a moment like someone in King Arthur's court. I thought I should be kneeling, that I was being dubbed by royalty. She said, "Toad, I make you a frog. Frog, I make you a prince. Prince, I make you a hippie, a beautiful flower child." I relived that just lately. I'll always remember the beauty of that child's message. I had a notebook and wrote that down as soon as I left her. But I didn't need to, for it was in my heart and I could recall it, as I do today.

The first years I retired, I got a subscription to the theatre and another to the ballet. I found I didn't need so much of that as I like mostly to observe people, to watch them and to make such memory trips as I have described and to be active with the Gay 40+ Club and the gay caucus of the Unitarian Church. I think this day is so magnificent. I think there are many advantages young people have today over the generation I was part of. I've already touched upon the honesty. There are many homosexuals arriving in this city each month and we are already tipping the scale. I hope that we don't feel too cocky and tell other people to go to hell, saying, "You've kept us down and pushed us around so now we're going to show you by bringing to office those politicians that will favor our way of life." I think that would be a terrible mistake. At least for me, I want to see the world as a mixed bouquet. If you look at a field or at a garden you'll find many colors there.

A woman once asked me if I would landscape her garden. Since she was a wealthy woman and said I could pick the plants I wanted, I looked forward to it. Before we sat down to make sketches she took me through her house. Every room and all the walls, rugs, and furniture were of one color—white. She said, "You see all of this? I have only to change an evening gown when I am having a dinner party and add sofa cushions to match my gown and a flower arrangement. I am the important one and all of this is background. I want a garden that is all white. Every shrub, every annual, every perennial, every bulb must produce a white flower or I don't want it." I said, "What a challenge, it's so unnatural. Nature isn't like that." She said, "Do as I tell you." And I did. I shopped when the plants were in bloom. She was very pleased and paid me well. There were others who did the maintenance, the watering, the pruning, and so on. I later met her at a party and she told me, "You pleased me until this last year. Then you let me down. I have blue camellias outside my terrace, the fuchsias are shades of lavender and purple, and there's color everywhere." And I told her, "I let you know it was going to be like that. Nature is not monochromatic. Nature is many colors, many cultures, many races, many different kinds of people—homosexuals, heterosexuals, a lot in between, a lot you don't know what they are. Hummingbirds coming over your garden wall and bees—they're cross-pollinating. You couldn't keep that garden white. And I'll bet it's more beautiful now than when I planted it." Well, she had grown older and mellower and said she'd have to think about it.

I'd like to travel sometime. I've had a problem with my weight which is often the problem with people who like nice things to eat and who can cook well and reach retirement. I've gone away to fat farms a couple of times. I take off weight then come home and run with people who like to eat and drink. I gain it all back. I haven't paid a single penny but right now I'm benefiting from a free nutrition course given at the public service hospital. I'm attending lectures there. I'm getting it free and getting better results.

Young people stereotype old people. They think that we're crotchety and forgetful, incapable of keeping up with the wonderful changes of the time. But that's a crock of shit. There are no people so varied as older people are. They've had more years to develop their idiosyncrasies, their greatness or their weakness. And they are very different from one another. The people who are cloned and similar are the very young people—teenagers. If it's in vogue for a girl, as it was some years ago, to wear a kerchief on her head, the knot fastened on the chin, it would be unforgivable not to have the knot fastened under the chin. And she wants her parents exactly like the parents of her friends. She wants to be accepted. But as people get older they want more of their individuality. And that's what I would say: "Live it your own way."

I've looked for contentment and found that contentment was the death of ambition. I found that people climbing the corporate ladder were not contented people. Their eye always on the next rung, they were the achievers and the people who worked under stress. I know there's a need for people like this in our society, but I've lived in this little apartment for twenty-five years and I never needed to have a big car or drag a boat around behind it or have a country estate. I've lived as a working man all my life and had a rich, full life. Oh, sometimes I was cocksure of myself and later reversed my thinking as I've gotten older. But my life has been sweet. I just hope there's a little more of it.

I met a little boy who was waiting for the bus and looking in the direction from which it would come. Like seagulls, we were all looking in the same direction. I didn't want to make conversation with him because children are always taught not to talk to strangers and older people. But he walked in the gutter with one foot up on the walk and the other down in the gutter. Well, I went right behind him, doing the same thing. He said, "Do you like to do that too?" And I told him, "Yes, I do, but it's been a long time since I did it." He said, "How long?" I said, "I think about sixty years ago." He said, "Wow, I don't have grandparents but I guess you'd be older than them. What does it feel like to be old?" I thought it was a very remarkable thing for a child to ask an older man. I told him I was glad he asked me that, for while I have no pain, and my body works, I know the answer. A gerontologist was once asked that same question and said, "Take a little cotton and put a little in each ear, take a little vaseline and smear it on each side of your glasses, and put a little pebble or stone or sand in your shoe. Then I think you'll know what the limitations are as you get older." But the mind has a collection of vast material from your youth and middle years. And if you haven't become soured with life, your old age can be beautiful too.

2

Todd Grison

Todd left his native Alabama when he was nine years old. Much of his life was spent in the Midwest and his home base is now a two-story house on the outskirts of San Francisco. He is animated and his voice rises and falls against a musical background of Beethoven. He has short salt-and-pepper hair and speaks positively of his fifty-odd years. "You have to put something into life in order to get something out because later on you won't have shit; you'll just be an old fag with nothing to fall back on." Todd has worked for the same company for 25 years.

I WAS BORN IN ALABAMA, DELIVERED BY A MIDWIFE. BACK then black kids, and even some white kids, weren't born in a hospital, a midwife came in. I didn't have a birth certificate; the only record of my birth was in the Bible. Eventually my mother had to go to a notary public to certify that I was born. There were three of us. I'm the oldest and I have a brother and a sister, also a half-brother and half-sister from my father.

I left Alabama when I was about nine. My mother wanted me to go to school in a Northern state, so in 1939 or 1940 I went to live with my father in Detroit. I didn't stay with my father too long, though, because he was living in a ghetto. Believe me, in Alabama I didn't live in a ghetto! I wrote my mother a letter and told her that there were roaches running all over the house and bedbugs so bad I had welts all over my back. Mother said I would have to come back but I didn't want to go. I'd always heard there had to be something better than Alabama. I guess I went to the movies too much and saw the way other people lived and decided, "That's the way I want to live too." She called my aunt in another part of Detroit and told her I wanted to leave my father's house so I moved in there.

My aunt was the type who couldn't be bothered with kids. My mother warned me to be on my best behavior, to never worry Aunt Cammie. When Cammie had left Alabama she went to Cleveland and after five years moved to Detroit. She met a man there and they got married but he was killed in the first world war. She made it on her own selling real estate. She and I got along beautifully. I stayed with her all through my childhood and whenever I was on leave from the Army. Even lived with her for a while after I was married. She died four years ago when she was seventy-six.

I volunteered for the Army in 1945. I was seventeen and had just flunked twelfth grade. A good friend of mine, Wilbur, and I went down to go into the Navy but I can't swim and when I heard about how the Navy pushed you into the water I said, "Let's join the Army." On the day we were supposed to report I went down to the bus station but no Wilbur. They said, "Okay, Grison, get on the bus." When I finally heard from Wilbur I was in Italy. The Army wouldn't take him and he just couldn't tell me.

They sent me from Michigan to Alabama for basic training. At that time there was eighteen weeks of training and infantry training was *hard*. I was lucky that my platoon sergeant was from Detroit, so I had it a little easy because most of the other guys were from the South. We were all black; there was no integration back then.

One day this guy and I were pulling targets and he said, "Hey, Grison, come here, I want you." I said, "Man, what are you talking about?" He said, "I want you." I said, "Hey, man, let's cool it." I couldn't run anyplace. If I so much as stuck my head out on that target range I would have been blown away. So he picked a good time to come on to me. Afterwards, he and I pulled guard duty together on some empty barracks so I said, "Why don't you meet me down at those empty barracks tonight?" He said, "You gonna be there?" I said, "Yeah, sure!" Shit, I didn't go any place near there that night. Oh, that fool! I'm sure he would have raped me if I had gone.

After eighteen weeks training we went overseas and I was sent to Pisa. When I arrived there I was promoted from private to corporal and ended up in the supply division. The supply officer liked young boys and I was the youngest one in my company. I was petrified anytime he would come near me. Hell, I wasn't even shaving yet! One day he came in the bathroom and said, "Soldier, they issue you a razor, use it." And I did.

One time we were renovating a place for a USO about two blocks from camp. I was drunk on near beer and this guy Solomon said, "C'mon, Grison, let's go back together, okay?" and I said okay. About halfway through the weeds, he said, "Hey, Grison, come on, I'm waiting for you." All of a sudden it dawned on me what was happening and I thought, "Oh, no, I can't." At the time I was a sergeant and he was only a corporal. I think it must have been in my mind all the time that he was gay, but I never fooled around. I used to see guys and think, "God, he's good looking," but I'd always drop my eyes. I told Solomon, "Look, if you *ever* approach me again, I'll have you court-martialled." I saw him the next day and couldn't even look at him. I don't think I would have gone to bed with him anyway because he was chunky.

There was a drill sergeant who did have a beautiful body. He used to come into the supply room—my private quarters were in the back. I guess I was gay then and didn't know it because I had them all fixed up. You know, the iron bunk beds? Well, I had mine all boxed in, real fancy. Anyway, this drill sergeant had to come back to my quarters to turn in his pistol and he would always hang around and bullshit. At that age we were playing, horsing around and shit like that. This guy was about 22. Once I threw him and pinned him and there was no way I could have done that, me at a hundred and twenty-five pounds and him with a great body like that! I pressed against him and all at once I could feel something, something real hard, and I jumped up and said, "Oh, come on, let's quit this horsing around." Later on I found out he was married. He used to tell his wife he was protecting me from the other guys. Hell, he was protecting me for himself. Another time I was drunk and I remember him bringing me home, undressing me, putting me in bed and kissing me, kissing me on the cheek. He was so good-looking. Hell, maybe I just dreamed it. But it was nice. I'd have no reservations about the situation now.

I almost got married while I was in Italy. But I got three letters from my mother saying, "You are not going to marry no white girl and bring her back here to Alabama." When I was growing up my mother was the authority in the family. I came back to the States in '47 and went to Alabama to see my mother. I also knew this family there with fifteen or twenty kids. I had sex with one of their girls, Marlene, and she got pregnant. Only had sex one time. But all it takes is one time. My mother asked me, "What are you gonna do about this?" and I said, "I'm going back to Detroit." She said, "I think you should think about it 'cause you got your sister here and you wouldn't want some boy to do that to your sister." So we got married and stayed married about five years. Married life is not what I wanted. Meanwhile, I had only really fooled around once in gay life, in Switzerland. I was there on leave and a waiter at the hotel where I was staying kept feeding me drinks and saying, "When are you going to come to my place and see my glazings?" At the end of the night he said, "Well, my chauffeur should be around soon," and I was just drunk enough to believe all this bullshit. What eventually came around was a damn cab! We drove for a long time, and in my drunken stupor it still seemed that I knew what he wanted. When we got to his house we went to bed, had sex and both passed out. I don't remember much, but I remember it did happen.

One day I told my wife, "I don't love you and you don't love me so why don't we just split up." She agreed. So I moved back in with my aunt. After I left my wife I started hanging out in some of the clubs in Detroit. They used to have what you call a "Blue Monday" there. If you were a hustler or prostitute or whatever, Monday was the night for you. The clubs would be jammed. When I started going out, some of the black gays would come in and be buying drinks right and left. And I thought, "My god, how could they live like that?" Well, I found out that with most of them it was just a front. Eventually I got into that little group and started putting on this big front too. You had to be seen in a certain lounge on Saturday night. Back then all the gays in Detroit went to church on Saturday night, and when church was out they'd go to a certain cocktail lounge and sit around and greet everyone, you know, like gays always do. I thought they lived very nice.

I remember a book came out around this time called something like *One Year of Gay Life*. I read it and I thought, "I'll try that." I was twenty-two and hadn't grown out of my attraction to men so I figured this was the time. The first guy I asked out was very nice, and our "date" went very well. But I saw him two or three days later on my way to work. We were about to run into each other, to meet face-to-face, and I couldn't do it. I crossed the street before I got to him because I had guilt feelings.

I kept reading books to find out where I was coming from but that didn't help very much. They only helped me reach the conclusion that I never wanted to get into female clothes because, to me, that would be demeaning. It would take all my feeling away if I had to go out and get dressed up in drag and be like a woman. If I wanted women, I would have women. But I want a man and I want to be a man. Don't get me wrong, I love females, I love 'em to death, my mother, her sister. I respect them. But going to bed with a woman, or drag queen, no, I don't think I could. You see, when I walk out of here, out of this door, I have everything that a male's supposed to have and I want to sleep with another male. I used to say to my wife, "If I want something with a dress, I want no imitation."

While I was hanging out at these bars in Detroit I started seeing prostitutes and basically I learned I'm a street person. Prostitutes are wise and most of them are good people. I knew one in Detroit and she knew I was gay. When I'd stop by her bar, she'd say, "Damn, I wish you'd come in earlier 'cause we could've made twenty bucks apiece." She'd say some trick had been in and wanted to watch me fuck her while he beat off. At the time $20 was good money, too. I used to take $10 and go out and have a ball and still have some change left. But I never did any hustling, never had to. My aunt made really good money and she always kept $100 in her purse. If I needed money she'd give me $10.

I was working at the time too. When I came out of the service they gave me twenty-six weeks of unemployment so I said, "I think I'll take that 26 weeks." But my aunt said, "There's nothing wrong with you; go back to your old job," and she shamed me into going back. Fact is, I've never drawn unemployment insurance, ever!

In Detroit I got into a group of about eight or ten gays. We all had a cashmere suit and everything, the whole wardrobe. We'd get together every weekend, but we were always going home alone. All we were was a lonely little group. I said to myself, "I don't know what it is but something's wrong here!" Then on Halloween, on one street there were four or five gay bars, so they blocked the whole street off and the gays promenaded. I decided to go see what it was all about even though all of those bars were white because we didn't have integration then. Instead of going to my regular bar I walked into a white bar. I really got the cold shoulder, no one would even talk to me. But I went back the next week with another guy. We weren't set up in cashmere, just dressed casual. Some of our friends said, "Oh, I see you're goin' hiking on us, down to a white bar." I said, "Look, I'll go anywhere I want to." That's when I more or less broke away from the group and found out how vicious black queens can be. All they do is gossip. That's not my bag, I couldn't care less about who's going to bed with who. All we did was sit around talking about everyone, what she is wearing, all this, "Oh, dear, I see you got a new jacket." How boring!

One day after work I stopped by one of my new-found bars and met this large, tall dude. He bought me a drink and I bought him one and we started talking. I hadn't had anything to eat so I started feeling good real fast and invited him to my house. We went to bed, this tall Texan and I. He was a disappointment, but I thought, "Well, since I've got the man here we might as well do *something*." I was sitting on the edge of the bed, thinking how to entertain him. I leaned over to put on my house slippers, and, before I knew it he struck me across the head with a whiskey decanter. The blood started flowing and he stole about $10 from my wallet and a $300 watch. After he took the watch and looked in the wallet he asked if I had any more money. I said, "Yes, in the bureau drawer," and he said, "Well, give it to me." He was so stupid! I had a .32 in there that I had brought from the Army. I never kept it loaded but when I came up, I drew it and cocked it. He said, "Oh, man, don't shoot," and I slapped him across the face with the gun. I said, "You son-of-a-bitch, give me back my wallet." I didn't think about the watch. At this point the blood was nearly blinding me. He ran out of the house and I got the blood stopped and went after him. I put the gun in my pocket. I looked all around, but he had gone. I never saw that man again. He was such a cool, nice type of guy, but besides robbing me, he was a lousy fuck. From then on I was always cautious. In gay life you're going to get burned if you don't watch it. I always figured I was gonna have gonorrhea or something like that, and I used to be deathly afraid of syphillis. Now it's AIDS.

After I was robbed I met Lynn at one of the white bars. He had just moved to a town about fifty miles outside Detroit where he had a job playing piano in a church and teaching. We were together five years. We moved to California and both got jobs: he was teaching and I worked for an insurance company. In about a year I was able to go in on buying a gay bar. I worked at my regular job during the day and behind the bar at night.

Then one time I took a vacation to Alabama, and when I came back earlier than planned, Lynn had a black guy sleeping in my bed. Lynn said, "He got kicked out of his apartment," and I said, "I don't care what happened to him, he shouldn't be here." Things got a little cool. Shows how stupid I was, too. But I felt if you're together, you're together. I wasn't trickin' around on him, and the whole time I was pushing my ass behind the bar, trying to make something for us. The relationship fell apart because I didn't understand enough about gay life at that time.

When Lynn and I split I thought, "Oh my god, what am I gonna do?" I was away from home with no family. But then I thought, "What the fuck are you thinking about? Hell, girl, you can make it! It's not like he was taking care of you. I was thirty-five at the time and I met Dale about a year after that. I don't think I was truly in love with Lynn when I look back at it now. Actually, I never thought that two men could be in love until I met Dale. I didn't believe in love; every guy was just a trick. But with Dale it was something that just grew. When we had our last fight and he was leaving, I begged him not to go. I made up my mind at that point I would never feel that way again, that I would never have another lover. Dale and I had been together six years. I don't know what happened, what we fought about. Over nothing, probably.

After that I said, "You know, I think men should be able to deviate," because you get tired of doing the same thing. Like on a job, it gets to be a routine. You stop by a bar, you have no intention of doing anything, but you see someone there and you start talking. I can understand that now but then I couldn't. There's a difference, also, because when I met Dale he was ten or twelve years younger than I was. He was going to college and didn't know that much. He stayed with me until he wanted to get out and find out things for himself. If I had realized that then, I could very easily have said, "Hey, go on out." I think you can't set certain rules for people to go by, and if you find something better out there, you should go get it. But you better know what you've got at home. I don't want to know who you went to bed with, but you better make sure that when you come back you are clean because we're together in this home as lovers. Two males who have been together for five years don't have two- or three-hour sex. It dies down but it's not gone. And sometimes you have to go out and see what's there.

When I told Dale he was the last, I meant it. Too much had happened, too much hurt. For instance, when I was in the hospital Dale would come by every day and one day he didn't show up. When he came the next day I asked what had happened. He said, "Oh, I went to a bar and got drunk." When I got out of the hospital some guy told me, 'The reason Dale didn't come to the hospital that day was because he was with me." It was just too much. But we still slept together occasionally until about a year ago. Then I got so upset with our "relationship" I went to Vancouver on vacation.

I was in a pub there one night and this guy Mike came up and said, "What part of the States are you from?" I told him San Francisco. Well, Mike was a really good talker, he'd talk your ass off. He started asking me if I'd seen Vancouver, Queen Elizabeth Park, the zoo. I said no, so he asked me to go to the zoo with him. We ended up in bed instead of at the zoo, which was fine with me because I had actually been to all the places he asked me about. After we had sex Mike said, "Mr. Grison, I want to tell you something. I am a married man." I thought, "Oh, shit, here's another one who's got a gay lover." I said, "What's his name?" He said, "No, a wife is what I have." Well, we had a very hot affair. I went back home and he called, so I went back to Vancouver and had another "vacation." Between Western and United, I gave the airlines a lot of money. He also came down to see me. The second time I went to see him, he had told his wife he was gay. Anyway, our affair went on for about a year. Mike was a very good long-distance lover. He lives down here now.

After Mike and I were through, I met Rick. Rick was shacked up with Phil, an old friend of mine. One day Phil called and asked me to stop by for a visit. Rick and I started talking and all of a sudden Phil pulled me aside and said, "I won't have this kind of thing going on in my house." All we were doing was talking! Well, I started being an evil bitch at this point. I said, "Fuck this shit," and I made a point of paying even more attention to Rick. I was ill and was in no mood to go tricking but I wanted to prove that I could. Rick and I left together and he said, "Todd, you're nice, but I'm not going to get carried away with you." As soon as he let me know he was going to play hard to get I told him, "I will *make* you fall in love with me." As it turned out, I fell in love with him. But it was a nice friendship; he has always had trust in me. One time he borrowed $3,000 from his credit union to help me consolidate my bills. And I paid it all back.

When I first came to California I had a rough time finding a job. I worked making rope for a dollar an hour but I could only take it for four days. I was ready to go back to Detroit. One night Lynn and I went up to the Top of the Mark and coming back I slid down the hill and skinned my arms. I said, "I'm going home, I'm definitely going home." But Lynn said, "Todd, give it a chance. Wait at least four months before you make a decision."

They didn't have integration or fair employment then, none of that. I went to an insurance company for a job, a clerical job I thought, since I had worked as a clerk for the government in Detroit. I didn't know they had a kitchen. When they showed it to me I thought, "Why are they showing me this?" Then I got the picture. I said, "Why not?" I ended up working there for twenty-five years. Within a few weeks I was cooking for the president of the company and after ten years I was working in the computer division.

Later I opened a gay bar where the Embarcadero Center is now. It was deep in sawdust and most of my customers were blacks from Oakland. Eventually it became black and white. Gay bars were changing so fast back then, if you stayed open a year without being busted you were lucky. When the bar was just beginning to pay off, after three years, the redevelopment people came through and said they'd have to move me to another location. But the timing was bad because I had become anemic from the long hours and had to pass up their offer.

About homosexuality . . . I do believe that recognition is where we're coming from. But flamboyancy, throwing your head back and saying, "Well, *girls*," and, "Let me tell *you*, honey," I don't go for that kind of shit. I don't see where all that is necessary. No one has ever invaded my privacy or questioned what I do in the bedroom. And I don't act like that with all that "May" and "Mary" shit. It shows so little discretion.

I remember when my Aunt Cammie first told me she suspected I was gay. One day she said, "Sit down, I want to talk to you." She was concerned because she'd heard rumors. She said, "Sonny, maybe you should see a psychiatrist." And I said, "Why should I do that?" She hesitated and said, "I don't know; I don't understand about that life, but I want to say one thing and I'll never mention it again. Whatever you do in your life, be discreet about it." We never mentioned the subject again and I did not say to her, "Well, look, I *am* a homosexual." I was on the verge of speaking, but I thought better of it; I let it drop.

I think my whole family knows, but it is something that they have never brought up. One reason is that I always covered myself. And I have always helped them financially. Behind my back they probably say, "Well, you know, he's a fag." But one thing's for sure, I have never embarrassed them because what I do in my bedroom is my own personal business. I often thought that if I brought shame on my family I would do away with myself. Discretion is very important to me.

The younger gays put too much emphasis on being gay. Even if you're gay you still need to have some means of support unless you're going to be a robber or you're going to sleep with someone my age and get whatever you can out of them. I thought once, "When I get to be fifty years old, I'll be supporting some cute little number." Well, they're cute but there's nothing in their heads. They're so stupid, some of them. You have to put something into your life in order to get something out of it. I always tell the young ones, "Go to school, get an education, so you'll have something to fall back on because later on in life, you won't have shit. You'll just be an old fag with nothing to show for it." I've seen many of them, older than I am, still hanging out in the bars. It's the most pathetic thing. They're making silly asses out of themselves. Perhaps if I was rich I would have a harem but that would probably be a bore too. I just believe you should enjoy your life because that's all you've got.

I was very fortunate to make it to forty-some years old and still be able to get lovers. I've always been choosy about my lovers, and I've always had very good ones. We're still on good terms, still very concerned about each other. I think we have to look around at our partners, the ones we have had for two or three years, and start to evaluate and say, "Look, man, look what we have together." Because we don't know how long it's going to last. We just don't know.

I think we're trying to crowd tomorrow into today a little too fast. Too many of us burn out before the age of thirty. I bought this house because I was working and I wanted everything at once. I never was a person who would say, "Wait until tomorrow." I was an alcoholic, but until last month I haven't touched a drink in years because I could talk myself out of the booze. But the older I get, the looser I get.

I don't think I regret being a homosexual. At first I did. I more or less hated myself. But I've never had hang-ups about sex or if my partner was black or white or whatever. There's something beautiful and attractive about everyone I meet. It doesn't have to be a physical attraction, it may come from within. Perhaps if I hadn't lived in San Francisco for twenty-five years I might feel differently, might not be so open-minded. But I love this city, all that happens, all the love affairs. One thing's for sure, though, I've never regretted even one small part of my life. Never.

3

Alan Williams

Alan lives in a spacious second floor flat in San Francisco's North Beach area where the California Beat Generation flourished. He is 60 years old, a tall husky man with the profile of a Roman warrior. As Al speaks he moves slowly through his museum-like home, crowded by art and antiques collected during his adventures abroad.

I CAN REMEMBER MY FIRST INTRODUCTION TO GAYNESS. I WAS hiking with my family and we went into a canyon. We had to go under a bridge. There was a big ugly sign under the bridge that said "Dirty Queer." Well, subconsciously I could feel something. I was in grammar school and had already fooled around with a little girl—I was very confused. I definitely remember the comments of my four very straight brothers; I can still see those words, "Dirty Queer." And I thought, "My god, I don't want to be related to that." I think that that's a part of the continuous struggle; we're so much a part of our conditioning.

I had a powerful father whose company built some of the biggest buildings in San Francisco—the Palace of Fine Arts and so forth. I'm a fourth-generation San Franciscan. My father had an 8,600-acre ranch in Arizona where we spent our summers. I loved it because I had a horse and could scrounge around in Indian cliff dwellings and that sort of thing. In high school, when it came time for sex, my father simply hired the housekeeper's daughter to sleep with me. All of a sudden it was, "Here, here is a sex partner." Another time when my father was driving, he stopped the car and said, "Look at that; that's a whorehouse. Go." And he sat there while I—a young boy—walked up to the door. I rang the doorbell and an enormous woman answered. I can still see her. Her bed was next to a window and the window was open. I wanted to climb over that mountainous woman and jump out the window.

After high school I received a scholarship in Fine Arts and later won a year's fellowship from the Mexican government to study art. Shortly after that, I met a wonderful woman, one of the best-known artists in the country. We were both involved in sculpture. I was teaching it and she was teaching pottery and ceramics at the same university. We got married when I was twenty-four years old. It was a sexual marriage, it wasn't superficial. I really had feelings for her but it wasn't right. I wanted to love women, but I felt I should be sleeping with a man.

Thank God, something guided me to the right woman. It would have been horrible to have married someone who wasn't a thinking, sensitive, logical person. It wasn't long after I got married that I knew it wasn't really my trip. The struggle of not wanting to hurt someone, and all that bullshit, followed. The marriage lasted eleven years before she died. My wife had a small child when I married her and I helped raise the child. She's one of my best friends today. We go to the flea market and the beach together, really enjoy each other, so it's worked out well.

At the end of that period I met a man with whom I've lived successfully for twenty-seven years. So it can happen. But first of all you have to love yourself. I've had plenty of relationships but only one with a man before my present lover. And that man was so neurotic that I thought, "Oh, my God, is this what homosexuality is all about?"

I taught sculpture for four years in Berkeley. I had a good class, a marvelous, interesting group of people. They kept asking me, "What is modern art?" I thought, "God, if one more person comes up and asks me that I'll quit"—well, I was about to renew my teaching contract when I had a chance to sign on a freighter. And because I was married (I'm sure that had something to do with it) I didn't renew my contract. I just got on the boat and sailed away.

We went up the Columbia River, picked up some lumber, sailed down the Panama Canal. Then I jumped ship and went off to see the San Blas Indians. That was an interesting summer; I really liked it. When I got back to the freighter most everyone on board was drunk. I suppose I was the only one sober – I've always had a prejudice against alcohol because it hurts so many people. There was an old-time union organizer aboard – I think he was called Old Wobbly. He spent the whole trip talking and loved to have anybody listen. He talked and talked 'til we ended up having a strike after we got through the Panama Canal. It was a slow bell strike where everybody keeps painting the same spot, keeps doing the same job over and over until terms are reached. We just floated and floated. It was really interesting.

After the Panama trip, I went to Africa several times and became a compulsive traveler. I got into primitive art from farmers with no art background. We used to call all African art "primitive" because it was thought of as secondary art. It isn't, it's a traditional art, older than any other culture.

My collection of African art, artifacts and sculpture kept growing. I helped start the very first African historical and cultural society. I was the only Caucasian on the Board of Directors and was elected three times. This was in a period when no one was offering any African history. But all of a sudden there were demonstrations and universities agreed to sponsor black history courses. They looked around and said, "Well, first I guess we'd better get some black history together." Today we have the largest African history library in San Francisco and the San Francisco African-American Historical Society is a respected organization. I'm proud to say I helped clean up an old grocery store to create the community center – I got down on my hands and knees and scrubbed the floor.

I eventually got involved with many projects, mostly dealing with civil rights. I worked with Dr. Martin Luther King, and I'm proud to say I was the first Freedom Rider recruited by Ralph Abernathy. I've been in five prisons, mostly for civil disobedience. I have a straight brother who asked me never to tell his grandchildren these things because they are such a downer. My God, if I've done anything to be proud of, I'm proud of my social involvement. I was a guilt-ridden liberal at first, but, thank God, I worked for the right causes. I worked for prison reform and for civil rights because I could relate to them. I also worked in the office of the Mattachine Society in 1950.

I was involved in getting Caryl Chessman released from prison and worked for general prison reform. I've also spent forty-five days on death row in Parchman Penitentiary because I sat next to a black person in a train station. Being a prisoner is frightening because you don't know how you're going to react—to walk out of a train into hundreds of people shouting at you is an extremely tense experience. When we got to Parchman I couldn't use my legs because my back had been screwed up from another confrontation. They took all our clothes away, made us sleep on steel ramps, and just hosed us down every once in a while. This was the same penitentiary where, shortly before I was there, six inmates had taken sledge hammers and broken their legs as a protest against prison brutality.

I remember a beautiful happening there. Though we were segregated in the prison, the black and the white people sang together. I've never been able to become part of any organized religion, but I always respond to group energy. If I ever felt like I was in a cathedral, it was in that penitentiary where the whites sang to the blacks, "We Shall Overcome." All those corny civil rights songs had real feeling to them. We sang back and forth to support each other—same way as gays do now. These people knew something positive had to happen. The social conditioning had to change. Ah, social conditioning . . . we're all part of the past. Every generation can do a little something. The frustrating thing is that it takes so long for mankind to come around.

All this makes me think about how culture shows the history of life. Once I went to New Orleans to photograph. In New Orleans there was a period when black craftsmen were free to work. Although the architects were French, the craftsmen, the men who forged the iron, were African. They were close enough to their original Nigerian culture, where bronze originated, to have mastered it. And as they worked with the French plans, their own sense of design came out in the beautiful wrought-iron balconies. But the white workers complained, "We can't get paid for doing our work because the blacks are laboring for nothing." So the blacks were put back on the plantations and all that know-how was lost. It's really sad how minorities are exploited. I think the blacks have also been exploited by the church. The only way a black person could survive was to go to a church and be away from whites. But at the same time, from learning the Bible too well they became crippled. I think gay people have been exploited like this by the bars. Just to relax, to be openly gay, you go into these dingy holes which foster alcoholism. I think that's another form of exploitation.

I became involved in the whole McCarthy hearings baloney. I was called a communist because I went to a public meeting about what was happening. I was pulled down the steps of City Hall by the cops and thrown in jail. I'm a non-violent person; I've never been in a fight in my life. But I was pulled down those City Hall steps trying to go to what I thought was an open meeting to hear Joseph McCarthy. The cops threw me on my back and ruptured a disc which I still have a lot of trouble with.

Somebody said to me the other day, "How come we don't see your sculpture in museums? Don't you do art work anymore?" I've exhibited in museums and galleries all over the country, won lots of awards. A big piece of my sculpture was once in an art center in front of San Francisco's City Hall. Then one day in Hunter's Point, a policeman shot a young boy and there was a lot of controversy that eventually led to a riot. The whites and blacks in the area were afraid to come out of their housing projects. So I wrote a poem and told the community they could take the sculpture from City Hall and put it on the boy's grave. I think that helped stop the riots for several days. All the people came out of the projects and held hands. It was really an inspiration.

I've come to think social change is like doing a piece of sculpture: it's creative and it's a lot of hard work—like organizing the National Gay March on Washington. That was very hard to get going, then all of a sudden you see it on the front page: gay people in Washington. That was a creative happening.

I thought it was important to have the support of the San Francisco Board of Supervisors for the march on Washington, but at first they didn't want to support it. Unfortunately the person blocking it was a black lady I knew twenty years before who gave me a party once when I got out of jail. To make a long story short, I sent her red roses and went and talked to her, talked about old times and emphasized that it was still the same struggle. You know, in the media they try to split blacks and gays—divide and conquer. After our meeting I got a letter from the head of the Board of Supervisors saying that he thought the march was a marvelous idea. And after lots of talk, at the last minute, the Board voted unanimously for it.

I knew Supervisor Harvey Milk pretty well. The great thing about him was that he could smile, not in a silly way, but with a sense of strength. It came from within–like he loved himself. In the old days we were taught not to love ourselves. But Harvey Milk had common sense. He could talk straight, debate, exchange ideas and there was a real joy about him, and that *is* a gift. So often things seem impossible but, thank God, once in a while you see a little humor. Sometimes things are so outrageous that if you didn't laugh about them, you'd have to cry. And life's so short, let's try not to be a drag about it. Try to change something–or walk away from it. Harvey Milk had a wonderful elation in his face. Though he was gay, he accepted it, he was using it, working with it. The last time I saw him was a couple of weeks before he died. I can still see his eyes. The last thing he said to me was, "We'll go to Washington for the march."

Oh, I remember the great people I've met and known. I considered Harvey Milk a really strong person, a beautiful, positive person. And Dr. King, César Chavez, they're great spirits. They've all had something in common. I think they felt they were in the right place at the right time and they allowed energy to gather around them. They weren't pretending to be gods, that wasn't their trip. They took the energy from the crowd and gave it back.

A few years ago I was selling buttons for the gay march on Washington and someone asked me, "Well, when did you become involved in the gay struggle?" And I said I was born in 1924 and I became involved in the struggle from the very beginning. We are a sum total of our whole trip on this planet, you know. You learn, you feel, you are a part. The young can have the courage to go further than I have gone. And that's why it's good to get uncrippled. I think we should know our history and learn from it. Young blacks, like young gays, have a sense of strength; they can stand up straight and have courage and be healthier people.

Getting real images of gay people through to the media is important because the media can cripple people. The last time I went to a gay parade 100,000 people came. Proud people, electricians, gay parents, plumbers–a real cross-section with a noticeable lack of alcohol or drugs. I came home thinking, "God, things are really unfolding!" Then I turned on the television, and they only showed one guy, one nelly guy with beads all over his head. I mean he has a perfect right to be that way but he doesn't represent everybody in the gay community. Yet the media shows him as the symbol of the whole gay parade. It was the old Amos and Andy thing again: twenty years ago they would not allow you to show a hard-working black bank executive; they'd always show some Amos and Andy image. Have things really come so far? We're just now leaving behind the image of beaded men camping it up. It's a shame it takes so long to let go of this image. I think people have a perfect right to be as nelly as they want, but to say this is the sum total of one of the largest minorities in the world is a crime! A family, a healthy kind of family, is important. It's a shame that we don't feel more a part of each other. When we walk down the street in the morning and can't even say "good morning" to each other! I saw a lot of different kinds of families when I played Santa Claus at the Emporium. That was one of the most pleasant things I ever did. I liked to wear a mask and forget myself. But I would not have let my child go see Santa because he's usually some poor old guy who's underemployed and probably hates children. He's scared of them. I actually saw myself as that child. Nobody in my family ever told me I was wonderful so I have this mad urge to tell children they're wonderful, that old Santa Claus loves them. Then the kids straighten up and relax. The places I've worked told me I never had to take a crying child, but just by going slow I got the kids to trust me.

But what I'm leading up to is how the family conditions a child. I looked at every single child's eyes—I didn't look at the family—and I could see the conditioning of the child. A Jewish child would come to me with a competitive religious thing, wanting to participate, but the parents would stand there and say, "We don't believe in you but . . . ." A black child would come and never cry, never be forced, and the mother would walk away holding the hand of the child. A Japanese child would almost never be frightened of Santa Claus because in their community they have a place for old age; they were familiar with the beard. The Arabs were interesting: the father would stand back and laugh and enjoy his child being frightened of Santa Claus. He wanted the child to be frightened of a symbol of Christianity. Once with a German child I said, "Well, do you *really* want that gun? You wouldn't want to kill your friend, would you?" And the parents went to the manager saying, "How dare you tell my child he shouldn't have a gun; I'm raising him to be a hunter." Another product of conditioning. And I think it was a Buddhist child who came up and asked, "Oh, are you God?" I said, "Well, I think I'm just a nice old man who likes you, loves you." The mother said, "No, in our culture we consider Santa Claus as another saint or a god." Yeah, Santa Claus is one of my secrets. And the funny part is I really enjoyed playing him.

At this point in my life I'm mainly concerned with being good to Alan Williams in a healthy, balanced way. I'm trying not to eat myself up with activities. I've worked hard for causes. I don't want that anymore. Now I enjoy going to the country. I have some friends who have a small farm and I love to work in their vegetable garden, go for hikes and swim nude in a little lake near where they live. I want these things but at the same time I know I'd never be satisfied doing *just* that. I'd have to come back to the city and lick a million stamps for the old people or gays or something. That's part of my life. For me that's creativity. I have no urge whatsoever to send my paintings to a museum.

I don't think "gay" and "homosexual" are adequate words. I think we are the "homophile community" that represents gays, parents of gays, our neighbors—a way of life. We have to stop constantly torturing ourselves by comparing ourselves with our brothers with four children and a house in the suburbs. The word "homophile," to me, speaks of family. Our close friends, I think, *are* our family. I'd like young people to accept a family concept that includes older gays. I also feel that we should have our fair share of public housing—there's no reason that two men or two women shouldn't be able to live together in a housing project. We should get our fair share of services and our fair share of the tax dollar.

I realize now that I'm a totally gay person, although I used to think that I was bisexual because I was able to function on both sides of the fence. But not now. I was just ignoring that little voice in my head that was saying, "You are homosexual." It was always, "You are bisexual." I couldn't relax enough to accept the truth. But I doubt this word "bisexual." Kiss a woman and kiss a man and right away you know which kiss has the electricity to it. It's just that simple if your head is cool.

Recently I ended up in jail again. I was part of a group of about three hundred people arrested while protesting the nuclear energy issue at Livermore Laboratory. I've also become an ombudsman for a center that provides counseling services to inform people of alternatives to nursing homes and institutions when they reach that stage of their lives where they need support. So I'm still involved.

I share this house with the same man I've lived with for twenty-seven years. He works for the government and he's aware that he could be fired if they knew he was a homophile. He's an excellent photographer. Four years ago he climbed the Himalayas, and the year before that he went to Machu Picchu. Every year he takes fabulous trips to the back country. I think we have a healthy relationship because we are so drastically different and yet give each other the freedom to pursue our interests. He's hung up on opera and, personally, I can leave most of it alone. But we have a marvelous honesty toward each other. I think it's a great luxury to have a strong, consistent love. But you must love yourself before you can offer yourself to others.

4

Bob Basker

Born in East Harlem and formally educated in Hebrew schools, Bob claims his real education came through the contacts he made in subway station bathrooms. "Classical music, ballet, opera, I learned about these because the older men there would take me home with them. I'm the only 'cultured' one of five boys in my family because of these associations." After exploring several European ports, Bob returned to the States, got married, then divorced. He first became active in the gay movement in Dade County, Florida, and established the first Mattachine Society in Chicago in 1965. He is sixty-five, a full-featured, compact man with a vibrant delivery.

I WAS BORN IN EAST HARLEM IN 1918, THE YOUNGEST OF FIVE sons. I was brought up in a primarily Italian neighborhood. My mother and father had emigrated from Poland, then part of Russia, so from the very beginning we spoke Yiddish at home. I was enrolled in Hebrew school when I was five although my mother lied and said I was six. Hebrew school was ridiculous because they just taught the Bible. By the time you got to the second page you couldn't remember what the words meant on the first page. I was also a cantor, conducting services in Hebrew on Friday nights when I was eleven or twelve at a place called the Harlem Hebrew Institute. My mother and father were extremely orthodox, not fanatical but pretty extreme. My father never worked on Saturday, never carried money on the Sabbath, and a lot of the family's activities revolved around the synagogue. Also, my father was a very well-educated man as far as Jewish tradition and Hebrew were concerned but not at all worldly so he was never able to make a living for the family. He always went out looking for jobs but was incompetent as far as keeping them. A loving father but a man always dominated by my mother, who had to take responsibility to see that things worked. She always put him down; it seemed to me she screamed at him a lot. He was a real timid soul, a Casper Milquetoast. I remember following him down the street, making sure he didn't do anything to self-destruct.

We were a welfare family. On Passover we'd line up for our Passover suits. My brothers Izzy and Morris and my father and I sold newspapers on the subway, and I remember once being put out on the street with our furniture. We were so poor that when we went into the subway we'd wait until the train was arriving and my mother would put her nickel in and shove me under the turnstile. We'd get in just before the door closed so the agent couldn't stop us. And the home relief people would come around and look in the icebox to see if there was food — because somehow or other if you were poor you weren't supposed to have food. During the Depression, even with as little as we had, when people would go from door to door asking for food, my mother would always share.

My mother was the neighborhood Florence Nightingale. When people were ill they would call on Pearl. She had sort of a medical bag. She would do cupping, rows of little glass suction cups to draw blood to the surface. It seemed to work. She was always helping others. Perhaps I get a little of that from her. If I can reach out and help someone, I do it. I do it many times as an unsung hero but I do like to get credit for it. Some people resent that and think it's a weakness on my part.

Throughout high school I didn't know how to wear clothes the way the other kids did. With our Eastern European background we just didn't have any taste in clothes. We were lacking in social graces too. One time I went to an afternoon tea at the high school and a student said, "Do you want cream or lemon?" I didn't know how to answer because I had never had cream offered with tea, so I said, "Both." She served both, put the cream in, then the lemon and the whole thing curdled. But I drank it.

When I was about four or five I took the neighbor girl somewhere and unbuttoned her clothes. I don't think I took them all off but I got behind her and bumped her because I heard you were supposed to fuck women. When we went back to her place her father realized that her clothes weren't buttoned and he bawled us both out.

My oldest brother, who was fifteen at the time, forced sex on me when I was five years old. He fucked me. I didn't want him to and he had what I considered a monstrous penis. Since he was ten years older than me I said, "It's too big, it won't work." His argument was, "Well, when you take a shit it's wider than that so there should be room." He was completely ignorant of how to do it and on the theory a stiff prick has no conscience, and using no lubrication, he fucked me, really hurt me. He raped me. At first I allowed him to, then I protested but it didn't do any good. Later, when my folks came home, I complained to them about what had happened. That was the last I heard about it. But recently, in talking with my brother Jack, I found out that that brother had been tied to the bedpost and whipped within an inch of his life as a result of my complaints. We never got along well all our lives because I resented what he had done. I had nightmares about it. Later in my life I went through some psychotherapy and one of the nightmares I told my doctor about involved this big husky Negro coming at me with a sword in his hand. When we analyzed it, it was my brother, the face of my brother, and I had camouflaged his penis as the sword. So I was apparently very disturbed by the incident.

Later on all of my brothers and I had sex with each other. Four brothers, and I had sex with each one of them. Aside from that one experience there was never any forced sex. We did everything, though. Sometimes singly, sometimes all together. I am the only one that ended up being gay. But all of us were involved. We fucked, we sucked, I don't think we rimmed. Rimming wasn't a big thing in the United States until after the war.

In grade school I was in a class taught by Miss Gugliamo. She was having an affair with one of the other teachers, Mr. Denmark. She used to meet him during school and she'd have a class monitor be in charge while she was gone. One time the monitor stuck his head in the door and said, "It's okay, fellas." All of a sudden about half a dozen guys in the classroom opened up the buttons on their pants, took their cocks out and started jerking off. In public! I was shocked, absolutely shocked. I was fascinated but shocked. I remember two of the boys very vividly. Over on my right, one seat ahead, was Mario, a beautiful Italian boy. I still remember his cock. It was thin, almost like a snake. There was nothing wrong with him, though; he was just a beautiful olive-skinned boy who was always friendly with me. And then there was Clay, a boy about a year or two older than I was, and he had this sort of reddish hair around his cock and a sort of very pale, reddish-pink penis. I turned to him and said, "How could you do such a thing? And you go to Hebrew school too!" I was very righteous. But Clay said to me, "Hey, why don't you try it?" and I said, "I would never try such a thing." Well, that night, at home in the bathroom with no lubrication, I remember looking down at my little penis with no hair around it, just the rolls of tummy. I don't know how long I jerked off, I guess until I had that feeling of climax. Of course, I was too young to have a real climax. I didn't have any semen show up for several years, until I was about thirteen and a half. I started masturbating from then on, though.

When I began selling newspapers at night, between the ages of eleven and fifteen, I was exposed to a lot of sex in the tearooms. They were open all night. On the subway, around one or two in the morning, you'd do a round trip. You'd have to get off at a station where you didn't have to pay to get back on again. I'd get off at 110th and Lexington and I'd go into the bathroom. You'd meet people having sex with each other, not always, but often all through the night. Sometimes you'd walk in and they were in the midst of having some kind of sex and they'd look up and say, "Oh, it's only a kid," and go right back to whatever they were doing. I was serviced regularly and once in a while I would do the servicing. I met some really nice people who were afraid of being involved with a thirteen, fourteen, fifteen-year-old kid but I did manage to go home with some of them. I was generally the aggressor. It was from spending time visiting them and going back and back and back that I got to learn something about classical music, ballet, and opera. I am the only "cultured" one in the family, whether it has to do with reading or the arts, and I think it's all because of my association with gay life, when these older men took me home with them. They occasionally took me to a concert or to the ballet or opera. I used to cruise the back of the Metropolitan Opera constantly or the back of the ballet in order to meet these men and go home with them. It was never a question of me taking money. It was just a matter of going to a nice man's home and being treated to some food and to an occasional shot of rye whiskey.

I couldn't wait to get into the bars when I turned eighteen. Before I came of drinking age I used to hang around the parks in New York City, especially the Goldman band concerts at the mall in Central Park. Those concerts were wonderful—a lot of cruising. Sometimes in the movies I'd be picked up by older men, even before I was old enough to have climaxes, and we'd go somewhere and I'd jerk them off. I was fascinated watching them have a climax before I could have one. I'd look at that stuff and wonder, "When is it gonna happen to me? When is it gonna happen to me?"

I graduated high school in June, 1936. I was active in the student movement in high school. My parents were not educated but they had been politically victimized in Russia so they were natural rebels. I was involved in the National Student League, the American Student League, and in the student peace strike for which I was suspended from high school. Later on, in college, I was suspended for the same thing.

After high school, whenever I went out looking for a job, I couldn't get one because my name was Solomon Basker. When I changed it to Robert it made a big difference because in New York City, in 1936, there was still a lot of anti-Semitism. I finally ended up working for the National Youth Administration as a carpenter, rebuilding ferries on Staten Island. Then the war broke out and I enlisted.

For several years, from '41 to '44, I was stationed in the New York area and then I went overseas to Plymouth, England. I really enjoyed it there. I loved the gay life in England even though the people there were very uptight as far as gay life went. After a while my unit moved to Antwerp, Belgium, where we were under the rocket bombs and V-2's. I was buried alive twice in buildings that collapsed on me, but I never got a scratch so I didn't earn a Purple Heart. Never could get a service-related disability either.

One time in Wales I had sex with some nineteen-year-old kid in the YMCA. It was really great. He shipped out on a merchant ship and the next day I found out I had gonorrhea. I felt terrible because I might have given it to him, but I had no way of getting in touch with him. At that time the way you got rid of it was to have your urethral canal irrigated and then take sulfa pills. It was a lot more complicated then than now.

We were never taught about VD in the proper way back then. We were taught to avoid sex because we'd get VD, and I'm sure many of us developed psychological problems about sex as a result.

A medical student in Paris once taught me, with his finger, where my prostrate was. He taught me where the saddle point was and if the pressure is applied right, it's quite sensuous, sexually stimulating. I learned how to finger someone's ass after that. Learned that in Europe when I was twenty-six.

I had sex with different people three to four times a week, starting at the age of fourteen. So if you figure out three times a week, fifty weeks a year, that's at least a hundred and fifty partners. Over a period of twenty years, three thousand partners. That creates a tremendous amount of sophisticated sex, if one is sensitive to the needs of others. In a way it gives us an advantage over straight people, our ability to have this multiplicity of experiences. For instance, one time in Paris with a young Frenchman, we had sex in a private box at the Paris Opera. Afterwards I couldn't remember what opera it was—we used to laugh about that. Another time we had sex in the garden of Versailles. I think straight people rarely have or take advantage of these types of situations.

During the years that I was with my army unit, of the four hundred men in it I must have had sex with a hundred of them. But I never developed a reputation of being gay. Sex was on an individual basis, in the shower room, in different ways. There were a few gay ones among them, but most of them were straight yet willing to play. How it worked was you'd get in the shower, around one o'clock in the morning after you'd been out on the town, taking a shower before you went to bed. My technique was to say to the guy next to me, "Hey, would you do me a favor and soap my back?" And the guy would soap my back and I'd say,

"Thanks" and then I'd say, "Here, let me do your back." I wouldn't ask, I'd just assume, and start to soap his back. If he didn't flinch, I'd start soaping his chest and if he didn't flinch then, I'd start soaping his stomach. Then I would do one leg, then the other, then start soaping his balls, then maybe his ass. Generally, by this time, they'd have a hard on. If they flinched anywhere along the line, they'd say, "Thanks," and move away. Only one time did someone come to me who must have heard something from someone else and approached me to have sex. Other than that I never had any problems.

During the time I was stationed in Antwerp I became acquainted with an older group of gay men. One night at dinner I was introduced to a man who was much older than I was. I was twenty-six and this man, Pierre Rhinehart, was fifty-one. He was a restaurant owner and he fascinated me. Apparently I fascinated him too, being an American soldier who spoke several different languages and was interested in his culture.

Pierre not only had an apartment in Antwerp, he had one in Brussels, too. I went to this apartment and I was overwhelmed. The apartment was full of flowers, the most beautiful flowers, gladiolas, everything, trays of liquors, and this beautiful music playing from Samson and Delilah, "My Heart at Thy Sweet Voice." It was very romantic and I was *really* overwhelmed. We had sex and I enjoyed it very much. We were very compatible . . . he loved to fuck and I loved being fucked. And the guy was just insatiable at fifty-one. Well, not insatiable but capable of a tremendous amount of potency. And he loved to suck. He'd suck me all over. I don't think I ever sucked him, I don't remember. And when the sex was over, he made all these sauces and exquisite food. He was a real French chef and he really spoiled me.

But the first time we were together one of the things he did was shove a bunch of bills into my pocket. I was highly indignant, I was insulted. I didn't go there for money, I went there because the man had the right vibrations as far as I was concerned. I had a wonderful time and I enjoyed the attention I was getting. He insisted I take the money, though. I thought it was very rude of him to do that. But I kept it. And I got even with him. I thought, "Well, fuck him. If he's got that kind of money, I'm going to insist that he pay me as much as the Army pays me." So I told him how much I wanted and there was no problem. I think it was like four hundred Belgian francs . . . a month! That was about forty-four francs to the dollar back then. I made all kinds of money. I didn't have any expenses. The Army took care of one part of my life and I lived at Pierre's apartment when I didn't have to stay over on base. I'd send money orders back to my brother in the States to hold for me. Once in a while I'd do money conversions. I never dealt the black market, but I didn't mind converting currency from one denomination to the other and picking up a couple of bucks. By the time I came back to this country I had saved about $10,000 so I could go into business for myself.

Pierre offered to send me to medical school, which is what I wanted to do. He offered to get me a car and everything, but I finally decided to take my discharge in Europe and become an American civilian working for the Army. I was discharged in November of '45 and stayed in Europe until the summer of '46. Then my job ended, they closed up the Signal Corps supply part of the Army. After that, I had a great time. I went to Nice and Monte Carlo on vacation and took Pierre along with me. I did a lot of traveling.

Once, on a train, on the way back from Czechoslovakia to Brussels, I met a British soldier. When we got back to Brussels at one o'clock in the morning, I decided to stay over. The soldier was taking the boat-train back to London and that wasn't leaving until five o'clock in the morning, so I suggested that he share a room with me and he agreed. He and I had a few hours of sex and he said goodbye in the morning. I continued on that morning to my final destination, Antwerp.

While I'd been traveling around Europe on business I'd visited Pierre occasionally. At this time I hadn't seen him for about a month, so I decided to visit him. As I was sleeping that night at his apartment I was awakened by a smashing slap across the face. It was Pierre. He was screaming at me, calling me "Dirty Jew." After all the anti-Semitism I'd been through with others, I could never accept it from my partner, my lover. What had happened was he'd gone through my pockets and found the hotel slip from the hotel in Brussels. He'd gone down to the hotel, paid the desk man some money, and asked about the American who'd been there the night before, asked who he had been with. Then he came back and pulled this shit on me.

Pierre was a very jealous person. When he attacked me with

the slap across the face, that might not have been so bad, but calling me a dirty Jew, that was the last straw. I told him I was leaving for good. He said, "No, you're not. I have taken down the names of all your customers and business contacts all over Europe and your cousins in Brussels, and if you leave me I will denounce you as a *tante*"—the French equivalent for homosexual. He was blackmailing me to stay with him against my will. I couldn't turn around and blackmail him because everybody who mattered knew he was gay. So I got stuck there for a couple of months until one day I got hold of his briefcase and, sure enough, there was the list. I tore it up and flushed it down the toilet. The next day I moved out and went to Paris.

In Paris I ran into a very charming youngster I knew from before, a kid about twenty-five, Jewish boy, red cheeks, a real doll. I told him the story about Pierre and since I had to go back to Antwerp on business, I asked him if he wanted to come back with me. I wanted to show him off to Pierre. I really wanted to get this old bastard, so I called Pierre and asked him if we could visit, told him I had a friend with me. Honest to goodness, in one month this man had gone through a Dorian Gray. He was walking with a cane, bent over, shrivelled up; in one month he had become an old man. I felt sorry for him. But I didn't do anything to assuage his pain because I thought he had gone too far. I decided maybe I had wronged him in a way, although he had first wronged me. I'm sure he's dead by now because he was in his fifties in 1949, so it's been over thirty years. But that took care of Pierre and that romance.

I returned to the United States right after this incident and went into sales management with Encyclopedia Britannica. By 1952 I was offered a job as district manager for Chicago. By this time I had a feeling I wanted to have children but I had never developed any friendships with women.

I started going to psychotherapy. I didn't feel guilty about being gay, but I wanted some confidence that I could have a straight relationship. I'd had maybe four or five sexual encounters with women in all these years and none of them was great. When I was fifteen my brother took me to a whorehouse in Brooklyn. The madam was a fat, buxom woman who my brother wanted. I was lucky because there was a fifteen-year-old girl; she must have been from the country because she was real sweet. But I couldn't get a hard-on with her. We just talked for a while and finally I got it up and just as I was gettin' it in, there was a knock at the door and the madam said, "Get dressed, the cops are downstairs." I got dressed and the girl and I had to go over the roof to the next tenement to get out of the place. That was really *coitus interruptus.* The only girls I was ever with in high school besides her were Jewish girls and they didn't play with you. You couldn't even kiss 'em. Another time at an American Legion Convention I picked up a whore, a black woman, and had sex with her in a car. I don't remember any other experiences with women until I was in the Army and this fellow had a date with a girl he didn't want to go out with, so he asked me to take her out and tell her he'd been transferred. I made a date with her. I put my hand on her vagina and, Jesus, it was like a handful of cheese, it was unclean. That was another very unpleasant experience. Another time in the Army I was in Czechoslovakia and I went to bed with a Viennese woman. We were under the covers and the covers shifted and this smell came out from under the covers and it was so bad that my erection just collapsed.

When I was living in Europe with Pierre I had a pleasant affair with a famous female opera star whom I had met through a French actor. I had sex with her regularly. She was married and I liked her husband. I felt very strongly about going to bed with someone who had a mate, it was sort of hallowed ground to me; but she insisted that her husband, who was Jewish and had been in a concentration camp, had had an accident and hadn't been able to have sex with her for years. I took her at her word and our sex together was very pleasant. She was the mother of two daughters and oh, how she could sing . . . fifty-two different roles in four different languages! When I got back to the United States she wrote me a letter saying I had made her pregnant and her husband had found out, so she had had to do away with it. I thought at the time, "It's a shame I made her pregnant," but there was a feeling of pride. I thought, "Gee, I can be a father!" That's when I decided on the psychotherapy to try to get where I would feel really comfortable with women.

Before I really got into the psychotherapy, I was in Chicago, driving down Sheridan Boulevard, and I saw three or four gay guys. One of them attracted the shit out of me so I pulled the car over and started following them. They went into an art auction gallery. Little by little I worked my way over to them and started getting friendly, letting them know I was gay. They invited me back to their home and one of them, Joey Connelly, and I became very close for several years. Eventually Joey moved in with me. But it became an impossible situation because he kept attempting suicide. I had to break away from him. I used Sally, a lady who worked at Britannica with me, a lady who was to become my mother-in-law, to break away from Joey. One day at work she saw I was dispirited, and I told her about the situation. She said, "Where is he now?" and I told her he was visiting some people in St. Louis. She said, "I'll help you move," and she called the movers because I was just immobile, didn't know what to do. So Sally found me a place, moved me into it, introduced me to my future wife, and gave me confidence that I could make it.

Sally was a very domineering woman, an Englishwoman. She had been married twice. First she married a Dutchman, divorced him, then married a German. She was denounced by a Catholic priest for listening to the BBC in Germany and she ended up in jail with her daughter, Greta, my ex-wife. Eventually they got put into a concentration camp. They were not Jewish but they were political prisoners. Greta ended up coming to the United States where she met an American and married him. After a number of years in Chicago she had a son by him, and they divorced soon afterwards.

I didn't like Greta when I first met her. She didn't appeal to me at all. The next time we met was when my friend Martin asked me to be his best man – when he was getting married to Sally and Greta was matron of honor. Greta and I had a big fight that day, but after a while we got to know each other and started dating. We courted for about a year and then I proposed to her. Her mother knew I was gay but she thought I was a great catch for her daughter. As a matter of fact at one point she even thought I might be a good catch for herself, but then she decided on Martin. My wife knew I was gay before I married her but she knew I wanted a straight, family relationship. I fell in love with Greta, proposed to her, and we had sex before we got married. I was very pleased that I was so sexually successful with her.

During the seven years I was married I had very few sexual relationships with men. I did have them but they were random, just pickups.

We had two children and I adopted her seven-year-old son George because I felt it would be very awkward for him to have another last name when we had two other children.

Around 1960 or 1961, Greta and I became involved in integrating Skokie. We were both involved in desegregation before we met and the interest and involvement didn't stop when we married, it intensified. We became the nominee purchasers to obtain a home for a black couple in Skokie, Bob and Mary Smythe. All hell broke loose. Our house was firebombed, we had unending obscene phone calls and death threats, and all our bank loans were cancelled. Day and night, police patrols had to guard the Smythes and us, and my boy got beat up at school. The pressure wasn't on the Smythes—people could understand why they wanted to buy a decent home and get out of the ghetto—but they couldn't understand traitors like Greta and me, who were helping them do it.

I had recently been invited back to my Britannica position. One of the men I interviewed and hired as a salesman was black. The day I hired him my immediate superior called me in and asked me to let him go. I felt this was unfair but couldn't convince my boss. I refused to fire the man so I was fired. This was not company policy even though my boss insisted it was.

I ended up with a coronary and spent six weeks in the hospital. Greta separated from me soon afterwards, after seven years of marriage, and divorced me. One day she just pulled out of the house while I wasn't there, took everything—books, records, and furniture. She said she was no longer in love with me, that she didn't want to live with a sick man. She remarried within two weeks, and within a few months left with her new husband and the three children for an eight-year stay in Cuba. She has since remarried several times and divorced her fifth husband last year. She now lives in San Francisco and today we're pretty good friends.

After my divorce and my family's departure, which left me thoroughly shattered, I started getting involved in gay matters. I was instrumental in establishing the first Mattachine Society in Chicago in 1965. We called it Mattachine Midwest. I was founding president and delivered the founding speech which was reproduced in *Echo*, the East Coast gay magazine. I used the name Robert Sloane, my first and middle names. Then I was rehired at my old job.

At the end of the year, Britannica offered me a management position in the city of my choice. I chose Miami, hoping that the Cuban blockade would be lifted and I would be able to fly over for weekend visits with my children. I visited Cuba by way of a freighter via Montreal and St. Johns, Nova Scotia, a three-thousand-mile trip one-way from Miami. I stayed nine months and made my living by teaching English as a second language. I became reacquainted with my children and made arrangements with Greta for them to live with me during their teens. Being in Cuba for almost a year was just wonderful under the government of Castro, except for the official attitude on gay matters there.

During the sugar harvest that year in Cuba, I heard about these two teachers who were fired because they were lesbians. What happened was they were supervising a bunch of students at a country camp and some students had seen them kiss each other on the cheek. The students started telling everyone they were homosexuals and the word spread fast. In the middle of the night a bureaucrat came down from Havana and fired the two teachers on the spot without any due process. After much discussion with my colleagues, I went to our trade union and persuaded them to defend these women. The battle was successful and the teachers were rehired. After all the trouble I stirred up bringing this to a conclusion, I felt my ass might be in danger if I stayed, so I left Cuba and returned to Miami.

When my children got a little older, they came to live with me in Florida. They each became involved with the migrant farm-workers' strike, lettuce boycotts, all kinds of non-violent movements. Once when my son Don was arrested and I went to bail him out, he said some of the kids had said, "When my father finds out I've been arrested he'll be mad at me." And Don said to them, "When my father finds out I've been arrested he'll be *proud* of me." And I was.

I was active in the gay movement in Miami as long as I lived there. I helped to start the Gay Activist Alliance in 1971. At that time there were laws on the books against cross-dressing, laws so ridiculous they would arrest a guy for wearing an earring. We tried to negotiate with the police department but they ignored us, so we decided to have a demonstration, no, more like a parade. We applied for a parade license and were refused, so we had it without a license. The police had told us if we dressed in real drag, wore clothing that was "unbecoming to the sex," they would throw us in jail—so we wore ridiculous circus clothing and carried signs. We were still arrested. We got an attorney from the ACLU and took the police department to court for refusing us a parade permit. After a rather brief trial, the judge declared the cross-dressing law unconstitutional.

Besides being involved in the Gay Alliance, I was trying to make a living selling real estate over the phone, all over the country. Eventually I became a broker and was able to locate a building for and help establish a youth hall for runaway kids through the Metropolitan Community Church. But I continued to be involved in Florida's gay politics, or lack thereof. I saw what appeared to be successful efforts in New York, San Francisco, and Los Angeles for gay presence to be felt at the polls, so I convened representatives from eleven gay groups in July of 1976. We constituted ourselves as the Dade County Coalition for the Humanistic Rights of Gays. I declined the chair but was prevailed upon to stay as Convenor, and eventually gained the title of Coordinator. At this time I was getting deeply into debt since all this politicking had become full-time with no pay. Eventually they started to pay me $100 a week, then changed it to $300 a week when they changed my title to Executive Director.

Our coalition screened candidates, sent out questionnaires, made endorsements, and passed out ninety thousand endorsement leaflets at bars and baths. When the smoke had cleared, seventy-five percent of our endorsed candidates had won. At the same time we lobbied before the Dade Fair Housing and Employment Appeals Board, the mayor, and the county commissioners to amend the discrimination ordinance to add the words "affectional and sexual preference" to the existing categories that couldn't be discriminated against. The Dade Commission voted unanimously in favor on the first reading, but six weeks later, on the second reading, there was a furor. Anita Bryant was part of that furor, along with Phyllis Schafly. A lot of right-wing people came into town with their Bibles and filled the hearing room before eight o'clock in the morning. I tried to hold the line, and we lost several votes, but we still won, five to three. That's when Anita Bryant held the press conference and started the movement she called "Save Our Children." Eventually she gained so much support that the anti-discrimination law was repealed. I felt a little discouraged with it all, having come so far and then having it all lost. I decided to move to San Francisco.

While I was driving across the country, I read in a New Orleans gay paper that on Sunday, June 25, there was to be a giant rally in Houston at the Astrodome Annex, called Town Meeting I. It seemed like a good idea so I drove to Houston to attend, and brought some straight Houston friends along with me. As I sat there among four thousand enthusiastic gay activists and their friends, I heard repeatedly that their unity would not have been possible had it not been for the struggle in Dade County. You can imagine how I felt. I felt that these were my children and that what I had started in Dade County had resulted, ultimately, in this outpouring of four thousand Houston brothers and sisters.

When I got to San Francisco I figured I was not going to work in the gay movement for a while. The last few years of heavy involvement had put me very deeply in debt. I finally decided I should go to work for Britannica again. It was something I knew, so that's what I did. But then I became involved in the Alice B. Toklas, Harvey Milk and Stonewall Gay Democratic clubs. Each of them take me away from work, mostly in the evening, which always means when I attend the meetings I may be giving up *the* sale of the week. But I always need to make a contribution. I've made a big contribution to San Francisco and I'm very satisfied.

I've noticed that young gay people often worry about what's going to happen to them when they get older as far as sex is concerned, especially if they like younger people as I do. They are taught that they're not supposed to be sexually interested in people who are older. I tell them, "I don't have the same needs that I had before, but I still have needs two or three times a week, if I'm well." And I find that I can attract the young people I like without having to feel lonesome or put down. And I'm not talking about financing them. I don't feel that's a good relationship.

Since my wife, I haven't allowed myself to get into any really heavy commitments. I thought I would find a lover when I came to San Francisco, but I'm not free in the evenings to meet people. Sure, I'd like to find a lover but it isn't easy. I have to find somebody who's willing to put up with a lot of independence. I am now going to school to become a therapist and have even less time for a relationship than before. Maybe later.

5

Will Whiting

Born in 1926, Will moved to Phoenix, Arizona, from California two years ago with his lover who is suffering from cancer, the seriousness of which was not known at the time of this interview. They live in a rustic ranch-style home. Will projects a fatherly image accented by a voice that is opinionated yet sympathetic.

I WAS BORN IN 1926 INTO A FAMILY OF SEVEN. MY PARENTS divorced when I was seven years old. It was the Depression, and my mother supported us kids on Relief and WPA. Soon as we were old enough we had to start cutting out for ourselves, whatever way we could. This was in the Midwest, in Indiana. By the time I was eleven I was working summers in the park. I was tall and loud, so I was on the road that fall in a traveling carnival with a local gentleman. He *was* a gentleman, a college graduate from Rochester, New York, who wound up doing carnies for survival. He was happy in those years, though, and so was I. I had the usual sexual encounters of most youngsters. In the carnivals if you were fifteen and still a virgin, they'd buy you a black girl. So they bought me a black girl for my fifteenth birthday. And that was my first sex other than masturbating. I think I had my first homosexual experience when I was about fifteen, too, and that was with a Catholic priest. Then after that I had a couple of experiences with some guy who ran a gas station.

I worked the carnivals during the summer season and the good weather, up to about Thanksgiving—since the carnivals followed the sun and we worked until the weather came up against us. But I never became a carny because that gentleman made us kids come back and go to school. In fact, he saw to it that I studied while I was on the road.

During the school year, I did collections for a branch of the syndicate. They ran northern Illinois and northern Indiana. We collected from all the cigar stores where they had gambling in the back room, and brought the money back to headquarters. When I got older, I realized that the reason they hired us punks is that they thought we were just young enough and dumb enough so that if anyone refused to pay we'd shoot them—because we all carried guns. To this day I have a .38. I realized how stupid it was but how smart it was on their part, hiring fifteen and sixteen-year-olds. We drove a big black car, very gangster. But, anyhow, I grew up on the carnivals and then the war came along.

When I turned eighteen I enlisted. The service did a lot for me. I had a girlfriend I wrote to every day. I had no homosexual friends in the service at all, none. Which astounds me today because, boy, it was there. But I was *macho* and straight, never thought of myself as being gay though I had my cock sucked a few times, no big thing. That's all it was and it was fun. I never gave it any thought until after I got shot up pretty bad and lay in the hospital. I got to thinking, remembering when I was a youngster and fantasized about one of the kids on the basketball team. How I wished he would get sick so I could take care of him! That's gay thinking, right? I started to put it all together. I could never forget him. He was a beautiful boy, blond, and I had a thing for blonds. Anyway, after I got wounded I moved back to Indiana in the middle of winter and there were blizzards all the time and I thought "To hell with it, no way am I going to live in this part of the country."

I had a cousin, Frank, in Indiana—he and I had played around as children—and we got to discussing homosexuality. He was in school and he told me he had been playing up to a queer professor to get good grades. He'd tease him along. By the way, Frank committed suicide when he was forty-one and I'm sure it was because he was gay. I defended the professor, and told Frank I thought what he was doing was wrong. Either put out or shut up. Kind of made a joke of it. Anyway, I left Indiana and decided to come to the West Coast. I broke up with my girlfriend when I came back from the service and found four or five pictures of a classmate of mine in her wallet. So I went to California to go to school and ended up earning a living by working summers in carnivals.

I worked in Balboa Bay, in a "fun zone," because that's all I knew. I also worked nights at a little gambling joint in the wintertime while going to college in Santa Ana. I studied journalism and was the head of the press club. I was in a fraternity called the "Bachelors." One of my fraternity brothers was a boy called Lindell Ryder who lived on the Balboa peninsula. He was from a very wealthy family. I had a stinkin' little room at the time on the peninsula, and no car. So on some Friday nights I would ride back and forth with Lin and one night coming home he said, "What would you do if I propositioned you?" Now I'm six-two and Lin was five-nine. I said "I don't know, what do you mean exactly?" He said, "If I wanted to suck your cock?" He was scared to death, petrified. He'd become a good friend of mine by this point, a lonely little boy. His mother was divorced, remarried. Typical wealthy family. The mother never kissed her children. Anyway, I ended up spending the night with Lin talking till five o'clock in the morning and never laid a hand on him. This started a thing that was to go on for several years. Lin would call me up and say, "Would you like your back scratched?" That was a clue and we would take a drive somewhere. He would give me a blow job. This was a totally one-sided thing. I was trade, totally trade. No necking or nothin'. And he was satisfied. This went on until I got married.

Why did I get married? I was fucking around with girls primarily, never into the gay thing except for Lin once in a while and that was just doing a favor for a friend. He was like my little brother; being a veteran I was three or four years older than the majority of my classmates. I was running around with a couple of guys who also lived on the peninsula and went to school. One of them, Howard Penny, was talking about this girl he met over at the park in Long Beach. She was foxy and he was in love. He was a very sensitive kid and I was teasing him about it. I mean I was the carny *macho* stud. I was trying to protect him because I knew carnies and she was working for a carnival doing sketches. I said, "Howard, watch this. I can pick her up just like that, I'll betcha." I went over there and saw that she was cute and moved in on her. Well, since I was six-two and she was five-one, that was an impression in itself. I made out like a bandit. I slept with her that night and was with her for about six weeks. I'm very romantic, so one night I said, "How much money do you owe?" She only had a few miscellaneous bills, so I said, "Let's get married." So we got married just like that. It turned out that she had been married before and had surrendered custody of her son to the paternal grandparents. But she was all emotional over it and we had to do something about getting that boy back. I spent one summer in Oklahoma fighting a custody case. But the grandparents were beautiful people and I just couldn't win. The boy was only fifteen months old but a very happy child.

Not too long after that I got a job on the GI Bill where you both work and go to school. I was working for a newspaper and had been sent away on a weekend assignment to Pasadena. Well, it was Sunday and the guy felt sorry for me and told me to go home because I was "newly married," though I had been married for a year and a half. When I got home I found my wife in bed with another guy, so I immediately got a divorce. During all this time I had a lot of after-war problems: a bad skin problem, a bad leg, and gangrene. I was going in and out of hospitals three or more times a week. I was a mess.

After the divorce I started going out to gay bars alone. The first guy I ended up in bed with was a friend of my cousin's, the younger brother of the cousin who later committed suicide. I started going to bars in Long Beach on my own. I liked getting my cock sucked. I was still what they called "gay trade." Recently divorced, I was the hottest thing in town. Then I got into fucking which I like very much. You do that when you want to replace a wife. I got involved with the nelliest kid on feet. Those were *some* years. By this time, Lin's parents, who had a beautiful home and guest cottage, had me staying in their guest house. I was eating out every night at a steak house, when one of the waiters got a crush on me. He was another curly-haired blond, and had arranged that I sit in his station each time I came in. The piano player would play "Someone to Watch Over Me" every time I walked in the door. The waiter finally got up the nerve to proposition me. He asked me to go horseback riding. I said, "OK, but I can't ride." He took me to the stables at the home of a world-famous jockey. This at one-thirty in the morning. He hadn't told me that my horse was trained. He started giving it commands, and the horse would sit down, lie down, try to roll over on me, all kinds of good things. I was furious though he thought it was funny. We didn't make it for about a week; then we started to date every night and I moved in with him. He lived at home with his parents and our bedroom was just down the hall from theirs.

That was the first mistake I made, to move in with him. How we got away with it, I'll never know. We were fucking every night and all that goes with it. I don't know why they couldn't hear. Anyway I just couldn't take it. It wasn't right. I called my mother and told her to wire me from home that she was ill and needed me. She did. So I got on the plane and headed home and one of his friends, who was also on the plane, blew me. Oh God, under a coffee table, are you ready for that? I stayed in Chicago for the winter and lived with a kid who was a banker. I wound up in a hospital there and they sent me back to California.

I got involved in another bad situation with another very nelly fellow and Lin said to me, "C'mon, we're going to Hawaii." I told him I couldn't afford it. He said, "How much money do you have?" I told him I had about $400. He said "Well, that's enough. Just keep your $400 to help you get started and I'll pay for everything else." I had to get out of the scene I was in, so I said, "Why not?" We left in '51.

When I got on that boat, I figured no one knew me in Hawaii and this was my opportunity. I would have the chance to be myself. Fortunately, I've always had as many straight friends as I had gay friends. I could mix elements without any trouble. If it came up I always said, "I am gay, I've been married and had that, and thank you, I prefer what I'm doing now." And that was the end of it. Hawaii was liberal about most things, very little heat over there. But for a short time it got so bad they passed an ordinance saying that the drag queens had to wear a sign that said, "I'm a boy." What they were doing was hustling the soldiers. Of course, the soldiers were sometimes upset when they got into bed and found a dick between their legs. But Hawaii was very good for me. I met one of my lovers there, Steve.

Steve and I lived together just a year and a half before we came back to the mainland. Part of the reason we came back was that he got polio, I had met him just before his discharge from the

Navy and he didn't get polio until after he came to live with me. If he hadn't gotten it I don't know if we'd still be together or not. I'd have to carry him and everything else. They tried as hard as they could to help him in Hawaii, but finally they sent him to a paraplegic center in Akron, Ohio, not too far from his hometown of Indianapolis. I went out and bought a house that would accommodate a wheelchair, which isn't easy in Hawaii with all the hills. Try it sometime. But then Steve couldn't decide if he wanted to come back. He wrote that he was afraid; he didn't know whether I felt obligated to him and pitied him, or if I really loved him enough. He decided he ought to stay near the center because at the time he was told he wouldn't live more than ten years. It's been more than twenty and he's still alive.

The first job I had in Hawaii was working for a small retail store. They had a party right after I started and at the party I saw a very tall good-looking fellow looking at me. I thought, "I wish I knew him" – you know how you always feel about these good-looking guys. His wife came over and asked who I was. I told her I was new in Waikiki and she said, "Well, my husband and I decided that you were somebody we'd like to know." Well, Perry and I started talking and I found out immediately that he was gay. We found out we both had the same days off and he said, "C'mon out and help me scrape the windows, we just rented a new place and we're trying to get it ready." So every Monday for years, for fifteen years, even after I had a lover, that went on. I was his, well, we had a thing going. He's a big wheel over there now and has a daughter. We loved each other and still do, and his wife doesn't know to this day. We're just old and dear friends and I see him whenever I'm over there.

I didn't tell you but I had gone into the interior design field. The last thing I did was a seven-million-dollar building in Waikiki. But there was a lawsuit over it and I knew I couldn't stay there during litigation so I came back to L.A. to start all over again. That's when I met Tim. I was decorating at a place in the Valley. He was married to a lady at the time. He had two jobs. It was summertime, so he wasn't teaching regular school, instead he was teaching children to swim, in a day care center, and working nights at a newsstand. He had twenty minutes between jobs and on his breaks used to stop in at a little bar. I happened to be there one afternoon; I was pretty loaded and I cruised him. He had known he was gay ever since he was a teenager but he hadn't done anything about it, just fantasizing, buying muscle magazines and that kind of bullshit. The week I met him he had just started, one night a week, trying different affairs, seeing if he could make it work. But I started dating him and that was that. He drove a little Mazda. He's six-five so you'd have to see him to appreciate this, but his knees were on his chin driving this little thing.

We've been together ten years last August and we've paid alimony for four years. This is our sixth house. Tim was teaching most of this time and I was decorating. Then I came very close to a nervous breakdown and we decided I'd better quit for a while. So I didn't work for a year and a half. Then Tim got fed up with the politics involved in California teaching. He couldn't just teach, he was too busy doing programs, testing . . . and Tim's a *teacher*, so last year he decided he wasn't going to renew. He hadn't made any decision on what he was going to do, and I came to Phoenix on vacation. The bottom line is that we both liked it here so we relocated. I've been pursuing real estate and have begun work as an agent. I told Tim at the time, "We will follow your career because I can work anywhere. You're younger, whatever you want to do is fine because I'm going to retire as soon as I can. I was trained as a journalist and I will want to pursue my photography and do the things I want to do, okay?" We owned all this furniture plus we left a lot behind. I have a whole cabinet shop back there which I'm going to sell in the next couple of weeks. Tim got our house sold and did the whole move himself, about four trips in U-hauls.

KV: I'd like to put your work history in some chronological order, if possible.

Well, don't do that. I'll tell you why. I've had thirty-nine jobs in my life. Mostly professionally with interior designing and contracting, working with wood. I ran a trading stamp company for four years but I've always been in design as a sideline. I also majored in design at Woodbury College, after journalism; I knew I wasn't going to make it as a journalist because after I got shot up I had an awful lot of nerve problems and skin problems. Fortunately, I've outgrown it. But I used to have headaches so bad I couldn't see for three or four days and I was on medication for twenty-five years. About five years ago I was supposed to be taking three librium and two phenobarbital a day. I told Tim, "No more, I'm quitting all medication, I'm sick of it. If you can handle it, I can. I know I'm going to be a lot more irritable for a while than I should be." But he handled it. He's a beautiful guy. You know, you just can't take that many drugs, I don't care if it's prescribed or not, it makes you feel like a zombie. And I said, "Bullshit, I've got too good a mind, I don't like being fogged." So he agreed and I've not taken a pill since. I won't even take an aspirin. I've gotten over the skin problems. They told me as I mellowed and got older that it would pass. There's a lot of little things I'd like to do before I pass on. I'd also like to get into some more counseling—I do a bit of it now for the MCC (Metropolitan Community Church). There's a big need for it. You can be happy and gay; I've never been unhappy and gay. I can say that honestly. Even when my affairs were breaking up, I wasn't unhappy. It was the natural course of events. Most of the youngsters, the young men I've gotten involved with, outgrow me. They want me at the beginning for my maturity and what I represent and so forth and that's great. But then they grow and expand. They look around and realize that they can do for themselves, and they do. That's marvelous, that's why I have no regrets. They grow up. Then they do the same thing with their lovers that I've done with them.

I'm thinking of my ex, Paul. Paul was a milktoast who wouldn't say "shit" if he had a mouthful. She sat at a bar like this (huddled up) when I married him, right? Very possessive. Had eyes in the back of his head because I had a past. I knew everybody and she was terribly jealous. I'm domineering, very outgoing. He left me about five times. Usually when he left he'd call and say, "I'll see ya tomorrow." I moved him twice to L.A., I helped him set up his apartment and everything else. One time he set up an apartment and spent two days there though he paid one month's rent. But anyhow, that's Paul. I used to tease him about being a bad carbon copy of me. Because when he married this kid Jack, Jack was a little milktoast. He had very little worldly knowledge—he was only twenty years old. I used to laugh because then Paul was being dominant and bossy. Now Jack has matured and they're both in a good relationship. Paul outgrew me and then did the same number on Jack. But as you get older, as you grow together, you can make it work.

Tim has been tempted to leave me a couple of times. I don't blame him. But we talked it out. We have good communication and we'll probably be together unless something unforeseen happens. But this is what happens when you're older than your partner. Tim is in his early forties and I'm in my late fifties. We're both grown, adult, mature men. But when he was younger and new on the gay scene and I was in my forties and had been at it awhile, there was a big span.

When you're young—and I lived a straight life until I was twenty-eight—you look around and see gay life as a youth cult. You say, "What the hell happens to a queen who's over thirty or forty or fifty?" But when you're in it, you're not even aware of it. I don't feel left out. Of course, I was never young and gay. I missed that, thank God! I spent part of the last twenty years counseling a lot of young kids and I've never had an affair with anybody even close to my own age. Tim is seventeen years my junior. I've had four lovers and we're all still very great friends. In fact, on the first of next month we're going to a wedding anniversary and we'll stay with my ex and his friend who have been together for the same time as Tim and I have. I think being older when you come out is beneficial because you are more mature.

Another thing that makes Tim and me a little different is that we lead a Christian life. My relationships have always been Christian as well as gay. In our church, "We are Christians first and gay second." Because if you're gay first, forget it. I've always contended that if you have loved someone enough to live with them, you certainly think enough of them to keep them as a friend. Even my ex-wife and I are friends. Of course, I'm such a conceited ass that it would be an insult to myself to think, "Well, I don't want anything to do with them." I must have had some judgement when I chose them!

But being older and gay has its drawbacks. If you've got a relationship going, you've got to work at it. I do. Not only do I love my man dearly but I do it also for defense. I don't want to be alone at my age. If I were attracted to someone my age it would be different, but I've always thought young. I think men my age are stodgy, frankly, so I've never been with anybody even close to my age. Tim was married when I met him and I think that gave both of us, having been married, a better chance than most. By the way, I detest people saying "gay by choice," because none of us are. There's a commitment to your lifestyle in coming out, if you like, but that's different. I think that if you are in a mature relationship you are freer to come out.

KV: How do you feel about people going out in relationships?

That's a tough one. In our church, we have a "holy union." We don't call it a wedding because it isn't. It's a public commitment to each other. Our pastor set it up so you have to go to lessons six times. Tim and I are going now after ten years of marriage. We have an open relationship, though very little is done outside of it. Tim likes to go out to dance and play pool and he likes a little stray sex once in a while. I do too, but I don't look for it. Sex has never been very important to me in the first place. Which has been unfortunate for some of my young lovers. I think one reason is that I've had gangrene, so my sex drive is very low. I'm one of the few photographers who can take nudes all day and never get turned on. I think Tim may be ready for monogamy. He had syphillis from a "straight" trick and that didn't help at all. It was the only time he's done anything in a year and he got burned. We have no secrets. But I never need to know names or anything. When he comes in, I say, "Tim, how did you make out?" He says "Nah," and that's all. But there is a morality involved. This is a difficult point, but I will try to make it.

Gay love is Christian, okay? And lust is not. So it's morally difficult not to be monogamous but I see that you could have sex outside the relationship without lust. But usually it's wham, bam, thank you ma'am, which we feel is wrong.

KV: Do you mean then that it has to be with someone you care very much for outside of the relationship?

Well, not love. I don't know how you draw the line. If we make a commitment to each other, we're going to take it seriously. But if we decide not, no harm done.

KV: What would you do if your relationship ended for some reason?

I'd find another partner. I'm not good alone. I don't think anyone is. I would get into another relationship as soon as possible but I would make sure it's real; I don't believe in jumping. In day-to-day living none of us are really alone, but I won't get into the theology of that. So I'm never desperate. I may wind up alone if Tim's cancer becomes worse than it is. I may lose him. But you have to accept those things. I like companionship—someone around to bounce ideas off, to talk to, someone to share with.

Another thing about being a little older is the joy of being with a younger man—I guess it's a lot like being a schoolteacher. I've been all over the world and have always been a snob. I eat at the best restaurants, go where I want to go and so forth. It's such a pleasure to introduce younger men to cultural and social things. And it's easy to please them. Like Tim. He had been raised in Kansas, part of a large family, had never eaten an avocado—dumb little things. He didn't have any idea what a seven-course dinner was. I remember the first time I took him out for lobster and steak. Oh my God! You'd thought I had taken the kid to Maxine's.

I do my counseling at home, though I get my referrals through the church. The biggest problem with so many gays is the guilt trip they go through because of the culture they're in and organized religion in this country. But the scripture does not down gays. Christ never mentioned homosexuality. The only reason there were laws against homosexuality in the Old Testament was that the Jews had to populate in order to survive. To this day, an orthodox man has to have a wife so some of them are married and yet gay. Armies used to rape each other for the total humiliation of it. That's the kind of homosexuality the Bible talks about. The populace of Sodom wanted to rape the two guys who were staying with Lot to humiliate them, not for gay sex. But people take it out of context and say, "Whoa, that's an abomination to God." Bullshit! Gay love is real. And religion is love. That's what God is all about.

We built our new church here from the ground up. It's ninety-five percent gay. About ten of us built it and most everything was done three times. Nothing passed inspection except the electrical. We must have two miles of unnecessary electrical. The pastor's lover worked full time. We had work crews morning and evening. Tim, before he went in the hospital in July, was damn near out there every day.

We gays who are older, and have been through it, and have seen the evolution as far as it's gone, owe it to pass it on to the younger ones. Young gays would be much happier if they accepted their sexuality and got past the guilt trip. Instead of trying to be as gay as they can, they should try to be as human as they can. They get it all out of perspective. Their whole lives revolve around partying and the next foxy guy. Nobody needs that much sex. They talk it but they don't get it. They don't even pursue it that much. I don't care how horny you are, nobody could use as much as they pretend to pursue. They think they are proving themselves, but they are proving a negative, not a positive. And that's tragic. When somebody goes to spend the night at the baths to see if they can have 12 orgasms, it's tragic. So what have they accomplished? I don't care if you're nineteen or sixty, the only thing you've got going for you is dignity, personal dignity. When I see a youngster get led into the bathroom by somebody, if I've got a chance to catch him when he comes out, baby, I'll talk to him. He's going to feel like shit when I get done with him. Because he didn't need to do that. Everybody who saw him go in there knew why he went in. That's not necessary. What do you think of yourself? Are you a piece of flesh? Dangle your meat at anybody who wants it? Bullshit! And these kids, once they realize it, they stop it. But at the time it's fun. It's not fun. It's undignified.

I've been gay longer than it's been popular. I was gay when you had to wear red socks to be identified as gay. I walked into a bar in Chicago and had the place go absolutely dead on me because I wasn't dressed for that city. They thought I was vice. The piano player, Joy, recognized me from Hawaii and California and began playing "California Here I Come." I went to talk to her and that cleared the air. But I didn't make out that night even though I was a new face in town. Talk about harassment! They backed the paddy wagon up to the back door of one of those bars and emptied everyone right into the wagon. In those days we used to get a lot of heat and there was no such thing as entrapment. They'd just come in and bust everyone there. And get away with it! This town gets me mad too. You have to go in the back doors of the bars and there are no marquees out front.

I was over at MCC talking to the pastor the other day when a man walked in, maybe fifty years old, married, with two kids. His wife knows he's been gay in the past but doesn't think anything is going on now. He's still gay. He's doing the pickup thing, says he hates himself and is very close to suicide. He doesn't think he's got any place to go to. But he has. Instead, he's out there at the bookstores and tearooms. I don't see any point in dirty bookstores, I really don't. I think anyone who cruises and makes out in a tearoom should get busted. I think anybody who picks up a kid in the park ought to get busted. Now, maybe you think I'm wrong, but I do think this. I'm as morally gay as I suppose a straight is morally straight. But there is a tragedy in being old and gay if you have not declared yourself because the older you get, the more desperate you can become.

KV: Don't you think part of the problem is that there are so few places for gays to meet other than bars?

Not necessarily; I think a lot of it is the added element of danger.

KV: But where did that element come from? Can't that come from incorporating society's attitudes toward yourself that say you're wrong? Therefore you put yourself in that added element of danger?

Sure we incorporate those attitudes, but an intelligent human being should rise above that. It's self-punishment. The guy who goes looking for trade and rough trade is looking consciously or unconsciously to be humiliated. They humiliate themselves. They do a service. That's wrong, man. I don't service anybody. I'll join them! I've been to bed with straight men. Straight! Anybody who gets in bed with me is not straight. They may not be gay but they are entering into a gay encounter. That's the responsibility we older gays have. To be examples and I don't mean to be a lush or a dirty old man in a bar. That's a bad example and it's visible on the bar scene. They're the ones who haven't adjusted to their own sexuality. If a person *has to* hang out in a bar there's something wrong. If he's an alcoholic, he's got a big problem. If he's out there on the sex scene, he's a fool.

KV: What would you suggest for an older man whose lover has died, is looking to meet someone, and really didn't have that many gay friends?

That's a mistake isn't it? They should have more friends, be active in a church, be active in their business, etc. Real estate is the first field of work I've ever been in where being gay might make a difference. I have sold two properties so far to gays. My boss has asked me if they were gay. I said "I think they probably are. So what?" He said, "So nothing." See, I don't believe in deception because I think you have to live with yourself. If they ask me, I'll tell them so. I'm not hiding anything, it's just never come up that way.

We had a meeting one morning and had what we call a "want and need" session where we go around the table trying to match sellers with buyers. One of the guys had a new listing from some poor queen and started chuckling. Some gay guy had broken up with his lover and the house had been torn up in a fight. The guy was so despondent he was about to commit suicide. They started chuckling and the manager started chuckling along with them. I sat there and fumed and then gave myself hell when I got home. The next morning I went in before prayer to see the manager — it's a very religious-oriented business, we open every meeting with a prayer. I told him, "You know, I'm troubled. I'm going to tell you up front. I denied myself yesterday. You pulled a blunder I don't want to see again." He looked at me and said, "What are you talking about?" I said, "I don't care how many assholes we've got in the office, *you* are the leader. You can't open a meeting with a prayer and then laugh at a fallen brother. I don't care whether he is gay or what his problem is. Now there's a guy desperate enough to want to commit suicide and you people think that's funny. That is kind of tragic, isn't it?" He backed off and in the next meeting he made a public apology. He was wrong and he knew it. You can make your stand without affronting people. If they are homophobic, that is their privilege. If I am gay, that is my privilege. I don't demand their acceptance of my gayness but their acceptance of me. I don't demand it but I want it. If my being gay denies it, that is their problem. I haven't confronted it directly because it hasn't come up yet. They should have put it together by now because I do everything with Tim. Monday night I won a steak dinner for two, on the house. I didn't know it at the time but it is with the boss's wife. Well, you know who I'm taking. I took him to the Halloween party as well. If they don't like it, that is their problem. This may have nothing to do precisely with being an older gay except that you have to have the maturity to be gay.

Everything goes back to my fundamental philosophy. Whatever you believe, you have to believe in a supreme being. Everybody has to believe in that. I don't care what it is. I think this force is better for us being part of it. I don't believe that I have to write the all-American classic novel or anything else but I think this world has to be a better place for my having spent a little bit of time here. My time is like that (snaps finger) in the essence of time. But I've always felt that my responsibility for this life that I've been given is that the use of the force, soul, spirit, intelligence, whatever you want to call it, has to be more than it was when I took it, because I'm going to die and it's not. I am a product *of*, you are a product *of*, and whoever follows me is a product *of* it. We are the result of centuries of mankind. It's the same with being gay. We gays who have been through it and have seen the evolution, as far as it's gone, owe it to pass it on to those we talk with. If I can save one youngster some of the missteps that I made, then the place is a better place for my having been here. I mean, it's that simple. If I can draw one smile, the world is a better place for my having been through it. I believe that and I practice it.

6

Richard Von Berg

At sixty-eight years old, Richard has just recovered from his second serious motorcycle accident. Richard's self-proclaimed butch image contrasts with his love for chamber music and his gentle philosophy of "Hurt no one if you can possibly avoid it." He is a tall, rugged-looking man who lives alone in a simple apartment in Phoenix, Arizona.

I WAS BORN AND RAISED IN SYRACUSE, NEW YORK, IN A VERY conservative Christian family. There were four boys and a girl. This was 1915. By the time I was eighteen I had my first affair. I was completely, absolutely innocent, had no idea what was going to happen. A young, rich philosophy student came to have private study with a professor at Syracuse University whom I vaguely knew. The young philosophy student seduced me. His family came to pick me up to take me to a concert one night. The next night he was knocking on my door. We went up to a cemetery and on a flat gravestone he introduced me to the whole sexual world. It came as an absolute surprise. I had *no idea* what was going to happen. The gravestones were of two young lovers who had had a boating accident on the St. Lawrence River and were buried together. It was beautiful and very romantic. But I continued to see girls and double date and that sort of thing. I never had another sexual experience until I was thirty years old.

When I went into the service in World War II, I immediately went into personnel and became a sergeant major. And there, in Germany, the most sophisticated people seduced me. It was not a complete surprise, of course, because I had had that one experience, but I never did go back to girls. That was 1946, and from that time on I lived the homosexual existence: very sedate, never was flaming, never was screaming or nelly, that sort of thing. I've always been masculine and very butch. My sexual experiences became mutual immediately after the war in Berlin. But it wasn't too long before my appeal was what people called "a man," so I gradually became gay trade.

KV: Which means?

No kissing, no nothing of that sort, you know. This is a new terminology for you? There are new terms for these things today?

KV: I don't know, maybe. In some places the terminology is still there. In larger cities I think it is disappearing. I've heard the word several times, but I've never figured out exactly what it meant.

It is usually used to indicate the person a homosexual wants – in upper case letters: A MAN. It is strictly a one-way affair, either orally or anally in bed; there is no lovemaking at all. It's strictly a sexual moment and only one partner reaches orgasm, of course. And that guy is trade.

KV: Does he get paid?

Now you're getting into prostitution. When I was approached as a trade prostitute I sensed it immediately. And also, it turned out to be true that the little male prostitute, prick peddler, if you say, "Hmm, you're not what I'm looking for, fella, I like the fems, the ladies," they quickly find that maybe they could do that. Their legs go in the air so fast and they enjoy it so much, but that's another story. There's trade and there's gay trade. In gay trade there will probably be lovemaking, kissing, fondling. If you kiss another male, you're gay. By the time I was forty years old, the people who sought me out were effeminate – younger effeminates with the older ones. This has been my experience. But today, partly because the years have added up and partly because I've had two serious motorcycle accidents, the sexual drive is not that strong. The first accident didn't slow me down that much but the second only two years ago, did. I don't need it that much anymore. I had one last night and that was delightful. A young man that I've made the scene with many many times. This is the first in six months for me. The fact that we didn't get together didn't bother me at all. As it turned out he said, "Well, how come you haven't asked me?" "Be quiet girl, relax." So that's where it is.

Fifteen years ago, back in Monterey, I found that I could not make it with a man past fifty. And this was not a case of becoming a chicken queen. I've never had anything to do with them under twenty-one. But there are two sides to every coin. I never wanted young boys; they aren't developed as people, they haven't matured yet. Their personality is lacking. They haven't thought through problems, they haven't had to make adjustments, so they haven't any depth. And I've never gone to bed with bodies, I've gone to bed with people. That's important. Then there's the matter of the older man beginning to seek the younger person. It is very common in gay life and very common in heterosexual life where you hear of the male menopause which is a very real thing. Very real.

But I did lose interest in the older man and the reason I lost interest was not just the body. Though, of course, I'm attracted to an attractive figure and a pleasant personality and a nice smile. After they pass me on the street I turn around to look at their buns. I can't help it. You get the idea. I like to screw boys. This is my particular pleasure. One of the advantages of the ladies is that I know they're going to bring me a clean body. I want them to know how to prepare themselves so that there's no unpleasant physical aspects at all. That of course may be awfully wrong. We have people on the other side who go after truck drivers hoping that they may be a little bit dirty. But I suddenly find that I cannot have sex with an older man. He should have matured. He should have gone beyond that sort of thing. He should be the aggressor. And finally, I'm showing no respect for him if I go to bed with him. I shouldn't be screwing that man. I was approached by an extremely attractive man in a bar, about two weeks ago. He came and sat down next to me. He had lovely gray hair, just beautiful. It was so beautiful that I looked to see if he was using some of this stuff men put on their hair like girls do. No, it was absolutely natural. Plus he was physically beautiful—nice, trim, neat little figure. We were talking about five minutes and he said "Let's go home, go to bed." I refused as nicely as I could. That was wrong, I'm not going to screw him.

But I don't like to hurt people's feelings. So I avoid putting myself into the position where I'd have to say no. That's why it so disturbed me. I had no idea it was coming or I would have been aloof. I don't like to hurt people. You avoid hurt. I left the Christian Church when I was twenty but JC's teachings are still with me.

So what happens to the older man? By the time I was eighteen, chamber music was my great love and has been until this day. I'm going tonight to hear the new string quartet at the university, a remarkable group of four men. I'm also a reader. I'd like to be an intellectual. I never went to college, I couldn't. I was the one out of five children who stayed home and took care of my parents. I've read widely all these years. When I became sixty-four I had to wear a hearing aid because I couldn't distinguish words clearly. I had two cataract operations at that time so I have to wear the goddamned awful visors or I lose some peripheral and close vision. So what do you *do*?

If these things haven't limited your enjoyment in life, then you continue. But when age or accident begins to take things away from you that you need, then you take pills. I've got pills in the other room. I've never been without them. Never since that first motorcycle accident. I kept going back and getting more pills, saying that these don't work, you know the routine? So I've had them for some twenty-odd years. After this last accident I renewed them so that now I have all the pills I need to take a powder and when the time comes, I will!

I have to hold my glasses to get them adjusted because they can't do any better for me. They told me before the operation on the eyes that I would have trouble with close-up reading. I refused the implant because I felt it was not perfected yet. They have many successful operations, but I don't want to be the one which wasn't. And I won't wear contacts because I will lose them. Young people your age lose them, so you know damn well I will.

So I can still read and now I can drive a car. I couldn't for a long time. So I can get to the concerts at the university without borrowing a car or paying about $15 cab fare. As long as I have these two things, chamber music and books, other things are relatively unimportant. I've cooked for myself all these years so I have pretty decent food. Sex is not that important. When you begin to show your years, and I did after this last accident – before that I carried them much better – you don't have as much luck cruising bars of course. And I don't know where the little prostitutes are in this town. The fem prostitutes. If I knew where they were I could find a slim Mexican. I undoubtedly would buy occasionally.

KV: When you say "feminine" do you mean the role they play in bed or their mannerisms?

Mannerisms, yeah, they're ladies. Both. They think of themselves as ladies, they wish they were girls. They know they're not, but they're effeminate and this, of course, appeals to my masculine side.

KV: I'm asking because an outwardly effeminate man may be very aggressive sexually.

Ooooooooo! Didn't I find that out once about twenty-five years ago. Holy Moses! I made out with this queen who was an absolute doll. She cruised me, I wasn't cruising her. She said, "Let's go," and this bitch drag screwed me. "Wow, this doesn't happen!" I thought. She said, "Well, you're not the first one who got upset that I would want to screw." I said, "I forgive you, no hard feelings. But we won't go home together again either." We parted friends. I had a gay bar of my own and he was one of my regular customers. So I know what can happen and I'm usually a pretty good judge, and from that time on I was a better judge.

KV: Could you give me some more biographical information?

My father got wiped out physically and financially in the Depression, absolutely wiped out, and he went downhill fast. I was the one who stayed home. Two of the others went to college, one just wandered, he was the bohemian. And my sister came home one day and said, "I just met the most wonderful guy." She brought him to me and said, "We'd like to get married," and I said, "Well do." She said, "But that leaves you all alone." I said "That's all right, I'm a big boy and make a decent living and will get along. Go get married." Then Paul said, and God love him for it, "We'll see your father, then." But they cleared it with me first because I was the breadwinner in that house, the only one. I was the middle of five children, two younger and two older. Then they went through that old, old tradition and he formally asked my father for his daughter's hand. How beautiful! My father at this time was really not much with it. He wasn't crazy, he just wasn't with it. What a compliment, though. I still get affected by it.

I started out washing dishes in the Depression. From there I went into life insurance. Mr. Roosevelt promised he'd never send an American boy abroad. I thought he was the charlatan of the ages. But I was blessed in one way because it got me out of the insurance business. But in the insurance business I carried a book—I collected insurance monthly and weekly. I did all right. I should have done better but money has never been important to me. My friend was the assistant manager and one day he said, "Rick, you can do better." I said, "Billy, I'm making all I need." Finally the general manager called me in. We were close friends and I was his best man. He started reading the riot act and I turned and said, "I think that I best be excused." I told him that everything I was doing was fine, I had a good book, enough clients, I wasn't going to work any harder. "If you want me on those terms, fine. If you don't, I'd be very happy to leave, sir." Well, Billy intervened and I agreed to increase my sales by ten percent. So I made more money but I didn't enjoy it because who wants to work like that? What are you going to do with the goddamn money anyway? You're just going to spend it.

After the war I went to Washington, DC, and was going to take one of those government education programs in hotel management. I went into the steward's office which was my first stop, purchasing steward. We have two kinds of stewards in the hotel business—purchasing and banquet. I started training and really enjoyed it. However, I went home for New Year's Eve, '49, and had been promised the time off beforehand. A couple hours before plane time I was told I couldn't go, that they were short and needed me. I said, "I'm sorry, I'm gone," and that was the end of the job, of course. Then when I got to Syracuse I got a call and was given a chance to manage a restaurant for the YMCA. I took it but was soon offered a job at a Howard Johnsons in Albany. I went there but the number two man seemed to have a little monkey business going on financially. And you don't fool around with dollars where I work. Absolute integrity always, you know. So I left for Texas and after five years there, suddenly that was enough. Being single, you're not liable to be stable. Married men are far more stable, they have to be. So I went to Los Angeles and then got a nice offer in Long Beach. That's when I had my first motorcycle accident. Goddamned near got me.

KV: When you had your motorcycle accident were you part of a cycle gang?

Not a gang, no. I was one of the founding fathers of a gay motorcycle club. We started with about five people and became the outstanding motorcycle club in Los Angeles. They're not as conservative now as me and my friends who founded it. They've become a little bit "gay," but it's still a class club.

We enjoyed the social life together as motorcyclists. This was about '57. We had regular meetings every two weeks. At that time there were only two motorcycle clubs and just a couple of bars that catered to the motorcycle crowd. There was a lot of S & M in ours. The sort of people I'm talking about who are into the S & M are quite respectable, nice people. I don't know how much you're aware of this in your studies but S & M runs the gamut from the very rich to the very poor. More of it in the upper middle classes, by far, than in the lower classes. And the higher up you go, the more there is. You know, Ben Franklin was a member of one of the wildest clubs over in England. He was a welcome guest there whenever he went to England.

KV: You said you had a gay bar. Was it in this time period in Los Angeles?

Yeah, a gay motorcycle bar in Los Angeles. I had that for a year and a half with my partner. It was the same man that I lived with. I had gone to Los Angeles at his invitation, we got together and had a fine weekend. He said "Let's go into a bar." "What kind of a bar are you talking about, Luke?" "A beer bar, it doesn't take as much money as a liquor bar and a motorcycle bar ought to be a beer bar." I agreed on both points, I didn't have much money. Never have had. What he didn't tell me and I didn't know until we had actually opened the bar was that two young men in the motorcycle club were also opening a gay motorcycle bar. I had just about got mine under way when they opened theirs, and that was it for me! Of course, I still had a nucleus, you know, but I didn't have the motorcycle crowd which made the difference between profit and loss.

So I went to him and said, "Luke, it means we are going to have to change our operation." I offered several alternatives: "We're awfully close to a Mexican neighborhood. We could put in a couple of big-busted broads, Mexican girls, and I can get an orchestra for very little money and we'll make a bundle. I can get along well with Mexican people." They're such beautiful people – so kind, sweet, gentle, courteous – that is, if you're right with them. If you're not they'll screw you just as soon as you'll screw them. But he said no. "Well, another alternative is to make a dance bar, encourage the dance crowd." "Oh Rick, I can't stand those dance bars." "Well, I'm the guy who's here all the time, you're not, and I'm the one who will have to live with that, not you. We're losing money now and we're going to have to come up with an alternative." "It's already on the market." He had the guys right there to sign the papers, they offered me a reasonable down payment and later washed money out of that bar. I left town not too much after that.

I wanted to tell you about Monterey. I fell in love with it. I went and knocked on a man's door, one of the general managers of a hotel there – the biggest and I think the nicest, to this day. I went in and said, "I want a job as your purchasing agent, sir." "Well, what makes you think I need one?" I said, "I know you don't have one. I know nothing about you, sir, but you have the nicest place and quite frankly I'm a goddamned snob and I will either work in a nice place or in nothing at all." I told him about my experience and that appealed to him. He told me to go back to my job but that he would call me because he'd have to make arrangements first. He called me, and I worked for him for four years. So I had pretty much been a purchasing agent continually up to my retirement. I worked as hard as I wanted to, as long as I wanted to, and then I wanted to slow down.

Eventually I came to Arizona. I owned a little mom and pop restaurant for awhile but went back into night auditing just before retirement. I'm a figure man, I'm a buyer, I'm impeccably honest and I'm very masculine. My family has never been embarrassed by me. That is one reason I left the East Coast, because this is my life. I'm homosexual and that's that. I can't change, I won't try to change. There's no point in being uncomfortable. I don't need to. But I will not stay in my home town and run around to gay bars and that sort of thing and embarrass my family. I will not and have not 'til this day. No one knows except perhaps my eldest brother, the doctor.

I went back there and was visiting in '66. The women had all gone to the kitchen and John and I were sitting there in all our male dignity. John brought out his pipe and we discussed several things. He told me the story then of one of the other physicians in town. He was on the board and they had to lift his license because he'd been playing with teenage boys, patients. He got from me the shock that pleased him immensely. Because I was shocked! I think it's dreadful. I can't accept this, teenage kids – gads, that offends me. So he got the reassurance he needed. But he obviously sensed, though he didn't get the chapter and verse, that I was homosexual. A physician should be able to sense these things of course. But he also got that reassurance that I didn't play with kids.

I recall a man that I was living with for five years in California. It was a purely platonic relationship though he was also homosexual – he was as butch as I am. I remember one time, he told me about a seventeen-year-old boy in the neighborhood. He said, "This kid wants to make it with you, Rick. Don't you realize that?" I said, "Yes, I am aware of it." He said "Well, what are you going to do?" "Nothing." "Why not?" I said, "Because I think it's evil, I think it's the wrong thing to do." "But what harm can it do? You know he's gay." I said, "Yes, I know he has come out, but his little psyche could be damaged too easily by playing with an older man and then perhaps having the guilt of finding out it was distasteful after all. I won't do this to him, I simply won't." "Oh Berg, you're a purist." "Yeah, but one of the things we share in common, sir, is integrity. Integrity is not just a matter of dollars and cents. Integrity is our approach to our fellow man too, sir." That's been my attitude all these years.

KV: In the course of your lifetime have you had many lover relationships?

Hmm, let's see. There was one in Washington, DC. Then there's the tenuous affair going on right now. Unfortunately the younger man, and he is thirty-two years younger than I am, wants to get married. I told him when I first met him that this would never happen. I need a lot of privacy – I need to be alone a lot. When I'm reading I don't want conversation going on. When this first came up, I told him, "Look, I'm this much older than you. You'll end up burying me. You ought to have a younger man your own age or within four or five years of your age. You don't want to fool around with an older man like me." "No," he said, "I want you." "Well, you're going to be all alone some day and you ought to find a younger man who can give you a lot more happiness in the bedstead than I can." Even when I met him five years ago I didn't want it that often. Once a week was fine, you know. "You ought to get screwed every night." He still says he wants me. I think he's crazy.

KV: It sounds like he's made his decision.

I guess so and he has to live with it. He's going to school now, I pushed him into it. He's taking accounting, God bless his heart.

I did live with Luke for five years. I worked third shift and he worked days. So fine, I have no conflict there. But I have to have a lot of privacy. A lot of solitude. People used to ask me "Do you ever get lonely, Rick?" I went home, I didn't have a good dictionary but I looked the word 'lonely' up. It didn't describe or really define it. But I experienced loneliness once.

In '66 I went home to help my friend Bill, the same one that I was in the insurance company with. I was his best man when he was married, I was Uncle Rick to all his children, still am. He called me and asked me to come home to help in an upcoming election — he was very involved in politics. On the other end of the line was his wife saying, "Rick, come, Bill needs you badly." So I went home some time in March and stayed 'til almost December. I stayed with them a week until we had our plan of action all worked out. Then I told them it was time for me to get my own place. "But Rick, this is your home." "Bill, I cannot live with other people." "You'll get lonesome." "I don't think so." So here was my sister thirty miles away with her family and I love her children always. There was my brother with his three and I love them. Not quite as much then. I hadn't matured enough myself to appreciate their qualities. It was my fault. But I love them deeply now. All these people I knew from the early years were there with their children. After the election, which was successful, I helped Bill with his insurance business.

Of course, I saw quite a bit of my family and friends in this time. One night I went back to my apartment, probably two weeks or more after the election, and all of a sudden I was overcome by loneliness. They all had these lovely families, these fine children, they had homes that they had lived in for years, they had all these deep roots and I was *alone.* For the first time in my life I experienced loneliness. All alone in that apartment I bawled like a goddamned baby. Just bawled my fuckin' heart out. Experiencing it and understanding the definition of it are two different things, sir. Ooooo!

The pain of it was more than I could tolerate so I proceeded to get drunk. And I am not the type to drink alone at home. I have my martinis before dinner to this day. But get drunk? No. I got drunk all alone that night to ease the pain. In the morning I went to Bill and I said, "I have to leave. I said I'd stay a year but I can't. I've got all your insurance affairs in very good shape. I've got all the loose ends tied up from the campaign, so you can put your hand on anything you need and it's current. Tomorrow morning I'll be on my way. Don't ask me to stay because I'm not going to be an alcoholic or drunk or a lush. I'm not going to be like a lot of people we've had to work with in political life. I'm going home." So now I know what loneliness is. I don't ever want to experience it again. I've been alone all these years since.

When I had my last eye operation my brother brought over a television and said "There, you need that now." I couldn't go out of the house for awhile of course. I told him, "I'm sorry, I've seen that in other people's homes and I will not be insulted by some son-of-a-bitch coming in my home to sell me a bra or toothpaste or any other goddamn thing." That is why I always liked the theatre, only I can't go anymore because of my hearing.

I don't have a circle of friends here. I've never been widely known. One fellow though, Gus, years younger than myself. Such a fuckin' goddamn butch you never saw in your life. He was a farm boy and worked on the Tennessee Valley project as a molder. He and I became friends when I had that little restaurant back in '70. In fact, he's doing some work on my car tomorrow, which I bought from him. He doesn't understand why I won't go to the woods hunting with him, why I've never learned to fire a gun. I couldn't kill anything. I'm sorry, it's not me. We tried one camping trip but we don't fit together as campers.

KV: Do you have any philosophy on how you conduct your life?

Simply stated, hurt no one if you can possibly avoid it. This is fundamental. And live as honestly and ethically as possible. These are my two guides and they're both taken straight from JC. This is my reaction to him after all these years—he was a sweet son-of-a-bitch, you know. He was on the right track and this is the way life should be lived. We should be kind to each other, thoughtful, generous where possible and avoid hurting any other person when we possibly can. Philosophical systems? Up until about fifteen years ago I professed to be a materialist and I quite seriously held that position from about the time I was twenty-five. Then somewhere in the early '60s I met up with Teilhard de Chardin, *Phenomenon of Man.* My God, what a lovely mind that man had.

I can't quote, I don't have that memory, but the essence of the man comes through and I don't forget it. After reading him I began to question again. Chardin spoke of things one would like to be true. He spoke of universal spirit, but in a far higher level than I had ever heard of it spoken before. It made you wish it were true and wonder if he was onto something. Not at all like those German philosophers who get so damned wordy. He said something like, if this thing we're on were blown up and you and I were to pass on, the essence of us would become part of the universal essence and then form part of the One. This One is nothing like the god described in the Bible, the old man with the gray beard. The Jewish god was a vengeful god, the Christian god was not a hell of a lot better. He was still the old man with the gray beard and if I was a good boy he loved me, if I wasn't, he still loved me, but he was going to whip my ass. And if I was really a bad boy he'd send me down to hell. Well, I'm sorry, I couldn't buy *that* god. And JC divine? No more than you and I. I still have not accepted the idea of being immortal, but I wondered if perhaps there is that universal spirit and now it's time to re-read Chardin again, to become reacquainted with his lovely mind.

KV: How do you envision yourself in the future, say ten, twenty years from now?

Oh I don't plan to live more than three or four years. When the time comes that I won't be able to read, to drive — the pills are in the other room. I will not suffer a long illness, either. I had a cancer operation in '57. My doctor came to me and said, "Rick will you do something for society?" I said "Harry, what the hell are you talking about?" He was a teaching surgeon and a tough S.O.B., I loved him, we got along great, insulted each other regularly, but respected each other. He wanted me to take the examination again for the benefit of the interns, the one where they put the cystoscope up your dick and see what's up there. He wanted me to do it without the aid of so much as an aspirin because he knew I had a high threshold for pain. He did his best to keep my attention by talking to me while these young fellas are looking and playing around with that goddamned tool up my dick, Aaaaaa! All of a sudden, his assistant, who for the first time had seen the inside, got shook.

I was forty-two and in a double room with a man in his sixties who was damn near death. I had cancer of the bladder. So when Harry came down the hall and said he had to talk to me, I told him we'd best go to the room across the hall. I told him, "I don't want that old man to hear what you're going to tell me, Harry, because it's going to scare the shit out of him to have a young man get told what you're going to tell me." He said, "I think it's cancer." I told him, "Yeah, that's not news, why do you think I pulled you over here?" He said OK and operated and got it. I had asked him the alternatives. One was the operation and the other chemotherapy. And I told him he could shove the latter up his ass. I asked him, "What are the chances of the operation?" He said, "Fifty-fifty." I told him, "All right, on one condition, Harry, that you tell me after the operation, man to man, and not patient to doctor, whether you've gotten it all and whether I'm going free or not, because if not, I will not go through a long-lasting illness." "Fair enough," he said. "Now I will tell you something I'm not supposed to say as a surgeon, but I'm telling you man to man. I don't think anyone should have to. I think you're entitled to say goodbye when you choose to." And I plan to.

7

George Morrison

George was born in 1921 in Fort Worth, Texas, raised in Southern California, and now lives in the Midwest. He decided at age nineteen that he never wanted to marry but never really faced the fact that he was gay until he saw a therapist in the late '50s. George is a priest. "My own contention is that the religious life is a very good place for a gay man to be." We met at a small outdoor cafe in San Francisco.

I WAS BORN IN 1921 IN FORT WORTH, TEXAS. I WAS A CAESARean delivery as was my sister who is two years younger than I. My mother had TB when I was born so we both grew up with the realization that our mother wasn't very well. Rather than sending her to a sanitorium, my father made provisions to keep her at home. We always had help in the house with cooking, cleaning and that sort of thing. I was very close to my mother. My grandmother was around quite a bit, too, to help, and my father was home a lot in the pre-Depression years. I had a very happy childhood until my mother's death.

Her death was quite sudden. Although I was used to the fact that she was ill, I was absolutely traumatized by it. Soon after, my father moved us to Los Angeles. He had a better business opportunity on the Coast but hadn't moved before because of mother.

KV: How did your family fare during the Depression years?

It's kind of funny, looking back on it now, but my father was the type of person who protected his children from thinking anything was wrong. I found out later that he lost everything and didn't know where the next meal was coming from, but he kept it from us. I suppose he was well practiced at making light of serious problems because of my mother. So I didn't really know what the Depression was all about until I heard people talking about it later. But that was typical of my father. He also tried to over-protect our health, again because of my mother. He didn't want us to over-exert or catch cold. My grandmother was a good balance because she was more realistic and we could get away with things with her when my father was gone. She would let us stay out late and good things like that.

When I graduated from high school my father remarried a woman he knew in Fort Worth who knew my sister and me. He thought that if he was marrying someone we knew, that we would get along with her, but his plan backfired. Looking back on it, I wouldn't have liked anybody because I hadn't really mourned my mother. This woman was thirty-five and Irish and there was nothing about her I liked, especially her moving into our home. I felt it was an intrusion and very unfair. Of course it was unfair of me but my sister and I both had the same reaction – only mine was stronger.

I went to college in the Midwest and rarely went home. My father and stepmother eventually had a child of their own who currently lives on the West Coast, I'm not sure exactly where.

KV: Did you decide to enter the priesthood in college?

Well, I went to a Catholic university. While I was there I was enjoying life and was popular and loved dances and good times. It's really funny when I think about it, but in my sophomore year I met a girl I became very close to. She was from a Catholic girls' college and she was obviously more in love with me than I was with her. I wasn't aware of what that was all about. She began to talk marriage when I was only nineteen years old. Until then I hadn't really thought much about what I was doing or wanted to do with my future. I began to look into the priesthood and talked with the priests who were teaching at my college. The next thing I knew it was the end of my sophomore year and I was signed up with them. That was in 1941. So in some sort of backward way, my relationship with this girl was a blessing because it made me think about my life. I had a feeling at that time that I didn't want to be married. I wasn't sure why, but at nineteen I knew the institution of marriage wasn't for me.

I joined the order and in those days the training was rather strict, but I really enjoyed it. It is a thirteen-year process from the time of your interview until the time you are ordained. During that time there are three years of teaching experience required, and I taught sociology. I'm sure I didn't know what I was talking about but I taught it anyway, mostly to returning World War II veterans who were older than I was. It was a lot of fun and hard work as well, but I enjoyed that, too.

I was ordained in '54. If you're going to pursue teaching you have to go on to a graduate degree. I got mine in psychology. I didn't want to go on for a Ph.D. because after my Masters I decided I had had enough studying and enough classes. It turned out to be a good move; I was trusting my feelings. I ended up teaching psychology and doing counseling. It was during this time, in my early forties, that I began to become more aware of my sexual orientation.

What happened is that I began to drink quite a bit, not sure why I was doing it. After I had enough to drink I would head out to the cruising parks I had heard gays hang out in. I didn't really know their exact location but I found them easily. That was quite incredible, in a way, how I homed in on them. I was three sheets to the wind and I would meet anonymous sex partners and then drive back at two or three in the morning. That fact, that I got back uninjured, is amazing as well. I would wake up in the morning with these tremendous guilt feelings of, "What am I doing? I am a priest, a counselor, and I have this good reputation, and here I am fucking around in the night in these weird places." Looking back on it, I can see that this was a good experience in my slow development but at the time I was very scared and felt I couldn't tell anybody. I wasn't sure what was going on with me, it just *was*. That's the best way I can describe it. But then the universe took over, or God or somebody, and I got a telephone call from a psychologist acquaintance who wanted to have lunch with me.

It turned out he wanted me to give him referrals for clients from the religious community. He was interested in having priests and nuns referred to him. As a psychologist at a Catholic university, he figured I would have good contacts, and indeed I did. I thought to myself, "Well, I know who your first referral is going to be." I took a large sip from my pre-luncheon cocktail and said, "Doctor, I have your first referral and it's me." So I went into therapy with him which turned out to be a blessing.

He was a very good therapist and I wept with him in his office. We dealt with the sexuality issue but even more with my mother's death. He rightly saw that there was something else behind my confusion, and that was it. All those years since her death I had never properly mourned her. Only then did I begin to accept the fact that I was gay. Interestingly enough, as soon as I started accepting my gayness, my compulsive behavior became more modified and my drinking less heavy. It was all a very, very gradual process, however.

It became clear to me that I needed to do something about my sexual orientation and make some contacts with other gay people. It was about that time that Dignity had started on the East Coast and there were chapters being established where I lived. I joined the organization and began to feel more comfortable meeting other gay men and becoming friends with them. However, there was still a problem with drinking and seeking out anonymous sex partners. There were one or two students that I became interested in. I had a lot of good student friends but looking back on it now I realize that the closest ones were very handsome men. One that I was particularly interested in was gay, though he hadn't dealt with it too much, and he was alcoholic. One night he and I were out and he got picked up by the police for drunk driving. We were both arrested and had to be bailed out. That began to attract a certain amount of attention from the administration. Then there was another incident at an alumni gathering.

I had gotten drunk again and was talking with a former student of mine who was just married, and ended up kissing him. I had no contact with him prior to that, but in our conversation one thing led to another and, well, alcohol does strange things. His wife was practically right there, too. The incident was reported to the Dean of Students by a couple of the students who were running the show, bringing out the drinks and *hors d'oeuvres*, opening the hall and so forth. The Dean was my immediate boss because I was running the counseling center. Well, that event didn't set too well with him, but he was very good about it and we were able to talk. It was decided that because that sort of thing gets around campus very quickly, it would be wise for me to take a leave of absence. I had been working hard, so I welcomed the suggestion. I was offered time in a retreat house to see if I liked that kind of work.

KV: It sounds like banishment to me.

Well, it did sound that way to me at the time, but as it turned out I enjoyed the retreat house very much, spent six months there, and had a very moving experience. "A very moving religious experience" is the best way I can describe it. I felt that I was very much loved by God and that this love was unconditional. I forgave Him for taking my mother from me. Prior to that I had cursed Him for it at the age of thirteen and forgotten I'd done so. Here I was, forty-five, and finally coming to grips with it. I also forgave Him for my being gay. Then I began to like the idea. In fact I liked the idea so much that I wrote a letter to my superior saying that I was gay and that it was fine with me. I wrote him that I hoped it was OK with him, too, and that I would like to get into some kind of work where I could minister in some way to the gay community. He had a hard time with it at first until I explained to him where the idea came from—above. He couldn't bypass that since we're all in the same sort of business. He finally told me that it was probably a good thing but I should go outside of our area because I was too well known around the school. He asked me where I wanted to go, and I chose to work in another retreat house in the Midwest near a large city with a sizeable gay community.

I moved from the retreat house and began involving myself more and more with Dignity in the city. I met a lot of wonderful people and for the first time I could feel that I had some real good gay friends, close friends. Interestingly enough I got a lot of support from my superiors, probably because I was honest about the whole thing. Their point was to be discreet and not make too many waves, which is understandable. I appreciate that. Maybe this all came rather late in life, but as I view most things in my life, this was fine, too.

I ministered to gay people as a priest, but I also found myself being ministered to by them. Then I fell in love, which was the best thing that ever happened to me. It was the first time that what I felt was more than just infatuation. This guy was twenty years younger than I was. He was taking a Dignity retreat which I had put together. He came to see me in my room and sat right across from me. And I couldn't hear a word he was saying. You know, that kind of feeling. I tried to pass it off as nothing in particular but it didn't work. I called him over to my place one night about eleven o'clock and that was the beginning of the affair. It was great! I had never experienced that depth of feeling with a man.

He was much more sophisticated than I; he had been in other relationships and had just broken up with a married man when I met him. He was determined not to get involved with anyone for a long time. But I pursued him hot and heavy. About that time was my twenty-fifth anniversary as a priest and friends of mine in New York invited me to go on a Mediterranean cruise. I had a miserable time because I missed my friend, who I was just beginning to know. I wrote a letter every day on the boat when I was up in Istanbul, Cairo, and all those places. I remember writing, "Listen, you won't believe this, but this is the first time I ever wrote a love letter in my life." He was much more cautious about these matters but I had decided to go for broke. Gradually he began to feel the same way I did but was more apprehensive, for good reasons. After all, he didn't want to get involved with a priest, for God's sake! But we really did go into a deep love and had a very good relationship; in fact, we still do.

People at Dignity began to understand that we were going together, so to speak. I didn't move in with him or anything like that. First of all I didn't want to. Secondly, I didn't think it would be appropriate. That was three years ago this May, and we're still friends, though the hot romance part has worn off. Now it's me telling him, "Look, you've got to look for someone who has more of a future to offer you." And he says, "That's my business, I'll take care of that." I've learned to shut up and let things take care of themselves. Right now I'm on vacation and he's back home studying to finish up his graduate work. I talked him into going back to school because he has talent. He taught me about the love relationship and I put some guidance in his life. It's a nice byproduct of the age difference. Even though the sexuality is still there in our relationship, it's not prominent; it's nice but it's not the main issue.

We used to make a point of going to Dignity together and having dinner afterwards, but we more or less stopped that. I didn't need to go to another church service, you know, Sunday night after I'd been in church all day. He enjoys the Dignity meetings but is not too much into the church things. As it turned out, some of the Dignity members didn't like our relationship. I'm a priest and I'm not supposed to be human and have a relationship and all that. If they didn't like it I just told them to "fuck off."

KV: Do you think they objected because you took a vow of celibacy?

Well, that's part of it. There's a lot of misunderstanding about words, you know. They are used with lack of discrimination. We take three vows and one's called "Poverty." That's a misnomer because it doesn't mean we don't have things, you just *personally* don't own anything. The Order owns everything, they take care of you. So we're not poor in the sense of poor people who have to scrimp to make ends meet. It's a nice arrangement, I think, a kind of communism. Then there's "Obedience" and "Celibacy." "Celibacy" is a word that is terribly kicked around these days and misunderstood. What it means is that you give up your rights to marriage and a family. You take a vow not to marry; it doesn't have anything to do with sex. So when gays talk about being celibate because of AIDS, they're using the wrong word. Then there's another word called "Chastity," which is a virtue that has to do with modifying one's sexual appetite; it doesn't necessarily mean sexual abstinence. So there's a lot of misunderstanding. I've worked through all of that for myself so I do feel I honor my vows. I practice celibacy and I'm not married. I think it has its counterpart in the gay situation because I'm not involved in an exclusive relationship and I've let my friend know that. Celibacy then is the freedom from an exclusive relationship. I think it's a good thing for some people but not for most.

KV: Do you think heterosexual priests feel that way as well?

Those who are true celibates do, but most of them don't. It's a complicated thing. The vows have to do with giving up what you have a natural right to. You have a natural right to private property, to a marriage and family. You have a natural right to do what you want with your life. I could be told by my boss to go somewhere else and I'd do it. But in turn I get a lot of benefits – community, support, and the opportunity to do many things I want to do.

I think in Dignity there was some resentment of me because a lot of the gay men there have an underlying hostility towards the Church which they turn on their priests. Other priests have told me this as well. They don't mean to do it consciously, but it comes out. A priest gets along as long as he keeps his place, but if he happens to fall in love or have a relationship or be seen at the baths or something like that, well, that's wrong to them. That's why I tell them to "fuck off" because I didn't oppress them. I've had a lot of the same experiences they've had, so I tell them to go play their games with someone else. This is not true of everyone, of course, but many feel they've been dumped on so they take it out on people who represent the Church, which they feel has done this to them.

A lot of people get into Dignity because they are uncomfortable or want to change the attitude of the Church toward homosexuality. Well, I disagree with the teachings of the Church, too, on sex in general. But many of them are obsessed with their oppression by the Church. The original idea of Dignity was to celebrate mass and the sacraments in a setting that would be comfortable to gay people. Many of them are sort of looking for permission from the Church – I don't think that's where it's at. It seems to me that the real issue is not to try to change the Church but to change yourself. You allow yourself to be as oppressed as you want to be. If the Church officially gives in on homosexuality, they'd have to give in on the whole thing – pre-marital sexuality, birth control, abortion – and they're not going to do that. Those in high places in the Church hierarchy are up against the wall. Publicly they have to uphold the official teachings of the Church. My sense is that change takes place in people, not in institutions. In other words, it doesn't come from the top.

KV: I have talked to a number of men whose first homosexual experience has been with a priest . . .

Yes, it's very common. It makes sense because the priest is not married and has no outlet. My own contention is that religious life is a very good place for a gay man to be.

KV: That's historically true as well, isn't it?

93

Well, yes. I think there are a lot of gay men in the religious orders and it makes sense. You gave up marriage and family, but you didn't want to get married anyway. At nineteen I didn't know I was gay, I just knew that I didn't want to get married. I also have a theory about the celibate personality. Some people are better off not having an exclusive relationship with one other person and I'm one of them. I'm happier this way and so is everybody else. I think my personality type is fairly rare but valid. I have no desire to live with anybody, and I value my solitude. My friend knows this and accepts this about me.

KV: Were you aware of other gay men in your order before you came to the realization you were gay?

Yeah, because I was pursued by some of them. I didn't quite know what it was all about, but I liked it. The younger ones today seem much more relaxed about it. It's become a more accepted thing because it's so prevalent and because of the times we live in. I'm probably the oldest one who is out as much about my sexuality. Without my planning to, I've become sort of a role model for some. My order has been pretty good about it. As long as you don't make an ass of yourself, which is reasonable enough to expect of anybody, they're not going to worry about it.

KV: Do you have any philosophy by which you live your life?

Yes, as a matter of fact, but I want to tell you a theory I have first. I find that there is sadness among many gay men and I don't think that it's merely that they've experienced rejection from people who don't like them. You can get over that easily, and most people do. I think they are sad because there has been a loss and they haven't mourned that loss, the same as I hadn't mourned my mother's death. It is a loss of expectation. No one I know has grown up expecting to be gay. Parents automatically expect you to be heterosexual, the Church does, the state, the whole world does. If we lived in a more sane world people would say, "Well, of course, some children grow up to be gay and some don't, including my own." You can have an expectation to be a lawyer or a doctor and fail, but you don't become sad about it for the rest of your life. That's why so many people who have had the courage to tell their families say, "Now they know but they never talk about it. It's almost as if I never told them." It's because there's a mourning period with every loss that people must go through.

Many gays have not sufficiently mourned the loss of the expectation.

KV: Wouldn't those heterosexuals in the relgious orders experience such sadness as well because there is the loss of the expectation of family and marriage?

Oh yes, that's very true, except that loss is more manufactured. But the experience of this particular loss for the gay person is different from depression; it is more an experience of sadness. My contention is that we need to mourn it and get over it. If you can't mourn it I feel the same thing happens when you don't mourn the loss of a loved one. You drown your sorrows in drugs and sex and other addictions. At least that is my contention.

My more personal philosophy has to do with expecting things to be the same. People get attached to things such as cars or jobs that they think are important. But those things don't remain the same. They change. My sense is that most people's sufferings come from laboring under the illusion that this thing or that will go on forever. That's not real and it leads to disappointment. There are lots of things in relationships that change, too. What one must do is realize that the essence of a relationship will be with you in the future even though the relationship may have changed or be discontinued for one reason or another. The idea is to embrace change, and more than accept it, *love* it.

I had a dog, Samantha, whom I had to put to sleep this year. She was ninety-eight years old by human standards. We had an incredibly beautiful relationship. I knew someday that I would have to make that unfair, difficult decision about continuing her life in possible pain or putting her to rest. However, I am quite convinced her spirit remains with me in my home. There is a presence which has continued.

People have to be able to sort out what remains the same and what will change in their lives. Ultimately you can call what remains unchanged "God" if you like, because that seems to be what is real above all else.

8

Andrew Weiler

*At sixty-one, Andrew has made a remarkable recovery from a
serious heart attack. He was married for many years, had five
children, has been in therapy, and has lived in Guatemala. He now
resides in a neighborhood bordering San Francisco's Nob Hill. I met
him in his apartment in a multi-unit high-rise. It was apparent that
Andrew has struggled a long time to understand his sexuality and
has only recently considered himself gay.*

I SUPPOSE I'M A PUZZLEMENT TO MYSELF. I'M SIXTY-ONE AS OF
last August; I'll be sixty-two in ten months, going on Social
Security. I've had a serious heart attack, yet I consider myself in
quite good health. I play racquetball three times a week. My
heart attack was due to the stress in my life which maybe I could
have learned to control.

I think it all started with the fact that my mother told us many
times that she knew exactly how she would have raised girls. She
wanted a lot of girls and she had three boys. Her only girl died
two months before I was born in the World War II flu epidemic.
So she dressed us boys as girls for the first couple of years of our
lives.

I never grew up with girls, didn't know anything about girls.
Nothing! And moving around as I did, I missed taking biology
classes. I had no idea of how the reproductive organs worked. I

only knew I had a penis. I wet the bed until I was ten or eleven years old, which I think indicates nervous problems. My mother was very loving, almost to a fault. And to this day I resent her. My father couldn't express his affection and was considered to be a very cold man but underneath he wasn't cold at all. After my mother died he lived another ten years. That's when I learned he was really a warm person, but it was very hard to get to him. I really resented my mother because she was such a goddamn prude. She couldn't help herself, she was of a different generation, and I know this. She loved my father but I think the only thing they had going for them was their sex life. She never used the word sex, never in her life; but she always talked about love.

I don't know whether she brought us up to be sissies or not. My father, a very masculine man, was a great athlete at the University of Wisconsin at the turn of the century. He didn't dominate the marriage though. And he didn't encourage or discourage us about athletics. But there was something about the way my mother raised us – we were soft. As I grew up I was ashamed of that part of me. I didn't want to be called a sissy.

I'm not sure that I was interested in boys early in my life. From twelve to sixteen I was interested in girls but nothing sexual. I liked them – I liked to talk to them. I got turned off by them in high school, though. The freshman and sophomore girls didn't want to dance with freshman boys, they wanted to dance with senior boys. This is par for the course I suspect, even now. I wasn't a very good dancer and I was very proud. I got turned down a number of times at our high school parties by some of the girls I wanted to dance with. That turned me off on girls from about age fifteen until I was about thirty. I was really hurt by all this rejection, and I was also very ignorant. I had never been told about sex, I never had a sister, and, as I said, my mother was a prude.

I don't know that my mother was any worse than other mothers but she was *my* mother. Occasionally I'd scratch my penis, my "private parts" as she called it, and she'd always growl and say, "What are you doing there?" and make outrageous remarks. She actually made me believe that if I wasn't careful I would go insane if I played with myself. I suspect that billions of mothers over the years have said this to billions of sons. For most kids it probably goes in one ear and out the other, but it made quite an impression on me.

We were among the wealthier people in town so it was very easy to mix. I had access to interesting groups of people yet I was very shy. On one hand I was arrogant, on the other hand I was shy. I look back on it and kind of cringe. I didn't have any status. I don't remember ever having any great strong feelings for women. I never had any great lust for women like I have had for men. And though my mother told me I'd go insane, I didn't stop masturbating. I did it at least once a day from the time I was thirteen or fourteen until I was married at the age of thirty-one.

I used to admire all the boys in high school. I didn't ever have any sex with any of them, never even touched their private parts. I went into the navy a few years after high school. In training I met a young man about my age, twenty-two or twenty-three. He had a good physique, not great, but he was very kind. He was a second-generation Yugoslav and he was the first person who ever told me off. He liked me and yet was able to tell me I was a pompous ass. I grew to like him very much but I never knew just how much until we got our wings. We had a bedroom together with two single beds, side by side because the room was small. The first month I could hardly sleep a wink with him there. I had to face the facts that at the age of twenty-two I loved him, I loved that boy. We were separated for about three weeks after we got our wings and I came out to San Diego. He came out later. I was sharing a room with another officer. One time he was gone for the weekend, the same weekend my friend was to arrive. When we met I'm not sure that we kissed each other but we did embrace, European fashion, at least. It was quite obvious that he wanted to stay with me that night and he was going to take my roommate's bed. Then the damn fool, sonofabitch roommate came back early and my friend had to go down the hall to sleep. Three days later they sent him to the East Coast and we were separated for years.

He knows now that I'm gay but we've never sat down and talked about it. I believe that he might have been able to be in love with me but I suspect that he was basically heterosexual. I'm learning more and more that you don't have to be basically anything except basically human. We were separated for two and a half years. At the end of the war I went to visit him. We went up to Ocean City and stayed all night in a room, and my God, I couldn't sleep. I was sexually aroused just being near him, but it was more than lust—I loved him. He was a delightful person, a very kind, sweet guy. Not a great brain but a good friend. My God, I got up and masturbated twice in the water closet that night! Finally, about two or three in the morning, I got up and dressed and walked up and down the sidewalk along the beach. This fellow came up and talked to me. He was quite frank—he wanted me to go out in the sand and have sex with him and I said yes. Actually, I suggested the sand and he said that was too messy. He was rather effeminate. So we went over and sat on a bench in the damn light and played with each other. I was so embarrassed that someone would find us. It wasn't daylight, but it wasn't in the shadows either. I was twenty-five or twenty-six and that was the first sex I'd had with a man. It was most disagreeable. We walked down the beach after it was over and he said, "Have you ever been Frenched?" and I said, "No, I don't know what that means." Then he explained it to me and said, "It's delicious, you ought to try it sometime. You'll really like it." I went away thoroughly ashamed of myself, disgusted with the whole incident.

After the navy I went back to school and met the girl who eventually became my wife. She was an artist, diminutive, very sensitive. Interestingly enough she had a number of masculine characteristics but in other ways she was very feminine. I don't know whether I could have married anyone who was terribly feminine. We just talked a lot for a year or so. Then I went to New York for Christmas the next year and she happened to be there. We met and went to a play. It was a great evening for me. I walked her back to her aunt's hotel where she was staying and we went in and had a beer or two. I told her, "You know, I like you as well as any girl I've ever known. I don't understand why we don't ever kiss each other or anything." By the end of the evening we decided to get engaged. She'd had a tough sex life too because of her parents. They were more modern than my parents, lived in New York City, but they were also very prudish. We went back to college, a small art school, and told people we were engaged. They said, "Why, we've never even seen you hold hands!" Well, we hadn't, we hadn't kissed either. One thing led to another and I confessed to her I didn't know whether I could even have sex with a woman, that I'd never done it.

It took me four years to convince this girl to marry me. In those four years I moved to California and got a job but she wouldn't come with me, she was teaching. I moved back to New York City, to the Village, to be closer to her, but we had a fight and broke up. She would not marry me and it was broken off completely. She was mad at me, wouldn't write to me, was never going to see me again, and all that sort of thing.

Living in the Village and in New York City I began to experiment sexually. I was there for a year. Oh God, I'd go through the parks, and I was horny as hell, like everybody, and feeling frustrated. I got a lot more frustrated than I had been in the past; masturbation was not that satisfying anymore. I met a black fellow in the park and I saw him four or five times. I wasn't happy with the relationship, partly because he was so poor. I had to meet him in his basement. It was so horrible. My place was horrible too, although it was above ground in another part of town. But it was kind of spooky going into Harlem. I met another young fellow there and I think he was a hustler. He was going to beat me up but instead he robbed me and took my watch.

All the experiences I had seemed sordid because I hadn't learned to accept my sexuality. Today I do things that are very sordid, but they don't upset me. I'll think about them the next day, "What in the hell are you doing?" But it passes.

Next I enrolled in school in Baltimore to become a city manager. For the next year and a half I worked awfully hard but occasionally at night I'd go out prowling, just an old pussycat. I never found anybody! I was afraid of my sex and afraid of being beaten up.

An important thing happened to me around this time. I had lunch with one of the boys in my class. He was a soft-spoken, sensitive boy. He admitted he was going into therapy. I asked him why and he said because he was a homosexual and he didn't like it. He wanted to get married and have a family. And I said, "Well, I'll be damned! That's just about the same way I am." He said, "Why don't you go to a therapist too?" And I said, "Well, by God, maybe I will." So I looked into it and started going to a very good therapist.

I wanted to get married and have a family. At the end of a year and a half I had been helped: I had exorcised a number of terrible dreams that I had had. I discovered that the awful spider in my dreams was my mother. I never realized completely until I was in that therapy how much I really resented her. I'd always thought it was my father I resented. To this day—and I know this is small of me—I can't quite forgive my mother because I feel as though she warped my sex life in such terrible ways.

The girl who had written me off forever wrote me a letter right out of the blue and said she was moving within forty miles of me to work in a museum. We saw each other the next fall, kissed a few times and I kept asking her to marry me. She kept equivocating and it got to the point on New Year's Eve that I was angry about the situation. This was it. She was either going to agree to marry me that night or I was not going to see her anymore.

Just as the night I didn't sleep with my navy friend changed my life, the night this woman said yes changed my life also. We had sex that night, New Year's Eve, 1950, and because of that night we eventually had five children. We were married in February. I was almost thirty-one and she was almost twenty-six, both very inexperienced. I enjoyed having sex with my wife, but she didn't really enjoy it with me. I will admit that my sex life probably wasn't the greatest, yet I remember having sex every night for the first four or five years of our marriage. I'm sure my wife remembers it differently. I probably wasn't a very good lover in those days, but she wasn't very good either. It was so goddamned hard for her to climax, I would be exhausted. Also I don't enjoy sex at night when I'm tired. But when you have children, you don't have much opportunity for sex in the morning because they're always running in and out unless you lock the bedroom door.

After we started having children, we had a child every two years for ten years. We lived together eighteen years and ultimately she asked me for a divorce. Two years ago my wife told me that the reason she divorced me was that she never had an orgasm in those eighteen years of marriage. I said, "For Christ's sake, Donna, you mean to tell me you were faking it?" She couldn't have fooled me all the time. Anyway, that hurt my masculinity for a little while and then I suddenly realized, "Good God, is it my job to give a woman an orgasm? It's a physiological thing." I haven't let it bother me since. I do have some guilt that maybe I ruined her life. She did not know that I was gay, and she was furious when she found out.

From the time I was married in 1950, until 1959, I occasionally would have a lusty thought when I saw a good-looking man. And it was usually a much stronger feeling than I ever had for my wife, whom I really loved. But one night – God, it's really hard to say this – she'd had an operation on her throat and she was in the hospital. We had a babysitter and I decided to come into San Francisco to a movie. I was walking down Market Street and this very handsome black fellow passed me. I stopped and he stopped and one thing led to another and I didn't go to the movie. He invited me to his charming home, a lovely old Victorian mansion that he helped to manage. It was very elegant, and the sex was just the opposite of what I'd had in Harlem, in the dirty old basement. It was a beautiful room, with low lights, and he put on classical music, which I love. We had a fire and wine. I had hardly ever drunk wine. He proceeded step by step to undress me. It was very interesting and I enjoyed it immensely. But all the while my wife was in the hospital. The thought still makes me cringe. Sex makes me do the damnedest things. I see people who are addicted to liquor and gambling, and I can't judge them because I have the same problem with sex. I don't seem to be able to control myself. Anyway, I kept seeing this man once every nine or ten months. He really liked fucking me and I didn't like that, but I loved the closeness . . . and the whole relationship had a lot of spice.

I lost my job and we moved to Los Angeles, where I worked late a couple of nights a week. Then I discovered a gay bath. Back then we didn't call it gay, just a bath. It was kind of scary but I still enjoyed it. One night I met a French-American who was a waiter at a big hotel. He liked me and I liked him. He was quite nice, a very gentle guy. Sometimes he would call me just before I was ready to go home from work and ask me to come to his apartment. Sometimes I would and sometimes I wouldn't. I was so nervous and shy I would always have to have a couple of big glasses of wine in order to get comfortable. We had fairly good sex. So there I was sleeping with my wife and sleeping with this fellow. Yet if you were to ask me if I was bisexual, I don't think I was. Someone once said, "If you don't *feel* you are bisexual, brother, then you aren't." I really think I was homosexual, that I *am* homosexual.

When my wife divorced me I tried suicide two or three times. I don't know why I'm still here, I'm just lucky I guess. But I'm glad

I'm here. After the last try I went back into therapy with a marvelous therapist. I decided I wanted to be married again! There I was, back in the old path again. He was a wonderful therapist yet he didn't really believe that any man could or should be homosexual.

Then I started going to a singles group at a church. It was just a place where you could meet single people, whether you just wanted to talk or were interested in a relationship. I was so shy I didn't know what to do. The first night I went, on a Sunday, I felt as though I had a big sign on me that said, "I'm available," and I just hated it. I talked to the therapist and he said, "Good God, Andrew, you'll never get anywhere that way." So I screwed up my courage and went back the next week. I don't know what happened but while I was there I was standing behind this woman and—it wasn't the shape of her head or anything like that—suddenly I wanted to bite her ears! And I thought, "My God, I've never wanted to do that to a woman before! I better take a good look at her." When she turned around, she wasn't beautiful but she was a very sophisticated, very charming woman. So I screwed up my courage again and went over to talk to her. We had a perfectly marvelous evening. She was getting a divorce from her husband. She was ten years younger than me, forty-one. She had discovered her husband had been running around and had left him. It was six weeks before I even kissed her. In six weeks and one day we were rolling around on the floor and we were in love. She used to kid me and say, "For someone who's so shy, you certainly do move." She was an artist, just like my wife, but more tuned in sexually. It was the greatest relationship I've ever had in my life. I was opening up in many ways. But she finally decided to go back with her husband. I simply couldn't believe it. She didn't love him. It was just another accident in life, another twist of fate.

At this time I thought I should live in the Los Angeles area to be close to my children so I moved there and took a little apartment. The first night there I went to a small bath and a young man half my age came into the room and we had a marvelous time. I said, "Well, I've just taken this little apartment. Maybe one of these nights you'll come over and spend the night with me." And he said, "How about tonight?" Well, I laughed and he laughed and one thing led to another and he came over that night.

We had a wonderful night together and in the morning he suggested that I drive him home, which was thirty miles away. We
went to breakfast and then he wanted to show me his apartment.
We went to his apartment, took off our clothes, had sex again,
and I never left – I lived with him off and on for five years. It was
wonderful sex. I've never felt that way about a man since. I don't
understand the great affection I had for him. He wasn't terribly
handsome, he didn't have a great figure, and he was twenty-six
and I was sixty-two. He was a southerner, very bigoted and
narrow-minded. He was uneducated. He liked what I thought was
trashy television and I liked classical music. The only thing we
had in common was sex. I finally had to leave him because we just
had too little in common.

I had a massive coronary during this period that just about
finished me. Fortunately my friend was with me at the time and
he got me to a hospital. Suddenly I was facing death. A few days
after I knew I was going to live, I asked the nurse to raise the
shades at five in the morning so I could see the sun come up. She
said, "You can't see the sun come up from here." I said, "I can see
the reflection and that's good enough for me. I'm so glad to be
alive!" When I was in Europe I'd heard about a little town in
Guatemala that was supposed to be like a little Rome. As I lay
there in that hospital bed I said to myself, "I don't think I'll ever
be able to work again, so I think I'll retire in Guatemala." And I
did. It took me a year to do it, and I had to leave my friend, but I
felt that was for the best anyway. I packed up all my worldly
goods, moved to Guatemala, and stayed ten months. I made only
one mistake. I invited my friend to come down for Christmas. He
couldn't come but he said he'd pay half my way if I'd come to see
him for a month at Christmas. So I came up at Christmas time
and we lived together for a month. I'd had sex with only one man
in Guatemala and it was an absolute disaster. It was so marvelous
getting back with my friend. The morning I left, we had breakfast at the airport and he asked me if I would go to the starting
gate alone, he just couldn't stand the thought of seeing me off.
We were both almost in tears. When I got back to Guatemala he
wrote me a letter and said, "I can't take it anymore. Don't expect
to come back to see me like that again." I wrote him back and
said, "Don't give up on me. I don't know my own feelings." But I
didn't get a job with the Peace Corps in Guatemala as I had

planned, so I moved back to Los Angeles and lived with him again. I hadn't been back a month before I had another heart attack. When I came out of that, we took a larger apartment and he bought a king-size bed for us. To this day I miss sleeping with a partner. I enjoyed it with him much more than I did with my wife. I don't mean the sex, I mean being close and affectionate. He was an affectionate man when he was in bed but he had this need to be very supercilious. He was very bitter when I finally left him for good and I understand his feeling because that was how I felt when my wife left me – I overreacted much more than he did. Now he doesn't even write me. I don't know where he is.

After we broke up I decided San Francisco looked awfully good to me. I moved up to San Francisco and I've been in this apartment three and a half years. When I moved here, I realized I was having impotence problems with men in the baths, and I decided it was all psychological. I started going to a lot of gay groups, realizing that I knew very little about homosexuals. At the older men's group, G40+, I told them I wanted to meet people. I really thought it would be better if I met someone closer to my own age. The first day I went there an older man – he was sixty-one and I was fifty-eight – came up to me after the session and said he'd been quite interested in the remarks I had made. I looked at him, grabbed him, and gave him a big kiss. I really fell for him hard, the only older man I've ever fallen for. We had about a week together, off and on, and I was impotent. If it was anything this older man had to have, it was sex with a potent man. He was extremely potent for sixty-one, also very assertive. No, he was more than assertive, he was insulting. If he had given me a little time, we could have had a great relationship. Actually, no, I don't think we could have because I don't think he could have stayed with anyone.

I go to the baths now almost once a week. That's my outlet. My mores and cultural beliefs tell me that the baths are an awful way to have sex, but my intelligence tells me that it's better than nothing. My first few years here I kept thinking, "Well, I've got to meet people and I've got to go places where I can meet them." I kept thinking I'd meet them in these gay raps. In three and a half years I suppose I've had maybe five men stay overnight in this apartment, and almost without exception I've been impotent. The worst thing that could have happened to me, I think, was when that older fellow insulted me.

I went to a sex therapist who was a nice fellow. They tested me to see if my organs were all right, and yes, everything was all right. This didn't mean I was completely impotent. I could go to the baths and not be impotent and come home with someone or ask to see him again and be impotent then. More often than not, I really didn't want to see them outside of the baths anyway. I just don't understand why I haven't found someone who's turned me on like my ex-lover. I surely don't pine away for him. But I do pine away for that kind of relationship and yet I've lived alone half my life. I'm opinionated, I suppose. I really would like a relationship, but good God, I don't know whether I'd want someone who'd want to take that painting down or wouldn't like plants or would like cats when I like dogs.

I realize that two people can be in love, two men, and live in their own apartments and have a very good time. I'm still hopeful that this will happen. At sixty-one I'm hopeful but not as hopeful as before. Occasionally I will go to the baths and I see these old men, in their seventies or eighties or sometimes only in their fifties, with these great pouch bellies. Sex has to be beautiful for me. I'm sure I have a warped idea of it but when it is beautiful, when the person is beautiful and it is a beautiful experience, I can relish it and revel in it.

After the heart attacks I slowed down. I accept things a lot easier. I have no ideas now of becoming a great city manager, that's past me. I don't want any high pressure jobs. I've found, though, that I still want to work, so I volunteered for a whole year in the Gay Community Center. Five of us helped build that building. I put in all the windows with a friend, glazed all the windows, and I drew all the plans because I have a degree in architecture. I spent a full year there working every day.

I feel I'm fortunate because I've seen both sides of the coin. I never really felt bisexual, yet I must have been because I was operating on both sides. And I will support gay causes if they are reasonable. I marched in the Gay Day Parade. But I don't try to proselytize people to become homosexuals; I think that the way mankind is, it would be a lot better if a person were not homosexual because it's so difficult. On the other hand, I suspect that for whatever reason many men and women will grow up fond of their own sex, and I certainly will fight and vote for anything that makes it possible for this to happen. So, though I'm not a great advocate of homosexuality, I am an advocate of people being able to do what they want to do. I'm a gay man and I go to gay bars occasionally but I don't drink very much. I find myself not at my best in bars so I've concluded that I'm not going to meet people in bars. The bath scene is my main social outlet.

It could well be that I think I'm younger in spirit than most men my age. I don't feel old, I feel like a young buck. Physically I know I'm not, and yet, good God, I don't go to the baths and stay an hour. I go to the baths and stay all night. I very seldom have an orgasm but that is not what I go for. For me it's the warmth I get there, the feeling and the stroking.

My daughter's picture is on the wall up there, the one in the middle. She's my married daughter. She married a black man. They haven't had any children. My other daughter fell in love with a Chicano boy and this is a picture of my first grandchild by them—though they never married. Friday night I got a call from my youngest son, John, who's living with his girlfriend in Maui. They aren't married and they just had a baby boy. So I have a grandson and a granddaughter. And this is a picture of my other son a month before he was murdered. He was hitchhiking back to Iowa and he was picked up by a young man, kind of crazy. During the night—we only know what this man told us—this man thought my son attacked him and he shot my son through the brain three or four times. It was quite a traumatic experience for our family. This is a really nice picture that one of my sons took of him when he was eighteen. He was a disturbed boy, quite disturbed. But he was beginning to come around. It was a real problem for me that the two men in my life I had to make peace with, my oldest son and my father, both died before I'd made my peace.

Yet I did make it; I made it in psychotherapy. In the humanistic psychology group I was in I asked one of the men to play my father and I got it all out of my system, made my peace. With my son, I wrote him a letter two years after he was dead. You really have to put yourself into it. It's interesting that if you're willing to give, you can use a technique that can be meaningful. I now feel as though I've come to terms with these two key men in my life. I don't have that gnawing feeling of regret that I had.

I'm very fond of my children. I came from educated people, educated goddamned fools. I had a tremendous education but I really wasn't very smart. My children may be smarter than I am but I still felt very disappointed in them because they weren't interested in school. Now I feel they have to live their own lives. And they're nice people, good guys and good gals.

When I moved up to San Francisco, my integrity seemed to demand that the children know I was gay. I asked my ex-wife what she thought and she said, "Well, Stephen is dead and you don't need to tell Carla because she asked me last year and I told her you were gay. And the boys know." My son who's been dead for seven years told them. He was the most incredible son. Sometimes he'd look at me and I'd think he was looking right through me. If he had lived he would have seen me, at least for one year, with my lover. My lover and I never held hands in public. And we had two bedrooms. We didn't sleep in two bedrooms but we had them just for appearance's sake, for my children. I don't know if I was trying to fool the children or not. But, by the same token, my wife never brought a man home to spend the night when the children were there. She has a lover and he's been there for meals but he's never stayed the night. She has some of the same feelings I do about things like that. Anyway, all the children know I'm gay. Though I don't think they like it, only my youngest daughter was furious about it. Her church said that homosexuality was against the Bible. But now she's quit that church.

I'm in a state of transition. That doesn't mean I'm going to leave San Francisco or that I'm going to quit working. It means that I've got to come to terms with myself. I have to figure out, "Am I an old man who's going to die of a heart attack tomorrow or am I a pretty goddamned lucky sixty-one-year-old man who, after an almost fatal heart attack, can play a vigorous game of racquetball and beat most anybody and run around all over the place and maybe live for thirty more years like my grandparents?" The chances aren't too good that I'll live that long but I think it's helpful to think that I might.

How do I want to spend the next few years? And what's going to happen to me sexually? I certainly enjoy the baths, and thank God they're there for me, although they're not as good as a relationship. I don't brag about going to the baths. I'm not ashamed of it, but I don't brag about it either. I wonder what's going to happen to me when I'm seventy-one, because it's hard enough now. Obviously I'm going to get older. The teeth, the eyes, the hearing, they'll all begin to go. Death doesn't bother me at all. But the thought of being infirm or having a stroke bothers the hell out of me. Or not being able to be independent. I've lived alone a lot. How does an older gay man go into old age? I don't suppose it's a hell of a lot different from the way any older man does it.

I don't want to vegetate—I've always been interested in books. My health will gradually go downhill, I know, but what's going to be hardest for me is to accept less and less of a sexual outlet. Yet I really don't believe there should be such a thing as G40+ for older men. I feel, "What the hell has age got to do with sex and being homosexual?" Although I went, the group offended me. I stopped after two and a half years. But I go to the younger groups and I mix well. I don't feel old and that's good because it helps keep me young. I have to be realistic, though. If I were to read the tea leaves I would see that there are fewer and fewer baths here in the city that I enjoy. And I've gone to an awful lot of them.

I think it's incredible that I grew up in a conservative Republican family with prudish parents. I don't suppose my mother slept with anyone other than my father or that my father ever slept with anyone other than my mother. I would hate to tell you if you asked me how many men I've slept with in my life. My God! It must be fantastic. If my family knew what I do, I think they would be horrified. But I've had a few wonderful relationships. The greatest one was with that second woman. The sex was off but the relationship itself was superb because I never felt more myself.

The conclusion I've come to after dabbling and reading and being involved in the gay movement so heavily for four years is that, essentially, there isn't a goddamned fucking difference between heterosexuals and homosexuals. If people would just accept that you're interested in your own sex rather than the other sex— that's really the only difference. The rest of it is cultural. That doesn't mean there aren't a lot of differences on the surface. I can envision conservative trends sweeping the country that would make everything more difficult. Yet I've seen great changes in my life in anti-Semitism and the acceptance of blacks. I've seen great improvement in our country but I'm not sure I've thought very deeply about it. I probably suspected I wasn't going to live this long. The average man lives to be seventy-six, and with a heart attack, the chances of me living beyond seventy or seventy-two are probably not too good. I'm convinced that it's a lot more important and more healthy to feel that, my God, I might live another thirty years. I was reading an obituary the other night. My lord, this man retired at sixty-five and died at ninety-five. He had thirty years in between! Well, I've decided I'm not going to sit around here and vegetate, I'm going to do something with whatever time I have left. I'm not going to let another twist of fate change that for me.

9

Raymond Friedman

Raymond is 82 years old and lives with his lover, Joseph, in Oakland, California, where they recently moved to from New York. He has a medium build and grey hair. A former Wall Street businessman, Raymond retains an aggressive delivery and speaks in an old-fashioned but open-minded way.

WELL, I WAS BORN IN 1901 IN NEW YORK CITY. I CAME FROM what in those days you'd call an upper middle-class family with an income of $15,000 to $20,000. We had a cook and an upstairs maid and lived in a three-story house in the best part of Brooklyn. We had a little Dodge car and a chauffeur who would come in the afternoons and take my mother wherever she wanted to go. So I guess we were comfortable in those days, and in the Depression we got by.

My family was very strict. I never felt that I was a wanted child. My mother, whenever she wanted to punish me, would say, "I wish you'd been a girl." So the result was I was probably a *macho* fairy, but I really don't know. Others have had the same experience with entirely different results. But I always was careful, even as a kid before I knew anything, not to do anything that my parents would suspect, particularly my mother. So I was always a manly man. At the same time I was cruising toilets when I was eleven, twelve years old and hating gayness of course. I had all the contradictions. I would pick up some kid, we would play around and then I'd hate him. I knew I was doing things I shouldn't do, but why I didn't know. And I didn't know how to find out. During that period from 1908 to the war everything was so undercover.

There were no gay books to read. You didn't talk even about straight sex. So I began to hate myself. I'd become friendly with some young boy my own age, we'd have sex and that was it. I'd never want to see him again. That went on even through college and after. In the fraternity sometimes I would go to bed with some guy like Jack. We'd stay out late and then he'd say "Why don't you stay overnight?" I wish he were alive today so I could tell him about myself now. He'd make believe he was asleep and I'd make believe I was asleep. It's the old story, we'd play around – our hands would move over to each other and we never said anything about it in the morning.

That went on with Jack until one day I decided that I didn't want to have anything to do with him anymore. I picked some kind of ridiculous quarrel with him so I wouldn't have to talk with him anymore. I think it was different for other gays. It certainly is different for kids today who come out. I knew nothing of hustlers and such. By joining the fraternity I now realize that there were terrific contradictions there. I found out later in life that one of the fraternity brothers was expelled for being gay. I asked a fraternity brother years later, "Whatever happened to so-and-so?" He said "He was expelled for being a fairy." And that closed the subject.

Today I remember very little of my home life. I was always kind to my mother but never warm and she wasn't to me. A very cold woman. As I got older I realized that my mother was a very neurotic woman. People thought she was a little angel. She was, but not to me. My dad was a nice man who was dominated by my mother completely – what mother wanted, mother got.

I first worked for a big brokerage house on Wall Street. I did well and made a very good living. If you got $50 a week then you had a really good job. Then the Depression came and I lost my job and wandered around from job to job, but always making a living more or less. My parents died in the forties. I was left some money and spent it all, enjoyed it. Oh, what the hell!

Even in my thirties I didn't know anything about bars. I was just beginning to find them while cruising the parks, subways and so forth. I lived for sex. I was a sexy bastard. But sex was only for a moment or two and I never formed friendships. My friendships were with straight people. They are the ones I went out with, went to the theatre with . . . whatever I did. At that time I was very lonely, very unhappy.

I met my lover thirty-one years ago and we're still together. He never wants me to tell people, even gay people, but we met in a subway. In those days the trains were old and there was a little partition out front. All the gays knew about it. There would be twenty or so crowded inside and then the feeling around would begin. He was from out of town and it was the first time I ever fell in love. It was the first time I ever really knew what the word, everything about being in love, meant. We moved in together and have been very happy. Of course, we have little spats, but one thing we've learned from the very beginning is that when we had differences we fought the differences and not each other. We never abused each other in any way. If you do, the hurt can't be repaired the next day.

I was about forty-eight when I met him. The thing that worried me was that he was about twenty years younger. You never know if they like chicken or older men. So at first I lied to him about my age. He didn't say anything. But later when I talked to other people I found out that he never went with anyone younger. Maybe looking for a father. I like younger people, maybe I'm looking for a son. People my age never appealed to me unless they didn't look my age. I didn't care how old they were as long as they looked young.

I don't believe you can tell other people what to do. Each one has to do what he or she feels they have to do. If that's how they find happiness, fine; if they don't, they have to take another avenue. I think the most you can do — and I'm talking about gays now, not straights, because I haven't lived that life — is to work out your own life.

Many gays from the thirties and forties are so conservative now. Recently an older gay men's group brought up the topic of young gays flaunting their gayness on the streets. Half the audience had very strong feelings about that. I think it's rather obnoxious when you see two straight people feeling each other up on the street. This is only the way I feel: that the freedoms we want are not the freedoms we are going to get by antagonizing people. Sometimes I get mad and sometimes I say, "More power to you." Sometimes I think these kids are alienating people; then other times I think that if you're not yourself how are you going to get what you want? The point is good taste. To do it when it's right to do it. If two gay people meet and haven't seen each other and kiss, fine. Straight men do it in Europe. But to do it to purposely alienate straight people, well, then you come down to good taste and knowing when to do or not to do something.

I meet so many people who are so despondent about the gay movement. They're in such a hurry. They feel we haven't made enough gains. But when you consider the gains in the last ten years in the church, in business! Sure there's a hell of a lot to be gained, but you can't get too far ahead of public feeling. Marx always said the enemies of the people are those that are too far out, either too far ahead or too far behind. So the thing is to be just a little bit ahead of the people and bring them along, otherwise you get backlash.

KV: Could you tell me more about what happened after you met Joe?

Okay. I met him and it's really a terrible thing to really love something you hated for so many years. I hated gayness, I hated gay boys, but the sex drive was there. Maybe like the man who loves a woman so much he finally goes out and shoots her. It was very difficult. I was experiencing things that I should have experienced at eighteen or nineteen. So it affected that whole wonderful period where you should be falling into and out of love. The happiest years in my life were with Joe, particularly that first ten or fifteen. But to be honest, the sex drive begins to wane. Yet we have found a love that is still important. I meet many men who have no one and can talk from now until doomsday about their sex life, but I know that they have very little. They're lonesome unless they're very insensitive people. I know several men who are in their sixties and have the illusion that everyone is giving them the eye. I met someone from Georgia, a heavy, physically unattractive man who sat and talked about his love life as if he had a gun and were chasing away all these beautiful, young men. I wondered if he thought anyone believed him. I don't know how he feels towards himself, I have no idea.

After six, ten, twelve years of living together, you have to see life a little differently. You can no longer go out and fuck three times in a night and take on everyone in the place—if you're that lucky. You should grow with age and try to reap those things that are worthwhile at that age, like companionship, affection, love. I'll never leave Joe, yet we don't kiss every morning and every night. Years ago we sent each other a little anniversary card every month with a present. That's probably the answer to the question, "Are you happy with the person you're living with?" Does it meet your needs? At sixty, seventy, your needs are different. Are we meeting each other's needs? It's a sense of security to have one another. A feeling that we're there and will be tomorrow. If all goes well, we'll be there a long time, who knows, maybe forever.

KV: Do you have any thoughts on monogamy? Do you think it's important to have sex only with your lover?

No, though I think it's important for awhile. Definitely until full confidence is established. I've never frankly spoken to Joe about this. I think we've always understood that if you want to do it, don't tell me about it. I know that kind of sex is not love. I know you're going to go out and have sex, and whether you think it of people or not, they will. He's never asked me. I don't think that at this stage it's important. The element of sameness with the same partner enters into it too.

At the height of our first year together Joe and I had little fights. For instance he was taking a girl out at night, and he said he'd be home at eleven o'clock and wouldn't come home until two or three a.m. I'd get angry and wonder what the hell they were doing. Here's this guy—I love him with all my heart and soul—and he's out with this dumb girl when he promised to be home earlier and I'm waiting to go to bed with him. Maybe he doesn't care too much for me. One bad bit of reasoning opens all these other doors. I think men who have stuck together are intelligent enough to think things over before they jump to conclusions that are utterly ridiculous. It's no good for only one to have a mature approach, both have to have it. So long as the mutual affection and love is still there. A toss in the hay does not make for a relationship.

I think it's necessary to realize that he has his own life too. Joe wanted to go back to New York for a couple of weeks. If it's worthwhile to you to see all the shows, your old friends, then go, why not? I think Tennessee Williams once put it this way—people who love each other often eat each other up and destroy each other, destroy their love. There's a difference between good sex and loving someone. You can have wonderful sex and not really love anyone. You see that beautiful boy in front of you, that boy that you, yourself want to be, but after a while you think "Hey, what am I doing with this guy? He's stupid, he's dumb, he smiles at me." But with someone you love you grow with them. You become more understanding of them, more active with them. After thirty-four years we occasionally get in each other's hair but we're not tired of each other.

I would like to find another two-bedroom apartment, we've always had one. I retired first and I have the whole day free. When two people get older, even though they're still lovers I think they should have their own privacy and bedroom. You keep different hours and it's good to be away for some part of the time. It's important not to try to possess people.

The night I picked Joe up in the subway he said he was going somewhere but he'd see me tomorrow. I said, "You'll never see me tomorrow, I know how these things are." He said "No, I'll be here." And sure enough he came. At that time I had a little apartment and we became friends and lovers. He was a kind person, intelligent, and someone I could introduce to anyone straight or gay. I saw so much of what I wanted to be in him. Isn't that what love is? You see a reflection you admire or what you want to be or what you think you are. When you fall in love, after you've had sex a few times you know whether it's the sex or whether you're crazy about the person. However, you can get into a whole fantasy world. If you're really not happy with someone, you can fantasize for awhile that you are happy. But in the end you know you're not and it breaks up, usually violently. People have to know how much they can expect from life. We try to see that we give each other some pleasure and happiness and a feeling of confidence. At times we often say gently, "Are you all right?" It carries over to times of sickness and so forth. It's terrific to have someone.

One thing that is terrible is when you meet some gay boys who have a life of quiet desperation. They can't seem to move. They can't seem to experience. The kind who go to bars every night, drink, stand at the bar and drink more. I think they lead lives without any ups or downs. And I think many gay boys try to live on cleverness. You never get any deep reaction from them. It's always flippant, you know, very Noel Coward stuff. They want to think and they don't want to feel. They're afraid of being hurt but they'll be hurt anyway. We're all hurt at some times.

I feel I got most of my hurts during the best period of my life when I was young by not having any gay companionship. I was living in a world that was so suppressive it's hard to even imagine now. That's why so many in our age group had this *macho* kind of sex. In other words, like in the fraternity, my hand went over to his prick because he was asleep and breathing heavily. But we were both damned awake and it was never really consummated. That causes a lot of hatred. If I went out and picked someone up in a park at least we had some kind of real sex. Meeting Joe changed all that and I don't know why. I just fell in love with him. I was physically crazy about him, as I had been about some other people, but at last I wanted to see this one again.

Sex was a problem with us at the beginning. It was something I had to learn to understand. He is not as sexy as I am. I have to respect that too. Sometimes I would wake him up several times in the night. I had to learn to respect when he would say, "I'm tired now." You have to realize that it's not that he's tired of you but that he's just tired. You both have different needs.

There are two things I would have liked in my life. I would have liked to have been handsome and I would have liked to have been thinner. I've dieted all my life and it's been a problem. I've never gotten gross or fat, just always a little too much. At one time I would have liked to have had a great big cock. But a number of years ago I did meet someone who seemed quite unhappy. He was my friend and I had never had sex with him. I said, "What's the trouble with you? You are very attractive, you can go out and find and get what you want." He said, "This might sound terribly funny to you, but as you know (I had seen him in the men's room), I have a very big cock and when people want me I think it's only because of that. Sometimes it seems that nobody gives a damn about me or cares what I say, what I think, what I believe, they just want that penis." Anyway, the only two things I wish right now are that I might have been handsome and been able to eat without gaining weight easily. Actually, I don't think I could have had very much more than I've had.

I've been retired since 1965. Joe retired four years ago. I haven't been very active in the gay movement, which brings me to the question of coming out. If anyone had asked me ten years ago if I was gay, I would have denied it. If anyone asked me today, I'd say, "What is the reason that you want to know? Is it curiosity? Is it because you want to know what kinds of friends to invite? Or because you have feelings against homosexuals? If you give me a decent reason, I'll tell you yes or no, but I've never asked you if you go to bed with your wife or husband. If I had, you'd want to know why the hell *I* was asking." Today if I felt they had a good reason I'd say, "Hell, yes, I'm gay. Take it or leave it." I don't have to flaunt it, but on the other hand why the hell should I keep it a secret? It's just a question of good taste. I plan to become more active in the gay movement now.

Well over ten years ago, a group of younger gay people rented an old firehouse in NYC that was not in use. They were paying a good bit of money for it. The young kids would go down there and most of it was just dancing and having a good time. I had just retired and thought it would be nice to go down there and help. Then I read a letter in one of the gay magazines written by an older guy who went down there for the same purpose. He wanted to offer his services in any way he could. He ended up feeling terribly rejected. He felt rejected on two counts. One because it was just a good time club, and two, he thought he was treated like a dirty old man looking for something for the evening. When I read that, I wondered if it was good for older people to try to get in with the younger group. If one thing went the least bit wrong, people would imagine that a bunch of dirty old men wanted a cocksuck job or something. Maybe hustlers. And if anything were to happen, you know what the write-up would be.

I have a subscription to the theatre. Joe goes to the opera, I don't, I don't care for it. When I met Joe in New York he wanted to get into the theatre. He has talent but it's one thing to have talent and another to get into Broadway. He has a subscription to the symphony and I go occasionally to that. I have to consider my money more carefully and not be imposing by saying "Oh, he left me at home alone." I tell him to go. I can read at night or do anything I want. I can clean the kitchen. I do all the cooking and he does all the cleaning. If you're going to nag all the time, stop it.

I was with two lovers about two weeks ago and all they did was argue with each other. It got so boring I couldn't wait to get away. Instead of being a pleasant evening it became unbearable. Everything that one wanted, the other was against. And everything the other was for, the first criticized him about it. It was a night of critique. Why live that way?

I feel that the real enemies to progress are the ones from the lower middle-class. Not the very rich and not the poor. It's not even the conservative or the radical necessarily. It's that class that are not in poverty but have a little something—they're making $12,000 to $14,000 a year. They're the ones fighting all the progress, who will hit you over the head because you are gay.

Right now it's hard to go into a movement. You have to really think it through. There are people who change every month and think they get the answer by joining a different group. I would never join a religious group of any kind because I think they're a bunch of hypocrites. I'm not sure that they're wrong and I'm not trying to say they are. But I have yet to get a satisfactory explanation from any of the Catholics who join Dignity or the Protestants joining their own group. It is the very church that makes these groups necessary in the first place. The big fight in the Episcopal Church is that they don't want any gay priests; of course they have them, but no officially sanctioned, openly gay priests. Yet they say they welcome gays with open arms as parishioners. How the hell can you stay in a church like that?

KV: What do you have planned for the future?

The main thing I try to do is to keep my health. Keep my weight and blood pressure down. I'm in good health except for a little problem with high blood pressure. I have no great plans. Still going and enjoying life, still having ups and downs. But the downs are far less than the ups. My time is my own. I'm happy with Joe. I meet enough people, have enough companionship. I go to the theatre and we have friends who visit us. We have a car and are not in any financial difficulty. We can live at a very nice gait. We travel, not a great deal, but enough to enjoy it, to keep us from being uneasy. So I think at my age a happy present is a happy future. What the hell, I'm not out to conquer anything anymore. I'm out to enjoy fully all the things I can.

You don't have many plans at my age. Let me tell you. At our G40+ group, one fellow played two songs from a show I'd seen years ago. It was called "The Follies." The Ziegfeld Follies were a great thing in New York. Eddie Cantor, George Jessel, all the greats, Helen Morgan, Will Rogers. . . . You never missed the Follies. If you were poor you sat in the gallery, if you were rich you sat in the box in your evening clothes. I wanted to say that there was one song in the show, "This was Called the Follies." They were tearing down the old Ziegfeld Theatre and they had gathered a group there to meet once more for old time's sake. Yvonne DeCarlo was in the show and she's got this great big bellowing voice. She belts it out like Ethel Merman. She sings this song "I'm Still Here." And in it she talks about her life. The times she was up here, the times she was in the gutter, the guys she loved and the guys who didn't love her. The whole big scene. It was a tremendous moment. The refrain is "I'm Still Here." So when you ask me how I feel about the future I say that I know at best my time is short, that I've been through a lot, maybe not as much as some but a hell of a lot more than others, good and bad, and I'm still here.

10

Jonathan West

Jonathan was a child star in Hollywood's Golden Age. Despite serious medical problems, Jon continues an active social life. His commitment to David has spanned over three decades. One secret to this longevity, he says, is that they do everything together.

MY WORKING LIFE STARTS VERY EARLY, SO THAT'S WHERE I will begin. At the age of four, in 1924, I went into motion pictures after a studio had a contest for kids. It was fun for us children because they had us playing games and doing little things within the context of a story, but we didn't know the difference. I made about eight or nine films until my father had a fight with the producer because he thought $25 a week was too little money. That did it for me.

After that involvement with movies I went into school, took ballet and all the things you did if you wanted to be in theatre. At about seven or eight years old I was very well aware of my differences; I knew that I preferred male companions to female, although I got along very well with women and girls. But as I grew older I became terribly feminine. I believe I thought it was part of being a ballet dancer. My father was just furious at me—he said, "Why don't you be a man and go out and play football?" So I tried football. I tried to do all the things he wanted me to do, but of course you can just see me on a football field. But I didn't think he was right until I actually saw a film of myself dancing. I said, "Oh my God, that's terrible. How weird can you get?" I finally decided I would reverse myself and try to become more masculine.

While I was in school I met this very charming young man. He seemed much older than me, and he was a very strange individual. We had an affair one afternoon on the beach. I was sixteen and he might have been twenty. That was my first encounter. He knew the score all right, but the funny part is that I seemed to know exactly what to do, though nobody had ever told me. From then on I realized you could cruise the park in Santa Monica and get picked up and find some lovely things. I liked older men. I think I thought an old man was thirty or forty, but as a teenager you would. So my first year out in the parks, believe it or not, I met 280 people, all different. I've told many people this, and they ask, "Why did you keep track?" I don't know, but I wrote down a little bit about each one. At that time the danger of going to the public cans was great. Periodically the police would arrest a whole bunch of people. But they would take one look at me and think that because I was a kid I couldn't possibly be involved. Many of my older friends were picked up and some of them went to jail for five, six, seven years.

Then I went back into motion pictures at 20th Century Fox and played in a few films until they decided I wasn't the type they wanted. They called me "elegant." Well, just then the war was breaking out, and I got my draft notice—I had just gotten a terrific part at Fox when it happened. I refused to be drafted and joined the navy. Of all things for me, they put me in the construction battalion, the seabees, with all these rough, tough marines. However, I was stuck there—I had chosen my service. I had the most miserable time in the service because I was constantly being approached by the so-called straights. They thought just because of my weird ways I was going to comply with them. Finally someone reported me and I became a very desperate person—afraid they'd find out about my sexual life.

I was called up before the admiral but they didn't have any proof. I called my father and he advised me about what to do. I went home on leave and got married to a girl I used to run around with in high school, and whom I had been writing to. That marriage was consummated by a son.

About six months after I got out of the service my father died, and right after that my wife and boy were killed in an automobile accident. I moved to San Francisco because I didn't want any more motion picture work, I wanted theatre work. And I didn't want to move to New York. Anyway, I had told my mother I was homosexual and she accepted it beautifully. She said, "If that's your preference, that's it. We won't discuss it any more."

In San Francisco I met a beautiful young lady from Colorado who joined my cast – I had started a repertory theatre in '44, '45. We'd produce plays here and then I'd send them travelling. I did it for nearly thirty years. I married this woman because I felt we could really make it work out and also because it was a good front for me, even in theatre. We lasted exactly two years. She divorced me once and we remarried six months later because we decided we couldn't live without each other. The second time, I divorced her because I couldn't tolerate her drunkenness. I didn't drink and I'd come home and she'd be dead drunk. During that marriage I got fully into the gay life. On Wednesday, when we were free, she'd do what she wanted and I'd do what I wanted. I usually went to one of the baths. I could have fun there and she wouldn't know where I was – and no one else would either. That last marriage, incidentally, really confused my mother – me telling her one thing and then getting married. After the second divorce I got a call from Fox, and I went back down there for a while and worked in the story department. All I did was sit there and read books and write little synopses of the stories. It was very good pay.

I met many leading men of the era, and very few weren't at least bisexual. You'd be so surprised when they'd come up and feel your fanny. On the set before the lights went on, invariably you'd get a feel job. David got a real job by the guy who was in that old science fiction adventure. He was in the back of the set while they were shooting a scene with Jane Russell – way back in the shadows – and this guy came over and went down on him. Lots of directors cast not only females on the "casting couch" but males as well. I got two roles because of a certain prominent person there. He even said, "I've got several people I can cast in these roles, and it's up to you." I knew exactly what he meant, and I told him OK. He said, "Well, then, we'll have a different kind of role first." I wasn't adverse to it. I thought, "Why not?" But I was always glad my father never knew.

The gay life in Hollywood wasn't undercover at all. It was the studios that put men and women stars and starlets together. After they made their social contact, like going to a party or a premiere, then they could leave each other and do what they wanted. I went out with several starlets and they always had a studio car and a chauffeur. After we went wherever it was we were supposed to be seen, they always said "Where do you want to go now? Home?" I'd say "No, let me off at some bar in Hollywood," because Hollywood at that time was the main place. I mean I would call every bar gay at that time because you made out whether it was straight or gay. It got pretty bad for a while and the studios started to crack down; we had to watch ourselves.

David once had a fight with a famous male star who told him, "Look, I sucked cocks to get where I am today and I can still do it. So watch out!" Some of the very feminine, beautiful women of the time were lesbians. You'd have to say about two-thirds of them were either lesbian or ready to go either way. Now today, I don't know what goes on. I think most actors do swing both ways, at least when they get started. But if they continue with it, I don't know.

It was about this time that I met Dave. He was a lighting technician and in fact he's done many marvelous things in Hollywood. We got together and from then on stayed together. We built a home in San Jose and lived there for a very short time. However, we felt that we were very suspect – you know, two men living alone in a home. The neighbors would make snide remarks so we sold our home and moved to New Mexico. After two years the heat got me down so we moved back this way to Oakland and then back to the city. We've moved around quite a bit. But in the thirty years we've been together we've had fun, lots of fun.

After our first year together we decided we'd cruise and have fun together because this one guy relationship doesn't work with men. One or the other is going to step out, and if the other finds out, it's devastating. So we made the decision that if we were going to go out we'd enjoy it together. That's why we're still together. We still have a devotion for each other, and there's no jealousy. This is what you have to get rid of in gay life – this jealousy. I watch it all the time and I feel sorry for these people.

Especially the young people going together. I see it next door. Each one tries to pick up extras when the other is gone to work, and I think, "Wait until he finds out, it's going to be horrible."

KV: Do you have any other special opinions on how you two stayed together so long?

Well, it hasn't always been easy. Believe me. Like any people we have our arguments and we fight. I finally learned to give in sometimes and forget it. If it didn't agree with me, it didn't hurt me either. I'd just have to say to myself, "It's his idea, let him have it, I don't care." And, of course, our religions are completely different. I'm Methodist and his church is more fundamentalist. His people didn't believe in jewelry, pictures in the home, entertainment, no dancing, no kissing.

KV: He doesn't abide by any of those things, does he?

I hope not. But when we go near his family we have to be extremely careful.

Now I have two old aunts living up north, and about fifteen years ago this one old aunt said, "Now Jon, I'd like to ask you a specific question if it won't bother you." And I said, "I think I know what you're going to ask, go ahead." She said, "Are you gay?" I told her yes and she said, "Well, thank God, there won't be any more marriages." I asked her what that had to do with it and she said that she was just tired of sending me wedding gifts all the time. She told my other aunt, who called me to say, "Ruthie just told me that you're homosexual. Why didn't you tell us before?" I said, "I wasn't asked." They both have accepted me as I am and they don't care. And they love David tremendously. We go there for the weekends or longer and we all have a very good time. Once I gave a show up there for their senior citizens' group and took the whole cast. Afterwards my aunt introduced me and said, "This is my nephew, he's gay you know." I told her, "You don't have to tell people that." She said "I want them to know." I told her not to go around introducing me and saying I'm queer. She said, "Then how do you make contacts?" Actually, I have an immediate sense of whether people are gay or not, or even bisexual. I haven't been infallible, but as you grow older I think you know more what to look for.

KV: How do you socialize, mostly?

We have lots of friends of all ages. Sexually we stay mostly within the forty-five to seventy age group now. We have a lot of younger friends, too, but I find the majority of them don't mix too well with older people. I've tried to put the two together and invariably it's a catastrophe. If I give a big party, it's generally eighty, ninety people. We have loads of acquaintances—I shouldn't say friends, because as far as friends go you have very few. We enjoy having people in and we're invited out constantly. We make a lot of contacts like last Saturday night when we went to a bar and met a very charming man. He's forty years old and he just came over and started talking. He said, "This music's awfully loud in here," and I said, "Yes, let's go back to our apartment." So we walked up the street and he stayed the weekend.

KV: So that was a sexual thing too, correct?

Yeah, oh sure. If they're interested we have three-ways, we have four-ways, sometimes we'll meet couples who have ideas similar to our own. Sometimes one of us will take a vacation alone and be gone a week, and if I meet someone while Dave is out of town, I usually try to get them introduced later on. I think it's wise, too, because then there's none of this secret wondering about what it was like. After you see the person you know what it would be like. Usually the ones I haven't introduced have been from out of town, people I never saw again. Dave and I also go to the baths a lot together.

I find going to bed with a woman very invigorating at times, if I'm in the mood. I'm not too often in the mood for it anymore, but I'm not adverse. Not too long ago Dave and I picked up a very charming woman and brought her home and had a great time. She was like another guy, she did everything in the book and we just enjoyed it. She stayed the whole weekend. We'd eat, sleep, have a few drinks, screw, go back and eat, sleep. . . . She said that she had never found a gay man who wasn't the best lover in the world, and that when she wanted sex she tried to find a gay man who liked women. Maybe she's right, I don't know. I know what a woman likes, though, more than a straight man who just wants to stick it in without any foreplay. We never heard from her again and I was thankful because sometimes a woman will want to hang on to you.

There's nothing we haven't tried. We have tried everything as far as I know and we finally decided on the things we like best. Some of these new sexual activities are quite different and have

126

changed over the years, though sex is the oldest thing in the world between male and female, two males, two females. But I remember when I first came out, well, someone said, "Would you like to sixty-nine?" I didn't even know what it meant. When they showed me I said OK. It was like the first time I was shown how to French kiss. It was fabulous, I enjoyed it. Then I found out that with other people, if they asked you if you liked to French, it meant would you go down on them. One must keep abreast of the times and I think I have done my best.

Don't ask me what my type is because I don't know. It's whoever at the time looks good and is nice. I have particular ideas about the body structure but that doesn't mean that they have to be tall or short because that makes no difference to me. In all the gay magazines coming out, I'm so sick and tired of looking at huge meat. I finally read a letter in one of them saying "Why don't you show all the normal natural meat and forget this stuff?" Now Dave is built big but not like that. So what do you do with it? Love it a lot? Put your arms around it?

Years ago when there weren't any magazines in this country, Dave and I used to send to Europe to buy them. We'd get them under a separate name because you could be arrested for receiving them. And they didn't even *do* anything in the pictures. They would put both males and females in the pictures so it wouldn't be too horrible. I remember once I opened one up, in London, and there were actually two men doing something. And I said, "My God, if they ever opened this up at our post office that would be it!" If you got things from the same address too often, they'd open it right up to find out what the hell it was. One day I did get called by the post office. They telephoned me and asked me to come down to verify a package. When I asked where it was from and they told me, I informed them that I had no such package coming. So we lost about $25 because I refused it. This way they couldn't do anything about it. Had I gone down, I probably would have been in a jam.

Dave and I were arrested here in 1954, '55. We were down on Polk Street in a bar. A fellow came in and bought a whole round, and for some reason he picked Dave and me out. He sat down between us and we were all drinking up a load. He said "How would you guys like to come with me?" We said "OK. Why not for a spell?" So we left the bar and he said, "My car's right over here."

Just as we got to his car another guy jumped out and said, "You're under arrest." He told the other guy, "I see you got some goodies." We were picked up for being homosexual. He claimed that we were trying to make him. We went to jail and we ended up in the tank all night. They finally transferred us to the old Hall of Justice on Kearny. Well, we got one of the finest female attorneys in town. She was with the gay activists at that time, believe it or not. She's retired now and a very old lady. When she went there she said, "I have never seen such a report. What did you do, rape the guy right there on the spot?" I told her we didn't even touch him. She said, "This is not only complete harrassment but entrapment too." We went to court and were given a choice between trial with or without a jury. She chose without because she said she knew the judge. So the two cops were there, and she asked me, on the stand, "What did you do, practically rape the poor gentleman?" And I said, "Judge, take a look at him, I'm not that hard up yet." The judge turned and said, "I don't blame ya," and pronounced us not guilty. But it still cost us a thousand each. That was a horrible experience, and we were afraid it would be in the newspapers, but we were never mentioned. Dave was afraid it would be all over and his folks would find out. It's an experience I would never want to go through again.

And believe it or not, the cop who originally picked us up had the audacity, when the trial was over and we were going out, to say, "I don't know why we can't be friends." I just looked at him and didn't say a word. When we told our lawyer about it, she said, "Well, *don't* be friends." And I told her we had absolutely no intention to do so. I've often wondered what he had in mind. It was a really weird situation. The judge asked that we not sue the city, and we agreed.

I retired from local theatre two years ago when I got very ill and that's why I decided to manage apartments while Dave continues to work. This way I can keep my standard of living high enough. When Dave retires we'd like to do a little traveling, but so much depends on the value of money. Maybe we won't even be alive in a couple of years. You never know from day to day. I'm going to be dying one of these days but I just hope that we can keep going, keep meeting people, keep making friends, or shall I say "acquaintances." I'd like to continue to be very active. We will be travelling to England and Scotland in a few months. I hope to keep going as long as I can and if I can't then I'll quit and just sit back and take it easy. Reminisce about the old days. We hear a lot of these older men tell us of their experiences and some of them are unbelievable. Then you sit back and think, "Mine are just as weird!"

Five months ago I got hurt very badly. I had asked two prostitutes who were living in the building to leave. One night when Dave had gone out to pick up dinner two guys came to my door. I thought it was Dave, having forgot his keys. I opened the door and all I saw was their silhouettes, and I could smell this stuff. They drugged me, took me to the hallway and pushed me down the stairs. They stuffed me under a car alongside the curb in front and left me for dead. My arm was broken in three places and I had to have fourteen stitches, and my leg was so badly twisted I couldn't walk. The police asked me if it was gay-oriented. I told them I didn't think so. I was waiting for the question, "Are you gay?" I was going to tell them no because they won't do a thing the minute you mention you're gay. It was quite a horrible thing to have happen.

KV: Do you have any philosophy you live your life by?

No, not really. I've never thought too much about it, either. I never want to hurt anyone if I can help it either physically or by reputation – both of which have been done to me. Dave and I were maligned terribly when we were first together. People tried to break us up by telling each of us different stories because they were jealous of our relationship. I think it's an awful thing to malign someone's reputation; even though your story may be true, there's no need for it. My philosophy is just to leave well enough alone. If you don't like someone, all you have to do is walk away from them.

Anyway, I think you should talk with Dave too. He knows you're here and he asked me why I made the appointment in the afternoon when he's not here. I said that I'm apt to give you a lot more detail if he's not around. Well, he'll probably tell you things he doesn't want me to know.

11

David Bowling

David is in his early sixties and shares a large apartment with his longtime lover, Jon. He is a big man, with a mischievous smile, a comforting mixture of hospitality and light-heartedness.

I CAME FROM A FAMILY THAT WAS VERY UPTIGHT IN ONE sense but who knew the score in another. Most of my childhood was spent in the Los Angeles area. My father owned a restaurant, a very prestigious place. He ran with bankers and stock market men. My parents did not quite follow the strict beliefs of their religion—they were first-nighters at many theatre premieres, and that sort of thing—though they returned to being strict later on. I was used to my parents throwing parties where many gay people were present, and my first lessons in sex were not about the birds and the bees but to look out for some of the guests. I was told what went on in Pershing Square when I was five or six. I was never to venture through there, alone or otherwise. So I knew about gays before I knew how in the hell you had babies. However, when I first found out about the sex act I felt it was a wonderful, beautiful thing. I thought it was fantastic how we're made. I never had any interest in boys that I was aware of. I was girl-crazy. This in itself, a psychiatrist might tell you, is a signal. I was noted for lovin' 'em and leavin' 'em. I don't think I could ever stand a girl more than twice. I had the Don Juan complex. I was not aggressive with boys, yet I was not satisfied with women.

This was in junior high school. We were very precocious in Orange County. We had professional prostitutes in my seventh and eighth grade classes. We had beer bust parties. Gradually, as we found out our parents were getting uptight about some of these things, we stopped coming home and telling them what was going on. We learned to shut up.

In those days we didn't have sex magazines, we had what they called "nudist magazines," which were really thinly disguised sex magazines. And then there were the health magazines. When I saw the men I wasn't turned off, I was turned on. And yet I never thought of it in a sexual way, I just admired these guys' bodies— and I will say, I also admired the bulge in their shorts. But I didn't know why. In those days they'd take the unsold magazines, tear the covers off and send those back for refund, and the magazine itself became public property. A friend of my father's continually fed us a stack of all the current magazines without our having to pay for them. Mother used to try to pick out what she thought might be a little disturbing like the detective magazines. After finding a few I could see why she hid those in particular. They were full of violent, disturbing murders. This was in the thirties when it was pretty wild. I think I gained a subconscious fear of what might happen to me if I were a homosexual from reading those magazines—we had some really horrible crimes in Southern California that had been done by degenerates to both boys and girls. The Hearst papers picked right up on that, you can bet. I associated homosexuality with a great deal of danger.

I knew so damn much about gay life that when I finally went into the navy and a person made a pass at me I knew exactly what they were up to. I was feisty enough to almost break a guy's arm in the theatre for groping me. This guy would not leave me alone so finally I took his arm, grabbed it in two places and whammed it down across the arm of the seat. He left. I hope I really didn't do any permanent damage, but I wasn't interested.

Slowly things changed for me. I met a Russian officer when I was on leave. This was during the war and we had a lot of foreign naval men coming into this country. I met him at the USO. I took him home with me because I didn't live on the naval base. I had no suspicion of anything and considered him a friend. The first time I met him nothing happened. But the second time he was in port I brought him home again, and I woke up in the morning with him blowing me. I was very upset and yet I was so excited I wasn't going to stop it. So I closed my eyes and looked dimly under my eyelids to watch him go on with it. I never let him think I was awake. I suppose that's rather stupid because I don't think you could really have that experience and not be awake. Anyway, that was the end of that friendship. I was so disturbed over the whole thing that I never allowed him to come near me again. But it had broken the dam.

I kept thinking about it and realized if a girl had been doing it I would have loved it. So why did it upset me so? I knew how to go out and get picked up, so I kept thinking, "I'm going to try this again but with a different attitude, when I'm not taken by shock or antagonism, to see if I can enjoy it."

I was stationed in Washington, D.C., at this time and I had a leave that was too short to come home. I was walking by some square, and this other sailor said, "Hi," and I said, "Hi" back. He must have seen my camera and figured I was not stationed there. Next thing I knew we were going around to some of the bars and having a good time together. We spent all afternoon and evening together. I tried to make a girl in one of these bars, and almost did, but at the last minute she stood me up. We ended up in the wee hours of the morning, hungry, and went to have sandwiches. He said, "I'm stationed in Algiers across the river and I'd hate to go back at this hour. Would you mind sharing your hotel room with me tonight?" Just for a fleeting moment it went through my mind, "I just wonder if he's gay." And immediately I thought, "no," otherwise I don't think I'd have let him come up. I was still very uptight. So we went up to my room, I got into the shower, and he came in after me. He took me in his arms, slipped slowly down my body, and by that time I had an erection you couldn't imagine. He took me in his mouth, came back up and said, "You know what's happening?" I said, "Of course I do." He said, "Do you mind?" I said, "Of course I don't. I've been looking for this." We jumped into bed and you would have thought I had done it all my life. He couldn't believe it was my first time. We had a wonderful time.

The next morning he said, "You're going to get upset." "No, I'm not," I said. He said, "Yes you are. You're going to try to rationalize what you've done. But when you start thinking about it, don't. Just forget it." I told him it would never bother me because I had loved every second of it. But my God, he was right. I got very upset. I brooded over it for months. "What am I? Am I a queer? If so, why do I like women?" Because I did, very much. "And if I'm not queer then why did it come so naturally to me?" Incidentally, I never had any qualms about going down on a woman, which made it very easy to go down on a man. I've always felt that if a body was clean there wasn't anything or any part of it that you couldn't touch. Anyway, I went around for many months in this disturbed state of mind. Finally I decided the answer was to explore some more.

I went out and picked up other men and found out about all the different aspects of sex and finally decided it wasn't for me. But one day while we were swimming nude in the Pacific—we'd do that when there were no women around—things changed. I used to look at some of my buddies and think, "Gee, the lucky woman who has that on top of her." But one afternoon I realized I wasn't saying that anymore. I was thinking *I* would like to be under that guy. I was bisexual. I had a mistress, and she proved to be a wonderful excuse because seventy percent of the time when my buddies knew I hadn't shown up all night, they thought I was over at Estelle's. But I sure as hell wasn't. I was out looking for gay experiences.

I was also engaged to be married. My wife-to-be gave me a "Dear John" reception when I came home from the navy. She said afterwards that she thought if she saw me again maybe she'd forget this other guy she'd met, but she couldn't. I left her feeling very disillusioned. I was so hurt I couldn't stand the thought of another woman for months. I don't want to say that she threw me completely over into the homosexual world because I don't think there is such a thing as someone being able to do it to you. But if there was a decisive fact that was probably it. If this hadn't happened I might have gotten married and just occasionally gone out and got something. A lot of married men live that way.

I met Jonathan in San Francisco and we moved to Hollywood. Hollywood, at that time, had a great many gay bars. You found out that they were either predominantly gay or else the chances of making a connection were good even if they weren't. Most of these places paid off the police, so you felt relatively safe going to them as long as you behaved yourself. That means that any overt groping or kissing could get you thrown out of the place or could bring on a raid. Because of the payoffs the bartenders were usually warned ahead of time. If you were a regular customer they would usually tip you off so you could get the hell out of there. But Hollywood has always been flamboyant. I used to go up to Hollywood Boulevard and often you could spot a gay and they could spot you. That's one reason why in those days the vice squads usually hired gays. This is one of the dirtiest things that ever occurred in police history and maybe it still goes on, but they used to pick guys who had been dishonorably discharged from the service for homosexuality because they would be adept at entrapment. It's a vicious thing but they could break through the barrier where a straight cop couldn't. I mean you can't always tell whether a guy's commercial or not, but you can tell if he's receptive.

There was a lot of gay life around the studios and a lot of them wanted to find out whether I was gay or not. But I think it was less open when I was working there than it had been when I was a kid. If you didn't mind getting known as gay you could let your hair down and see how far it took you. I was the other way around, I kept my hair up and just observed. A rather interesting thing happened one night in our apartment in Hollywood. Jon & I picked up a guy and he tried to blackmail us. He said, "You have a pretty good job at 20th Century Fox and you like your job, don't you?" I said, "Yes, I do." He said, "What would happen if I told them you were gay?" Actually, I think he said "queer." I could hardly believe my ears. I said, "You can't be serious. There are a lot of big shots there who have been trying to put the make on me. *They* would pay *you* if you told them. You don't know the first thing about film studios at all."

There was another amusing incident concerning the studios too. We had this one guy, a great big guy, but very fem. He offered me a ride to the studios and back, and after a couple of times I started to refuse because I was afraid my reputation was going to really be besmirched just by being in the car with him. Anyway, a bunch of the guys decided that they were going to fix him good because they had sized him up as being gay. They were going to get him cornered in the showers. Gang rape. It so happened that the very morning of the day that they were going to do this we had to take a bunch of sandbags over to one of the outdoor sets. We had to load them into the back of a truck. For most of us it took all we had to lift just one. But this effeminate guy walks over, grabs two sandbags, and tosses them into the back of the truck like they were nothing. The guys just stood there with their mouths open. This guy who acted like a ballet dancer, well, they never had anything to say about him after that. They were scared shitless.

KV: At this time Jon walks in and joins David for the remainder of the interview.

J: Tell him about the Black Cat.

Well, the Black Cat was a notorious place. Even when I was in high school I had heard about this place up in San Francisco. However, when I had come out and was hitting places in San Francisco I would occasionally stick my face in there just to see what was going on. I would never go home with anybody I met there. It was supposed to be just the riff-raff and the dregs who went there. If you cared about your reputation you shouldn't be seen in there.

One night I came in and the place was packed. I was thirty-one and had already decided that I would probably spend my life as a loner. I'd accepted it and I was willing to live that way. I was no longer looking for a partner. Then I walked in and saw *this* (motions toward Jon) sitting on top of the beer boxes at the far end of the place. And through that smoke-filled room I looked at him and I said, "This one's for me, if there's ever going to be one for me." I pushed my way through that crowd, to get as close as I could, and I started working on it. I tried every trick I knew in my little book and all I got was insults, sneers, put-downs. But I would not give up.

Finally I got him to go home with me. We both had apartments and he was losing his wife, leaving his wife, however you want to look at it. I said, "Which place should we go?" He said "Let's go to my place," and we did.

J: It was much nicer.

Anyway, the first insult I got was when I took off my pants and he said. . .

J: I said, "Do I have to put up with this?"

Anyway, he put up with it. We had a lovely time except that in the morning when I woke up with the sun streaming in across the bed, I looked at his hair and it looked like a calico cat. it was red, brown, pink and grey all over. Black too, and there must have been a few more colors in there.

J: He took me home to his apartment and said, "Why don't you make a cup of coffee." Then he added, "Gosh, I don't think I have any coffee." I looked in his little pantry and said, "I don't think you have much of anything." Anyway, we've had these friends who tried to split us up and we're still together. At the time almost every queen you met had the great dream of meeting a partner and having a lasting relationship. This was the big thing, yet the minute anybody started to have one, the rest would converge like vultures and try to tear it apart.

We still know some of these people and they can't believe that we're still together. One of their excuses was, "He's not worthy of you." Who's worthy of who? I mean that's a matter of opinion. We've had other friends who tell us they've gone through the same thing. I don't understand this — how do two people ever start making it together unless they're left alone and given the opportunity? But it's no different than heterosexual marriage; you have to work at it.

I'll tell you one thing about being together thirty years — it takes a lot of forgiving and forgetting.

J: I'm a very difficult person. I will admit this. Dave is not very magnificent but I think of the two of us I am worse. And he has forgiven many, many times where I never would have.

Basically I'm not a very forgiving person.

J: No, he's not, but he is with me.

I hold grudges, at least I used to. But I can't imagine holding a grudge with you.

J: David and I have always been lovers and we still are. In our old age we still are lovers.

Sometimes it's almost like having sex for the first time. Maybe not quite, but it's wonderful.

J: I couldn't imagine being without him.

We do have some common interests, yet I could spend all day in an art gallery and it would drive Jon up the wall. I could go to the opera three nights in succession, and Jon wouldn't even want to go the first night. Not that he doesn't like opera once every three years. I talk too much, it exasperates him. I like to read, yet I can't while he's here. If I try he won't let me, then he wonders why I don't get anything read. But he's considerate in many ways.

J: I am? Goody, I'm glad you admitted it.

Well, I really do believe that when I saw Jon that night – I know this song, "One enchanted evening, you'll see a stranger across a crowded room" – it sounds like a lot of crap but I really believe there can be such a thing as love at first sight.

J: You liked my nose. It stuck out from everyone else's.

I will never understand this. I've been attracted to people and then, on knowing them better, there hasn't even been a survival of friendship. I don't believe there normally is such a thing as love at first sight but how can you explain to me that I could open a door in a crowd and suddenly spot somebody and say, "That's it?"

KV: I'd like to discuss more of your experiences in the last thirty or so years.

I'll tell you about an experience I went through, which I don't think most Americans today would believe, and that's the McCarthy era. I was working in Washington at the time. The man who set this whole thing going was gay, and his lover had been run out of D.C. There was a big party one night and the way the police were in Washington – what's legal or illegal was not their concern. They had what they called the fire laws, overcrowding in an establishment. They got wind of this party. Of course the way it was being handled was very typical of D.C. at that time. People at the gay bars would say there's going to be a party at such and such, and word would get around. The police heard about it, and instead of waiting for the party to begin, they arrested each person as they arrived at the door. They got about two hundred people that night. The next day everyone's name was in the paper and which government agency they worked for. Needless to say, this man's lover was one of the ones arrested. Actually the police commissioner owned several gay bars himself. Anyway this guy's attitude was, "If my lover can't get away with it here in Washington, nobody else can either." You'd be surprised how bitchy homosexuals could be. It was entirely a bitch retaliation. All of a sudden it became political and found to be a good way of getting votes. This particular man also had a pending case back in his home state of contributing to the delinquency of a minor, as well as a service record of his homosexuality.

It got so bad at one point that all they had to do was have somebody say that they doubted your orientation. I'm not joking, I had friends in Budapest, Hungary, and did not dare have them send their mail to me. Instead I had them send it to my mother. All you had to do was have somebody accuse you, and in the morning you'd come to work and there'd be a pink thing on your desk. You had absolutely no hearing or anything. You were dismissed. It sounds just fantastic but it's true. One day at work I had an argument with this fellow who wanted my job—I had been promoted over him. He suddenly twirled around and said, "If you don't like this country, why don't you leave it?" All this because I had criticized a subway station that had just been built in New York City. In that instant I thought, "Watch your tongue, boy, watch your tongue." All he had to do was to prove that I was un-American. It was that simple.

I went on vacation in Ocean City, Maryland, and ran into a fellow I had known in Washington. I asked him where he'd been because I hadn't seen him in a long while. "Don't you know? I was fired," he said. I asked him why. "Because I was gay. They put a watch on my apartment because my name had been struck off the list five times." I asked him what he was talking about. He said that the police had a list of suspected gays in Washington and every time they arrested someone for being gay they gave them this list and they were supposed to go down the list and put a check next to the name of each person they knew. When there were five checks next to your name they put a person outside to watch *your* apartment. "Are people given a lighter sentence for checking off names?" "Yes." I said, "You're kidding, what did you do?" He said, "What do you think I did? I'm going to drag every goddamn person down with me I can." I said, "You're really serious?!" He says, "You're damn right I'm serious. I checked off every name I could. If I'm going to be dragged down I'm not going to go alone." I tell you, I couldn't believe my ears. If it had happened to me I would have just gone down myself. I found out from others that this check list was real. Once you were checked off five times they would put someone to watch you to see if you picked someone up or went to a bar or something like that, then they would cancel your job.

But I'll tell you another thing. Although it was dangerous in that era and everything was underground, I still think we had more fun than the gays are having today.

KV: Why is that?

I know the element of danger always sparks a little something, but I really find it difficult to understand a lot of the flamboyance of gays now. Even though they're more accepted on the surface, the public is much more aware and much more difficult to ignore. We used to get away with an awful lot of gay activity and nobody—the average public was so stupid—realized it. Now that they know what's going on, they're censoring it and so forth. I don't think the public today is any more tolerant than they used to be.

I had a friend, Betty, who was the hostess with the mostest in Washington. She had buffets by the score and many people in every night. There was hardly a person there, male or female, who wasn't gay. And she wanted to marry me. We went to Bermuda together. I went swimming in the nude with her and afterwards she told me she was so ashamed to think she'd let me see her body. She was from an old Virginia family. Later she came out West to visit me and though I didn't realize it, she had been goaded on by some friends to get me to marry her. When I realized she was at the point of not taking no for an answer, I told her I was gay. Her first reaction was: "Who did it to you?" I said, "Betty, I thought you knew that everybody you know is gay." She did not know. She started naming names and I had to say yes to all of them. I said, "Betty, you know in D.C. everybody thinks you're the gayest hostess in town.

J: When we went back to visit her in D.C. she had a huge party for him . . .

Yes, about forty people. She got right in the middle of it and said "Ladies and gentlemen, I want you to know one thing, this is Bowling's new love, Jon. This is why he didn't marry me. He selected him instead." I told her, "Betty, how ridiculous." She ended up marrying a gay man.

KV: What do you anticipate for the future, Dave?

Well, I tell you truthfully, it's very hard to look far into the future because Jon doesn't have good health and I'm not getting any younger. What will happen to us is hard to know. One time we had thought that we'd retire and go down to Mexico and live there but for several reasons we've given that idea up. Whatever happens, we'll stay here in the States unless something very unusual occurs. The cost of living, the absence of medicare in Mexico, things like that make it less desirable. When I retire we'll probably either have a modest place near the city or we might stay in the city. The cost of everything has gone up so that most of our dreams have gone down the drain. I think the main thing as far as our future is concerned is to make each other has happy as we can. I've gotten over the idea of wanting and acquiring things. I think I'm getting more into a giving relationship. I think I've been a selfish person most of my life. I think most people are basically selfish even if they don't think so. But I do hope I can give more of myself. I don't see any radical changes in our lifestyle and I don't think I'm ever going to come completely out of the closet.

J: Dave has come out of the closet a great deal.

KV: Do you have any philosophy of life?

J: Yes, Dave does. Tell him.

I don't know exactly what you're referring to. I will tell you this. I am a Christian but I'm a gay Christian. I don't think God's going to cast me into hell because I'm gay.

J: Go on. You had more than that. He's taught me some marvelous things, made it beautiful.

I'm not entirely sure what you're referring to, Jon.

J: About our being together. You brought this up when I was in the hospital and so ill. You said so many lovely things; why don't you say them now?

As a philosophy of life?

J: Well, if you've forgotten, that's fine.

Who's being interviewed here, you or me?

J: When you thought I was going to die, you told me how much you loved me and all those things.

I think what you want me to say is how I feel about you.

J: You came in and said, "I love you."

I told you to remember that whatever happens, I'm with you. Then you asked me to leave. I told you I didn't want to and you said it was the hospital rules. And I said, "Remember I'm with you even when I'm gone."

J: And I said, "I accept that."
I really do believe that Jon and I will be together forever and ever. Perhaps it's not my philosophy but it is certainly my belief.

12

Al Hoskins

Al is in his sixties, lives in Berkeley, California, and has owned both a small pottery business and furniture shop. After his lover of many years died, he attempted suicide but was stopped by the police before he got over the rail of the Golden Gate Bridge. Internment in a military psychiatric ward during wartime set a pattern for return hospitalization throughout his life. He is a large man with short gray hair who moves slowly and with caution.

IT SEEMS TO ME LIKE THE LAST TEN YEARS HAVE GONE BY faster than the previous twenty. The older you get the faster they go by. When I went to the University of the Pacific Dental School I told them I'd had my dentures for about a year or two and it turned out they were done about six years ago. But I remember the house and the neighbors and a neighborhood boy that I used to play with quite clearly. All the adults had labeled him as deficient and he got me involved in sixty-nining with him around the side of the house. My mother came along and found us and the shit hit the fan. I was only four years old then.

I remember him saying, "Do it like you used to do." We thought it was the same thing as nursing and somehow equated the penis with the breast. This sounds dreadfully Freudian. Well, to us it was just play. There was no sexuality, as we know it, connected with that act at all. My dad walloped the pants off me and my mother chastised me tremendously. I could not understand why they were so upset and I told an older boy the story. He was about eleven or twelve and I thought he might shed some light on the incident. Instead, he got so excited he had me blow him. Meanwhile there was another boy watching us. I considered what I was doing as just playing. The other kids called it "turning a knob on a door" or initiated it by saying, "Let's go for a walk or climb a hill or something."

Later on, the boy who had watched me blow the twelve-year-old was eating an apple and had a bunch of other fruit with him. He handed me what looked like an apple, a sort of red thing. I bit into it and let out a scream in horrible pain. He'd given me one of the hottest peppers that exist. He said, "That's what happens to little boys who do the sort of thing you did." He was only nine or ten and very self-righteous. Anyway I was gradually coming to the realization that this is something you're very careful not to let anyone know about. When I screamed, my mother came running out of the house and asked what happened. Fortunately he didn't spill the beans because she would have gone trotting off to Dad again.

I remember one sultry afternoon sitting on the fender of the car, the old Model T, and sort of playing around with myself until it got hard. I wondered what that was all about. My mother caught me and I got punished for that. She and my dad had been raised on the idea that masturbation caused insanity.

My only knowledge of girls came when we boarded a girl, Kitty Arthur. She was five and I was in first grade. My father had to move often and do all sorts of work. My memory is of fairly shoddy apartments, whatever we could get, hotel rooms and so on. At any rate, Kitty and I always used to play "nasty" or something like that. She'd been boarded in homes a lot and had experienced everything a kid that age could possibly experience. One evening she was feeling around me and asked me to put my hands inside of her pajama bottoms. She said I could feel her and I did. There wasn't anything there and I couldn't imagine what the hell that was all about. That was my impression of the female until I reached adolescence and heard other stories. Even when I was told about normal procreation, why, that seemed pretty damn dull. It impressed me as a duty rather than a pleasure.

The next big explosion as a kid came when I was playing with two older kids down the block, ages thirteen and fourteen – one of them got an erection. It was at night and we were sort of wrestling on the lawn. He got his crotch right down on my face and took it out and made me blow him. He was built like an adult and I was about nine or ten years old. I rather enjoyed it. Then he told his friend who was fourteen and he insisted I do it to him, too. We'd all three go out in the summer evenings. There was a big water tower, about a hundred feet tall, and we'd climb up to the platform on top. The only thing I didn't understand was why those two didn't involve each other in the same sort of thing. I remember one time I got real obstinate and said I wouldn't do a damn thing until they did something themselves. I achieved only limited success with that. The older one used to fuck me once in a while and that was rather painful. The first time I ever saw semen, I thought he was urinating or something. It scared the hell out of me. One day we were over at the younger one's house and his parents were gone, so we had our usual experience. When I left I met my mother coming up the street. She asked where I'd been and said she'd been calling me for about an hour for dinner. I got scared and told her what had happened. Oh God! I got another punishment. My parents phoned the police department and they came out and had a talk with these kids. Then the two kids came over and my mother had a talk with them. I got sort of nervous and giddy. In the dining room there were these huge French doors that opened out to the living room. I sort of hooked my arms over them and started swinging on them. Mother said, "Excuse me," and walked over and pulled me aside and told me I was acting crazy, and she wasn't sure that what they'd done hadn't made me go off my rocker. This was just shortly after the Leopold and Loeb affair, so parents were very concerned about older boys getting connected with younger ones.

So my earliest experiences with sex were "thou shalt not." At ten I was fully developed sexually, and almost fully developed physically. I was five-five and weighed 197 pounds. It was about that time that I went with the family to visit some friends up in Susanville in the mountains. I crawled into an irrigation ditch to take a leak and started thinking about all those earlier sexual experiences. I started masturbating just as a matter of curiosity. Suddenly this strange feeling hit me and I practically froze all over, it was absolutely delightful. That was my first orgasm. So after that, every chance I got, I'd masturbate.

When I was eleven I went over to the bus depot to the men's room. So many men, straight and gay both, out of curiosity as much as anything, examine the equipment of the other person. There was a guy there at the other end of the place who was sort of masturbating. I immediately got an erection which prompted him to walk over to me and start feeling me. Well, that of course thrilled me no end. It turned out he was an elevator operator in the medical building. My mother thought he was the nicest person. I used to visit him every time I went down to the old Hippodrome Theatre. I used to go to the Plaza Park too.

The park bothered me a bit because there were so many men on the bum there—we were in the midst of the Depression. I remember one guy wouldn't have anything to do with me because he was a hustler and wanted to save every drop he had in him for something he'd be paid for.

In another park at Sixteenth and 'P' Street, I met a fellow, and we went out. I told him I was eighteen and bitched about some of my classes. It didn't occur to me that if I were eighteen I wouldn't be taking these classes. It turned out he was the principal of a school. When I finally told him that I was only fourteen, he said, "Well, that makes a big difference. I thought you were a rather stupid eighteen-year-old, but I think you're a rather bright fourteen-year-old." Later on, Mother mentioned the young pastor who had baptized me. He'd been involved in a scandal of some sort and had ended up working for the school system. It turned out the guy who was blowing me rather frequently was the minister who baptized me.

About this time, too, my mother walked into the bathroom, caught me masturbating, and called my father. He got a big rope and actually started crying because he was so upset. He chased me out on the front porch and started beating me with that rope. He was absolutely hysterical. That incident just reinforced my own puritanical attitudes about sex. My mother reinforced my thoughts about girls, that a boy should not show any interest in them unless he was finished with college, had a good vocation and income, and could provide a girl with everything she wanted. Actually, I'd say from those early years until my thirties I was a latent heterosexual.

In my mid-teens I found out about the whorehouses in Sacramento. I never had any experience in them, but my friends and I would go down there because we liked to visit the prostitutes. We'd go into the living rooms in their houses in the older part of town and they'd come out and talk to us. Once in a while they would fondle one of the kids until he got an erection. I remember one of them said, "If you've got a dollar and a half, you can watch me with a customer." We didn't even have a buck and a half.

When I was fourteen I joined the Order of Demolay, which I liked because we met in the Masonic Temple. It was the first time I learned about billiards and pool. I thought it was just a game for toughs or scum who went into pool parlors. I didn't realize that the upper echelon played, too, in these beautiful places with Chinese carpets and plush figured wallpaper. And I loved the formal dances. "Unc" Pollack was the uncle of several of the guys in the order. He had been a youth leader for years. I wish to hell I knew his story but he passed away years ago. One time he offered to drive a girl and me home after a dance. When we got to her home I did the obligatory hug and kiss and was glad when it was over. He drove me home and parked about a house away from where I lived and said, "Well, aren't you going to give me a good-night kiss?" With that, I got excited as hell. I kissed him and he started Frenching. He must have been in his fifties or sixties. The affection I got from him I enjoyed more than the sex. I was always interested in people who were much older than I was. To this day I'm not a chicken hawk.

I still cruised the parks. One guy followed me out of the Plaza one evening. We went into a men's room and I fiddled around with him and then he asked for money. He followed me out, told me he'd beat the shit out of me if I didn't take him to my folks. I went to "Unc" Pollack and told him the guy was waiting downstairs for me. He went down and called the cops. The cops took us both down to the station and one smart-assed cop said, "Come on, you are a tutti-fruity, aren't you?" He wanted to humiliate me. They ran the guy out of town and let me go; however there was a newspaper reporter there and I was afraid I was going to be in the papers. The next morning I got up early and hitchhiked down to Los Angeles. I left my folks a goofy note saying that I wanted to make a man of myself or something like that. I got plenty more experience when I got to L.A.!

I stayed in L.A. only a short time but I learned about the parks and to recognize when people were cruising me. There was very little use of drugs or alcohol. It was during the Depression; people were sleeping in automobiles in used car lots, trying to get jobs as extras in the movies. There were a couple of johns down there but I had very little tearoom sex except maybe for a quick blow job – *being* blown.

I found out to my relief that there was never anything printed about me back home so I returned there. One of my first sexual findings was that it's exceedingly common among so-called straight men to receive anally rather than anything else, particularly the more macho ones. Blowing or kissing, no. But once these macho guys find out about their prostrate – that it's something quite pleasurable – they'll drop their pants at a drop of the hat. They feel they're doing someone else a favor. I was old enough now to go barhopping and I got involved in the underground gay scene with magnificent parties thrown in hotels and apartments. It was so underground that you felt freer than I guess anybody feels now. The only thing you had to worry about were hustlers and thieves, but I think they were easier to spot then.

When I was younger I worried about being found out all the time. Worry, worry, worry, worry. I still believed in the things my folks told me about insanity and masturbation and such. I saw a man and a woman coming out of the medical building on Tenth Street. I said to myself, "I'll remember them," their feet in the air walking, like a frozen picture, "if any thoughts come to mind that are bothering me, I'll remember these people." For years I could see the man in his brown suit and the woman in her nurse's outfit, without a cap, caring for him. I picked this image to block out the darker thoughts.

I got deferments through the last year of college and then I entered midshipman's school. I quit, stupidly, because I was mad at the instructors. They were preparing us for a commission in the navy. If you were on a ship and disaster struck, you took over and everybody else was inferior to you. If there was a group of people starving and there was only so much food, well, you got the food and nobody else did. I felt that was wrong. But while I was there I made full use of that uniform. I was physically well off and attractive. I fell in love with one guy in the school though we never had sex. Then there was a blind girl I met, Sara, who I took to all the dances.

She was twenty-nine, and when you're young a few years difference and the person seems ancient. She looked very mature and friends of mine said, "Why don't you get her in bed?" If I like a person and feel a twinge of affection for them, I'd pay attention to it. Well, the first time I tried to get her in bed she pushed me away. A week later she came over to my apartment for dinner and afterwards just took her clothes off. I tried several times with her and finally one day got it up. I had made penetration and there was blood all over. I was shocked. That sent me into a migraine that lasted nearly a month. I nearly died from the pain. The affair with Sara threw me into gay life faster than ever.

Then World War II started. I was living in San Francisco and Sol Neiderman, a friend of mine from Sacramento, came to stay with me. We found out through another friend about the Top of the Mark. The whole town was drinking there. It was very crowded so there was a lot of excuse for kneeing and fumbling. If someone seemed offended you'd say, "I'm sorry, did I bump you?" Nobody wanted a scene so everything worked out well. In the meantime, somebody else would be practically unzipping and fondling you. At any rate, I met the underground on a level that I could accept; something different from the old Crystal Grotto in Sacramento, down in the lower part of town that I wouldn't be seen walking into.

I had one friend who had just quit Jesuit college. He had a beautiful body—muscle builder type, hung magnificently. But as soon as he had his orgasm he'd lie back and say, "Don't even move." And he'd break out in eight bars of Gregorian chant and start crossing himself. It was rather frightening. Then he'd snap back again and we'd part friendly and go back out to the gay bars. The bars were straight one week and gay the next. The underground knew. They'd find some bar owner who wanted to make a little extra money with the gay crowd. The word would get around and telephones would start ringing. We'd say something like, "Next Saturday we're going to christen such and such a place." And then the crowd would go there just as brazen as anything, dancing together. It was like a floating crap game. Of course, all the semi-closet cases would show up at the new place.

I used to go to the Rickshaw, in Chinatown. Naval officers were always looking for places they could find junior officers or enlisted men. I remember one young commander would come with his wife and a few friends. They just liked gay people. During the war the bars closed at midnight, not two o'clock. Afterwards we'd try to scare up some gin or tequila and continue the party somewhere else. Anyway, the army got me and I was stationed in Chicago as a serviceman.

I met a GI, a young English Jew who was over here on vacation and drafted into the American Army. Physically, he was well-endowed. It was a very average sexual experience for me, however. But as far as the mind and heart went, he was great. He didn't bring up the fact that he was Jewish until later on. He said, "What do you think I am?" And I said, "Well, you're English for one thing." Then he stammered around and said, "And what else?" I said, "Now that you mention it, or feel the need to mention it, perhaps you're Jewish." He said, "Yes." But he wanted to make that the perfect weekend, which we did. This is what happened frequently during the war. Single experiences encapsulated a lifetime, practically. We'd talk, talk, talk, make love, make love, make love. When the sex would wear out, you'd go on talking and continue with gentle lovemaking. Particularly if you were going overseas and you didn't know whether you'd ever be coming back or not.

San Francisco and Los Angeles in World War II were meccas of gaydom. Both cities had a very active underground where you could meet people. Even straights seemed to have a more understanding and tolerant attitude toward gays, because we were all pushed for time and nobody knew whether he was going to be bombed the next day or not. There was already talk around the university in Berkeley of the atom bomb. I will never forget someone saying to me, "Al, they're making something, one ounce of which would blow the entire city of Berkeley to smithereens."

Then, while I was stationed back out west, I contracted San Joaquin Valley fever, *scopsidia mycacosis,* and wound up in the hospital. I had built up my weight previously, but lost it all. I got horribly depressed. I refused to eat. I would sip something or drink milk, but I wouldn't eat anything solid. Finally they sent the head nurse around, a navy captain. She said, "Private Hoskins!" That always frightened me. I had my degree and I was still a private, and being called private just fried me.

At any rate, I said to her, "What good does it do to eat? It's like a bunch of cattle in Chicago at the slaughterhouse being fattened up for the kill!" She said, "Oh, that's the way you feel about it, is it? I think you belong on another ward." With that, they transferred me to the neuro-psychiatric ward where I still wouldn't eat. Finally, I became good friends with a psychiatric nurse, a wonderful woman. I don't know if she was gay or not. She was like Sara, in a way, who held herself like a man, not at all gentle or feminine. She got me a grounds pass and I became a total vegetarian.

It seemed to me that meat, and slaughter, and everything in the war were all tied together. I'd go to the PX and get a pimento cheese sandwich and some nuts, things like that. They would march us over to the dining hall from the ward but I'd duck under the stairs on the way and hide so I wouldn't have to eat. Of course, I went down to about 137 pounds or so. Then there was the patient review board.

Of course, they asked me about homosexuality. I said, "No, man, unless you mean adolescent mutual masturbation and that sort of stuff." I wasn't about to declare myself and be a martyr. I felt that I was hurting no one by denying it, only protecting myself. Then the colonel or general, whoever he was, took one look at me and said, "Soldier, why haven't you shaved?" They had shaving sessions every two or three days where they would supervise the psychiatric patients and their use of the razor. I hadn't bothered going. I told him, "I don't know, I really don't know why I didn't." At first I thought I'd be taken off the ward and thrown into jail. I was very upset after the hearing and came stumbling down the stairs when someone came along and asked me what happened. When I told him he laughed and said, "It's the best thing you could have done, not to shave." Right behind him was the captain, and I told him, "I'm sorry I didn't shave." He said, "You don't have to worry about it now, they've decided to CDD you." Certifiable Disability Discharge. An honorable discharge.

Looking back on it now I wish I had had the guts to declare myself to that review board. I think if I had, it would have given me the strength and the motivation to go straight into graduate school. I think I would have gone into social service on the executive level rather than ending up being an old pensioner. Most of the guys I knew were people who had either declared themselves before and never gone into the service or were people who had gotten discharges for being apprehended or declaring themselves while in either the army, navy or marines. Many of them were resentful of me because I had a decent discharge.

I had the opportunity to declare myself even before I went into the army, when I was an undergraduate in college. A special research program in the psychology department had recruited a bunch of gay people for "reprogramming," and I joined — in one of my bouts of frustration with my life. They were giving the participants testosterone treatments, male hormones, at Cowell Hospital. The only thing that happened to me was that I developed mastitis, my left tit swelled up like a rock. A doctor named Adams said that if I wanted to stay out of the army, he would stand behind me. I was so closeted that I ended up denying being gay at the last minute. I realize now that it would have been far better if I had spoken out. It would have made me a stronger, more confident person.

After the army I became interested in left-wing politics. I did cruise quite a bit, was always looking for somebody that I could have a somewhat permanent relationship with. I wound up cruising a john in Berkeley with a glory hole. Cops and God knows whatall were hanging around there. I met the second person in my life named Tom. I was always meeting "Toms," and he was a teacher. He protested mad love for me and I was rather slow in responding. About the time I did start responding, he gave up and went his own way. I sort of cracked up over the whole thing. I turned on the gas one day hoping someone would come in and find me. Someone did come in through the window, a dyke friend of mine. I got into the hospital in Menlo Park and spent almost two years there undergoing insulin shock therapy among other things. All I can say is, insulin shock therapy can be a beautiful experience. The nurse comes along first thing in the morning and tells you to roll over. They give you a shot of curare to deaden the nerves. I ended up transferring to Winter General in Topeka because I had heard all these wonderful things about Menninger. Also I'd been beaten up once by the attendants in California. Finally, I ran into a wonderful doctor who was experimenting with methedrine, which is now used as speed by young folks. It was like being born again. I got out of my routine of hospitals and became interested in going back to school again, but not social welfare work. I went into pottery making at an arts school in

Oakland.

I had been wondering over and over again, "Am I or am I not?" Finally I decided there was no such thing as being or not being gay. It's something else again. I had two or three gratifying relationships with women but I still had the puritanical attitudes I grew up with. In order to consummate emotionally, I would have to be very successful financially. I stayed mostly with gay relationships and developed a wide circle of acquaintances at the White Horse in Berkeley. I'd invite people down for after-hours parties, but I remained off to the sides. It was not that enjoyable when compared with the way it had been before the war in the gay underground. Things were gradually coming more into the open in the fifties and sixties. For about ten years I had a pottery shop and later a Scandinavian furniture shop. I kept moving the business from place to place, getting smaller and smaller, and more and more into debt.

I ran into another fellow—named Tom, naturally—who was walking down Telegraph Avenue drunk. I thought someone might take advantage of him so I drove him home. We had satisfying sex. That grew into a relationship of about twenty years. He became exceedingly fond of me and declared his love. I returned the sentiment when I became sure of my feelings. But he constantly accused me of having relationships when I wasn't. He wanted absolute and total fidelity. I gave it, but he didn't believe me. I had to give up all my friends but he still wouldn't believe I wasn't having relationships with every Tom (ha), Dick and Harry under the sun. This reached tragic proportions several times. I'd never been violent before, but I blew up and beat the shit out of him several times, breaking his ribs and my own hand one time. He drank excessively and I tried to keep up with him. Eventually some of these incidents occurred in public. He started accusing me in the bar and it somehow got back to his employer who asked him to resign.

When I met him he was getting a divorce, and he told his wife that he'd found someone that he loved dearly. He introduced me to her and that went pretty smoothly. However, every time we had a fight he'd always run back to her. Then the next day he'd come back to me. He finally realized that things were getting too destructive between us and he cashed in on an early retirement and went to Germany. He wasn't there long before he came back to live with me. He finally got used to the idea that it wasn't being disloyal to someone you cared about to have an experience or two, that there were different kinds of relationships. Never again was I involved in the so-called gay underground or anything like that. When he returned I stopped going to the baths and going out. We became like one person though we were still fighting about his heavy drinking. He spent about two or three months in the hospital drying out, and then, as soon as he was released, he got arrested for drinking. He resented his dependence on me and tried to become more independent. But our sexual relationshp soured one day when he told me that I was using him. He did start making some money at last with his writing, but by that time his health was getting worse. Eventually he became an epileptic alcoholic and wound up dehydrated in the hospital. He passed away two days later during the night.

Well, I was never much of a housekeeper and I let the house go to wrack and ruin after his death. For months the kitchen remained exactly as Tom left it. I went to the Golden Gate Bridge and sat on the rail contemplating jumping off. The cops picked me up and put me in the hospital. Recently I've been undergoing dental surgery so I might be fitted for dentures, and my angina is bothering me.

A stranger wouldn't notice the changes I've made in the house little by little. From my suicide attempt and hospitalization I was put back on 100% disability again, retroactively. With the money I was able to buy my house which had been up for sale and now I pay a small mortgage check. The house was built in 1872. Somebody put the most awful brick facing over it, but it still has wonderful gable and gingerbread all over. I'm not going to do too much until I get the house paid off, but in a few months, after I get the place cleaned up, I'll invite company over again.

Currently there are four people I've met in the park that I see. One is immensely kind and I've gone over to his place a few times because he enjoys doing me. But I find it very difficult to be stimulated unless someone else is stimulated – unless I find someone who's a size queen or something like that. Then I can respond and make a penetration or ejaculation. On prescription I've been taking thorazine as an aid in sleeping and as a sort of emotional cushion during the day. I only take a little bit at night. I used to take four or five tablets at night but no longer. But with teeth trouble and the angina, I've been thinking of how much time I have left. There is longevity in my family, which means that I may outlive these problems. With the removal of my teeth I got a juicer that lasts a lifetime, to liquefy everything.

13

John Hall

John is sixty-three years old and lives in San Francisco's "Tenderloin" district, typified by low-income elderly housing, social service agencies, drug pushers, and prostitutes. His second-story two-room apartment is practical and meticulously neat and has a window from which he can watch the telephone booth across the street. He sometimes calls the booth if he sees a young man walk by whom he can invite up to his apartment. John is a short, spruce man with white hair whose even tone of voice becomes sharp when he speaks of his fixed income, the unfair treatment of the elderly, and the laziness of unemployed youth.

I'M JOHN HALL. I WAS BORN IN SONOMA COUNTY, CALIFORNIA, in 1919. My mother wore the pants in the family. My father was a gambler and chased around with other women. He would never bring any money home to support her and so one day she packed his suitcase, put it on the front porch, and that was that. She got a divorce and worked at a creamery across the street from the apartment we lived in—my grandmother was taking care of me during the day. Then my mother met my stepfather at work and the next thing I knew they got married. I had just turned seven and was going to grammar school. I never played with girls, I always played with boys, always the older boys.

I used to get a big charge out of going in my mother's closet and getting all of her old dresses and all of her old high-heeled shoes. I'd parade all through the house and just have a ball. She didn't mind me dressing up in the dresses and the shoes. She didn't see nothing wrong with it. But she didn't like me getting into all of her perfume and cosmetics. She gave me hell for it. She told me that if I liked that stuff so well, to buy my own.

So that went on for a period of years and finally I grew out of the desire to want to do it. The word "sex" was never mentioned in my home the whole time. That is how I turned out to do all the things I did and turned gay. Actually I think I was born homosexual. When I used to dress up I wished that I had been born a girl instead of a boy. But I never did go through the stage of wanting to be a drag or get a sex change.

In grade school I started chumming around with the older boys. We would go off into the mountains and the bushes up in the hills and they would get the cigarettes. That's how I learned to smoke. We would sit around and they would get a hard-on and I'd get a hard-on and we'd start playing with each other. There were little gopher holes in the ground. We lined them with cotton, then as time went on we decided that we should do it to each other. We would get the vaseline out—in those days they called it "cornholing"—and would cornhole one another. I was about eleven.

I met a boy in grade school that I just idolized, actually I fell in love with him. He was a handsome stud, had black hair, and the longest black eyelashes you ever laid eyes on. Men and women both went crazy over him; he had to beat them off with a stick he was so popular. He and I—we carried on. Fridays and weekends. We each had a towel and a jar of vaseline hid in our bedrooms. He was a year behind me in high school and became very popular with the women. He turned out to be a great jitterbug dancer. That was the days of the jitterbug. He and I drifted apart and I started going out with the boys. On Saturday night we would go to a dance and during intermissions we would go out to the cars and I would blow them in the backseat. This went on through high school until I graduated. One day I got home and my mother said, "Oh there's a letter from the government on your bed."

Yeah, there was a letter from the War Department and I thought, "Oh Jesus!" I opened up the thing and it said you are now cordially invited to be a member of the U.S. Armed Forces. I was inducted in San Francisco. That was in 1940, before Pearl

Harbor.

I was in the company of fifty-two men. Well, I think I had over half of them — even some of my officers. Oh, I got along beautifully in the service. I had no problems. Everybody was pleasant, nobody gossiped or talked or tattled. Everything was kept strictly private. That went on for about a year; then I met this staff sergeant. He was about twenty-five and a beautiful stud. We started to be lovers right there on the grounds and we would go off somewheres and . . . that went on for about a year, then all of a sudden we got transferred.

Then I was in the Presidio in San Francisco in the military escort and guard company. There was a coast guard station right next to us. A gay friend of mine and I used to go to that station every night and go aboard one of the ships. The sailors would sit around and play poker while Phil and I took turns taking these sailors one by one into the sleeping quarters and servicing them. We had a fabulous time until I got transferred to Arizona.

I was there for about a year and finally a line sergeant transferred into our company. He had been a drill sergeant stationed in the Phillipines. Over there they had what they called "benny boys," young Filipino boys that shine the sergeant's shoes, make his bed, do his laundry and suck his dick or he fucks them or whatever. He had a steady boyfriend over there and when he got back into the States and got transferred into my company, well, he found out I was gay. Next thing I knew I couldn't get rid of him. He was behind me twenty-four hours a day. He wanted me for his steady deal and didn't want me to have nothing to do with anybody else. He was very possessive. Well, I didn't like that at all. I tried to avoid him as much as possible but it was hard to do. So I had to have sex with him a jillion times, not because I wanted to but more or less because I was forced into it. I would go to town on pass with sailors and marines. I kept ignoring him and ignoring him until one night he went to town and he got drunk — I mean he got plastered.

He came back to the base about two o'clock in the morning, three sheets to the wind. He came in the door of these wooden barracks we were stationed in and started down the halls, screaming, "Where is that queer cocksucker? I want to kill him!" Of course, it woke everybody up. It scared the shit out of me. I was in bed and didn't have my clothes on. I jumped out of the bed and ran down the full length of the barracks bare-assed naked and out the other door. He come out behind me and chased me all over the company. The corporal of the guard, the sergeant and the officers, they were all alarmed about it. Finally they got him cornered and locked him in his room. They told him he had better shut up and go to sleep. They put me in the sergeant of the guard shack for the night.

They let me go get my clothes in the barracks and the officers and the corporal of the guard went off. The sergeant of the guard sat in his guard shack with a little cot next to him. The next thing I know I had the sergeant lying on the cot and I was servicing him. Ha! I had one hell of a good time for myself while I was in the service.

The next thing I knew the company sergeant got wind of it and the company commander got wind of it. I was called into the captain's office. I explained the whole thing—of course he knew I was gay—and he said I had better report to the medical doctor and have a talk with him. He told me I'd be better off as a civilian because you couldn't tell what any of these men might do, hurt me or something, and it was not good for morale. They transferred me to an air force hospital.

I was in there as a patient, but I wasn't confined to my bed, I could wander all over the hospital grounds. I figured as long as they got me in there for observation, they got me so screwed up that it really doesn't make much difference what I do. All the patients in that hospital were commissioned officers. About thirty-five or forty of them. During the day I would go bed to bed and write letters for them to their girl friends and then buy their toilet articles. They were short-handed on orderlies so I would give them baths and rub them down with massage lotion. They would get real excited. So at night after lights out I would get out of bed and fix it so it looked like somebody was in it. In my pajamas and my bathrobe I would go out the back door and into where the patients were. They had a row of beds on one side and a row of beds on the other side. I would start with the person on the end and go all the way down to the end and service every one of them and then cross over and go down the other side. I did that every night. I figured as long as I was going to get railroaded I might as well have a good time while I am at it.

Finally I went before colonels and majors and they had a

regular court-martial, with a medical officer. I had serviced this officer a jillion times and he liked me and wanted me. They hemmed and hawed awhile and a woman was sitting there recording all this stuff. All firing questions at me and just bugging me to death. I kept saying, "no, no, no," but finally I got to the point where I just thought, "Oh well, to hell with it." I said, "Yes, I am a homosexual. I suck cock. I sucked every air force boy's cock on the grounds," and I just read the riot act to them. That is what they wanted to know, so I told them. They kept me in the hospital for ten weeks after that trying to make up their minds. I finally got a blue section eight. Homosexuals, alcoholics, dope addicts, they all got blue section eights. It's not dishonorable and it's not honorable either. I lost $200 mustering out pay. I lost a number of things I was qualified for.

Two other homosexual friends of mine got discharges. They used to call us "the three musketeers." We moved to L.A. and were living in a rooming house. All three of us had jobs and, of course, going out to the glory holes and all the gay hot spots. I was having a ball when one night while I was getting ready to go out the phone rang.

My gay friend answered but the caller wouldn't tell who it was and I said, "Who the hell is calling me?" I went to answer it and would you believe it! It was that goddamned lying sergeant that caused me all this trouble in the service. He finally got discharged and had the nerve to call me up and ask me for a date. I said, "Well, you sonofabitch you, don't ever call this number again. After all the fucking trouble you caused me in the service, don't ever call this number again." I slammed the receiver in his ear and he never called no more.

I lived in San Francisco, Los Angeles, New Orleans, Houston, and San Diego. I would stay in one place for a certain length of time and then I would decide that I wanted to go somewhere else. In New Orleans I worked in the French restaurants down on Canal Street. I went to Houston and couldn't get a job so I drew unemployment insurance. I was going to gay bars and man, I picked up some of the most beautiful studs in Texas. They were gorgeous, not faggots, they were men, real men with great bodies and hung like horses. We'd do the works. In San Diego I was near the navy base and I would walk up and down Broadway. There were jillions of sailors and I would have three on this side and three on the other. They would buy liquor and be on pass for the whole weekend. I would take them to my room and it would be fantastic.

I came to San Francisco not too long after World War II and the gay bars were real nice and pleasant. You would go and everybody was nice and would buy you drinks. You would go home to bed with them and nobody was asking for money or causing trouble. I was working in hospitals and had the money. As time went on it got to the point where I couldn't cope with it any more. They all got so bitchy in the bars, all they were interested in was how many drinks you could buy them and if you didn't have any money they would forget you. I got tired of all that jazz. I don't go to nobody's house now. I just crawled in a shell, so to speak. I invite different ones up but all they want in this town is money. They are all too high and snooty. They think they are God's gift to the men and the women and the troops.

I worked in hospitals for seven years when I first came here. But I've been on disability now for twelve to fifteen years. I first started out on General Assistance. They give you rent orders and food orders and you almost starve to death on it. You live in cheap slum hotels. As time went on I got onto SSI (Supplemental Security Income). I lived in hotels all over and had a few good times. Then I lived in the avenues for a couple of years with a family and paid rent. I was working for the husband who had four hotels. Finally he gave up the hotels and went bankrupt. He had to pay or go to jail. He came home one night drunk and he and I got into it. He hauled off and clobbered me in the back of the head, split it open so I was bleeding. I packed all my stuff and moved down to the Adelle hotel 'cause I knew the French guy who was cousin to the owner. I moved in at two in the morning, bag and baggage.

I lived there five years and then moved to the Jefferson Hotel and then from there to here. I was doing some odd jobs for the landlady here but she and I had a falling out. Now when rent day comes up I just shove my $180 under the door and I don't call her on the phone and she don't call me.

I have one brother. Of course, he inherited my mother's estate when she passed away and I didn't get a fuckin' dime. When I read my mother's will I almost had a heart attack. She left her estate to my father first, providing he lived longer than her, which he didn't, then she left it to my adopted brother and if he passed away, then she willed it all to my step-father's nephew in Minnesota. At the bottom of the will she said, "I have a son by the name of John Hall but I do not wish for him to be included in the will." I was floored! So I called my brother and said, "What is this?" He said, "You weren't home half the time, you were always out drinking and carousing all over the country." I said, "Yeah, but how about when she used to drink? They had wild parties and they would get so drunk they would fall into the bathtub or pass out on the lawn." I would get out of bed and sneak into the kitchen and drink out of the half empty glasses and I guess that was the start of my alcoholism. Well, I thought he would be kind and man enough to say, "You keep half, and I'll keep half," but so far I haven't got a damned thing. I got so mad I hung up and I haven't called him since and he hasn't called me.

He sure doesn't need the money. He owns a barber shop with four barbers and has a shoeshine boy in one of those big office buildings downtown. He makes a fabulous income. I think he and his roommate are lovers. I really can't say for sure because everything is so hush-hush. Neither one of us says anything about that.

I am on SSI and the cost of living keeps going up. I go out on the street and see these young studs who are a lot healthier than I am come up and ask for spare change. That just burns me up. I've had to work for everything that I got. Half the time on GA I was starving, just existing. It seems to me the young guys I used to see at the welfare office were perfectly healthy. Nothin' wrong with them and half of them were getting bigger incomes than I was. All us poor senior citizens go to all these offices and get the runaround and lousy service.

I will stay right here until I croak or get cut off and have to go out and get a job. I've been on relief so long I don't think I'm going to get cut off. I don't have any plans. I was going to go back to my hometown but changed my mind since my mother died. I wouldn't go back now because the kids that I grew up with have all married and gotten families and settled down or else are scattered all over the country. The town is built up tremendously with a lot of beautiful homes and shopping centers. It's really changed from the one-horse town I knew. I just live one day at a time. I don't want to travel any more. If rent goes up I'll just have to find myself a cheaper place to live. I go for a walk every now and then to the beach and the Embarcadero. I have to go for my arthritis. I go up to see my foot doctor and my eye and ear doctor, I have to walk all the way up to the top of Hyde Street and my legs ache all the way. I walk about two or three blocks and stop to rest. The doctor told me to exercise but not to overdo it.

I'm just getting along the best I can. I sometimes stand at the window over there where you can see that pay phone on the other side of the street. If I see some good-looking stud go by, I call up and ask if he wants to come up for a little action. I'm not interested in men over sixty. No, over fifty. I wouldn't even want to touch someone's body my age. I masturbate three or four times a day in the hallway or at the mirror. As far as meeting gay people and visiting their houses, that doesn't interest me at all. I don't want to get tied up with anybody because as long as you got the booze and the food and the cigarettes and all, you're a swell Joe, but as soon as you got nothing, man, they drop you like a hot potato. I live on $317 a month. I just don't want to get involved, I would rather stay here by myself, I'm a loner type. Whenever I meet somebody and we have sex, fine, and if I don't have it, I don't have it. Outside of that I can't think of anything else to say.

14

Josh Holland

Josh Holland is a handsome, boyish-looking man of medium build with silver white hair. He possesses a controlled, thoughtful presence. I interviewed him while he was visiting friends in Los Angeles. He showed me pictures of his home in Atlanta; a large columned house on four acres with a meticulously manicured landscape.

I WAS BORN IN 1925 IN MOBILE, ALABAMA AND RAISED IN THE Southeast. I've lived in the Southeast all my life, mostly in Georgia. I think I realized I had sexual problems in grade school. I was a little bit different from the rest of the boys. I didn't take to games the way they did. Sometimes they would make fun of me. I wasn't physically coordinated and was made to feel inferior. That hurt me a lot. I really suffered very deeply as a child. I felt like I wasn't part of the crowd. I don't think I really realized what it meant to be gay or homosexual until I was a senior in high school. That's when I remember the other boys looking at the girls whose busts were expanding but I couldn't understand what the excitement was all about. I thought, "There is something about me that's not quite like the rest of the boys." And I always liked to watch the boys in the shower after gym class. I guess I really knew for sure I was different then. Occasionally I would run into boys in the same boat I was, future gays, too, I suppose. There was a very effeminate boy in our high school and when he came into music class one day, all the boys laughed and said, "Here comes Oberon, King of the Faeries." I thought to myself, "I'm really more like him, I understand him." The boys in the class never reacted to me quite that way because I guess I wasn't effeminate to quite the same degree.

After I finished college I started teaching school. Even in those days, in the mid-forties, I think people were aware that a lot of teachers were homosexual, so I had to contend with that in the communities I taught in. I think there was a certain degree of tolerance as long as everybody conformed to social mores and behaved themselves. I never had too much trouble.

I had my first homosexual experience with an older man when I was an undergraduate in college. It was a very bad experience and it upset me. The man was the type that preyed on younger men — I was really quite innocent. But I had told my parents I thought I was homosexual when I was about nineteen, so I got that out of the way early. It was quite a shock to them in those days, around 1945. Fortunately they were quite intelligent people and we never discussed it after that. I think it saddened them and worried them, but after the initial confrontation we just silently agreed not to talk about it.

I think I was ahead of my time in that I was very stubborn about being gay. I refused to alter my lifestyle, to play the game most gays did and get married just for social acceptance. I didn't flaunt my gayness but I didn't hide it either. In my first love affair I lived with my lover, Dan, for seven years before we broke up. We always remained friends, though, always kept in touch until he died a few years ago. Then for about nine years I was alone until I met my present lover, Fred, in 1963.

I moved to Atlanta, Georgia, in 1960 for two reasons: I wanted to get out of the teaching profession and my family had decided to retire here. That's when I really got into trouble with alcohol. I started running around to the bars, stopping in the bars after work. It was very difficult for me to live alone for those three years, from 1960 to 1963. By the time I met Fred I was an alcoholic. But he was patient and we went together about six months and then moved in together. We've been together ever since.

I have been promiscuous to a certain extent during our relationship. Fred hasn't but I have. I used to accuse him of stepping out because I couldn't believe he *never* did. Now I really believe it because I don't think he's all that interested in that kind of thing. I've had only two serious lovers in my life but quite a few one-night stands. I have a little shame, a little guilt about my promiscuity. I sometimes picked up people a little too easily, too casually. Maybe I was just under the influence of booze when I did it.

I met Brad and I became intensely attracted to him. Brad had had some very unfortunate experiences. He had just buried his last lover who had died of cancer. Then he had been going with a fellow he met here. I asked him once if he was in love with this guy and he said, "Yeah, it was getting to be that way." One night, unfortunately, this fellow called him at home and they got to talking a little bit too familiarly on the telephone. And would you believe it? Brad's wife was listening in on the extension! And she hadn't dreamt he had this side to him. He had three children, a job, owned his own home. Joe Blow, good citizen, good church man. You wouldn't dream he really was homosexual. He said he had had a strict religious background and could just never give in to being gay. He was a handsome man, raised on a farm in Wisconsin. Blond hair, blue eyes, strong and healthy looking. I was like a lovesick teenager over Brad. I told Fred about him and he said, "Well, I just don't want to hear about it. It's all right." I guess he knew it would pass. But I felt very sorry for Brad because his home life was ruined when his wife found out. He was reaching the point where he hated her. Every time he would leave his house on the weekends or at night, she would snarl at him. When he told her he was going shopping he would be meeting me. No matter what he told her, though, she wouldn't believe him. He told me he was going to get a divorce.

Brad said he always wondered what it would be like if he threw over his whole lifestyle and went into gay life. I don't know what ever happened to him. Sometimes I think I should call him but I can only call him at work. He was always very difficult to contact, very busy on his job, never free to talk, and that bothered me. And if I ever met him in the evening he had to make up some elaborate excuse for his wife. After a while I just thought it was better to end it, better for both of us.

I really belong with the man I'm with. He's seen me through a lot of troubles, like my drinking. He wants to be with me and I want to be with him. I guess we're getting into a comfortable stage now. Fred's about as kindly and sweet and gentle a person as you'll ever meet. There were a couple of times where he even paid for my hospitalization for alcoholism. My folks never knew about this, about my alcoholism being this bad. I think the reason I got into alcohol was that I was gay and lonely and the bars were where you met people. It just got hold of me before I realized what was happening. There isn't a history of it in my family and alcohol was never an issue at home, so I can't look at it from that angle.

I joined Alcoholics Anonymous in 1963. It was the weekend Kennedy was assassinated. Nobody worked for the next three or four days, they just watched the news. It was quite a dramatic thing and the perfect excuse to get drunk. And I got so *fucking* drunk I knew I was in trouble. That weekend I called up a very nice gentleman in Atlanta who's big in AA. He came down to talk to me and that's how I got started in the program. I know quite a few of the old-timers there now.

If I had attended the meetings I would have been able to stay dry, but I didn't. I fell off the wagon a lot between '63 and '69. Then one day in 1969 I started going into the DT's and thought I was going to fall apart. I came home and Fred wasn't here so I lay down and called him and asked him to take me to the hospital and he did. After that I didn't have a drink for nine years and two months, from July 14, 1969, to September of 1978. Then I had a terrible emotional crisis when I met Brad. I thought my obsession with drinking was completely gone but the encounter with him was just too much. Every day you see people you're attracted to but they are never attracted to you. With Brad it was reciprocated and it just blew my mind. I couldn't handle it, so I drank.

Sometimes the people you think will accept your sexuality don't, and vice versa. My first lover, Dan, had a brother who was a football coach, a very *macho* man. And he was probably the most understanding and kind relative either of us ever had. We always used to go over to his house on Saturday nights and play cards. Dan's sister was very kind, too. She would have us over on Thanksgiving and Christmas. She always said about Dan and me, "If that's the only kind of love they know, then they're entitled to it." His mother was always very nice to me, too. I don't think she exactly approved of our relationship, but she didn't dislike me personally.

Dan's in-laws were a different story. One time his sister-in-law had us over for Thanksgiving dinner and afterwards we were sitting around watching television. A woman's ad appeared on the television and she turned to me and said, "Well, you ought to know all about that kind of thing, shouldn't you, Josh?" And then she gave me this funny little look. I never really forgave her for that. I never went to her house again and never had anything else to do with her. Her stupidity amazed me, though, that she didn't realize her brother-in-law was the same way! I guess because I did all the cooking she thought I naturally assumed the female role, which in a way was true. But in another way it made perfect sense because Dan didn't like to cook and do that kind of thing. But her comment was so uncalled for, so unkind. She wasn't subtle or cute or anything. I wonder if she knew I couldn't have cared less what she thought. But I do miss the rest of the family. That's one bad thing about my relationship with Fred, we have no family contacts at all. I have a few old friends here but not very many. We don't go with the crowd at all. I've even given up quite a few friends since I've been involved with Fred, but it was worth it to me. They didn't care too much for Fred because he's not good at small talk or gay talk. He just feels it's unnecessary.

Sometimes I think we're our own worst enemies in gay life: the role playing we do in bars, the posturing as a certain kind of person, and all these effeminate terms we use for each other. Mind you, I'm guilty of this too. But it really is unnecessary. And it's turned a lot of masculine gays away from us, too, which is too bad. It's something weak in the movement—we don't always get along very well with each other. But I think the fact that there is a movement to make things better for us is an interesting social trend. Take the Negro movement. Even the most bigoted southerner had to see that the Negro was mistreated. He had to face the fact that there was no reason a lot of jobs couldn't be done just as well by a black as by a white. In our case, where gays are mistreated, it is much more subtle and much more difficult for people to understand. In certain job situations I feel I've been discriminated against but it's such a subtle, psychological discrimination I could really do nothing about it.

Several years ago there was a meeting at the State House and several gay people went down to try and press for the passage of a gay anti-discrimination law. One of the guys I knew who went told me it was just like a zoo with all the transvestites and such who went to represent the community. The quieter, more thoughtful ones didn't go. The people who could speak best for us don't, or won't because they're afraid. In a public place like that, no wonder the state legislators were turned off. That display just reinforced the stereotype they wanted to see and hear.

I've never conformed to any stereotype. But I also don't think there's ever been a place I worked where my co-workers didn't realize I was gay. There are certain gestures people notice. And they know you're living with another man and that you're older and that you've never been married. On the other hand I was never one to just deliberately talk about my dates with girls or about some football team or other things that men are supposed to talk about just to please other people. I just converse without talking about my personal life.

I've had only one bad work experience where I quit because of the anti-gay attitude of some of the people I worked with. But I think it had a lot to do with the kind of business they were in, the flower business. They were a little more sensitive about it than in other places. The people who owned the business weren't that way but the managers were very verbal on the subject. It seemed to me they were too conscious of gayness . . . they protested a little too much.

I've had a lot of miserable experiences with being gay in the course of my life, and I feel a little bit bitter. But I never dreamed that I would see a gay movement or public awareness and consciousness of it come into the open the way it has. In the early days we scurried around in the dark and were afraid. There is still a certain danger. I am still afraid because in some ways all this openness has made it worse. They know who we are and where we are now. And if they feel strongly enough, they could act violently against us. I don't think it's likely, but it's not impossible either.

I think all this public awareness on the subject is bringing lots of men to the conclusion, "I'm really this way too. I've been hiding it from myself for all these years so I'm going to go out and experiment and see what it's all about." Married men and men with more respectable positions used to be frightened out of their minds for even thinking about the subject. I've always been impressed with some of the married men. They can separate the two parts of their lives. In their own way they are faithful to their wives, they support them, and they get what they want: social acceptance, companionship in old age, children. They're not afraid of loneliness in old age, a fear that stalks many of us. They can go out and have their little side affair and it doesn't bother them; they're not hung up by the subject.

I'm happy with my relationship with Fred. We have a nice life here together. We know each other so well. He knows what he can expect from me and I know what I can expect from him. I just hope we can continue this way, take a few trips maybe. It's very, very comfortable and very satisfying. It's not perfection but what in life is?

15

Greg Aarons

Born around 1917, Greg lives in Phoenix, Arizona, with his lover of seventeen years. The walls are crowded with assorted nostalgia, pictures, and paintings spanning decades. George is a large man with a broad smile, fiery eyes, and a convivial manner.

I WAS BORN IN 1917 AND GREW UP IN THE MIDWEST. I DON'T know that I could ever say I "came out" then, but as a little kid I can remember always sitting on men's laps. I was looking through some old pictures about a month ago and found one of me at the age of seven. I was sitting in a canoe with a banner across me like a Miss America. It's the nelliest thing you ever saw. I thought, "My God, how can a kid at seven know what he's going to be?" But I must have. I can remember when I was about six or seven being groped by a guy who ran a construction crew. Then I remember falling madly in love with a kid in grade school. God, he hurt my feelings! I kissed him once and he started calling me a sissy.

I remember one other kid who was gay in seventh grade—watching him do the kid next door. Oh my God! It was just so great! I was sexually excited, so he had me kiss it. This kid he was doing was at first hesitant; I had to swear scout's honor that I would never say a word. We were in his house because his mother worked during the day. We always had the run of that house. I would sneak my mother's clothes out and we would dress up as girls. But when he let me kiss the head of it I thought it was just delightful.

I was the only son and had four sisters. My mother was from Ireland and it was a foregone conclusion that I would be a priest. I was fourteen years old when I went into the monastery. I was in for seven and a half years and when it came time for my life vows, I was a little leery and quite scared. I was going to be a priest ultimately but at the time I was considering whether to become a monk. Finally I decided to drop out. My mother was angry with me until the day she died.

At the time my sister was living in California and suggested that I go out there to live. I got to L.A. and there it was – Pershing Square, Hill Street, Slim Gordon's bar in Hollywood. I was only twenty-one but I just sensed where to go. Then I went into the army. That was a traumatic experience. Also, I think that's when my alcoholism started.

I was working in a shipyard and got a call from the draft board saying that I had to register. Suddenly I find myself on the third floor of the old P.E. station and there is a sea of cocks. Everyone was naked with a bag around their necks with their personal belongings in it. A voice said, "Go in there, take your clothes off, put your personal belongings in a bag. . . ." My God, it was like a smorgasbord. You go down a line in groups of fifty. You piss in a bottle, take five paces, stick your arm out for blood, take one step forward and there's a guy counting you off, saying, "Army, navy, marines, coast guard," like one-two-three-four. There were two guys who saw that they weren't going to be in the same service, so I traded places with one of them. It was that arbitrary. Then they dragged you through the gauntlet of psychiatric examinations. "Do you wanna fuck your mother?" "No." "How do you feel about women?" "I like them." And I do. "Do you ever have sex with a man?" "No." Well, who's going to admit it? "NEXT!" You get your clothes on and go downstairs and take an oath, and then you're on the bus to San Pedro or Ft. MacArthur.

When I went to camp I saw everybody sitting in rows on commodes or standing in lines at the community showers. I used to get up very early in the morning so I could shower and have my bowel movement alone. I just couldn't do any of that stuff with them, and I am sure they would have been very upset if they had to do it with "one of them." Oh God, I lived in fear.

I was so afraid of being discovered, yet in retrospect I can think of three times in the army that I "declared myself." First, I told a doctor that I was different, that men excited me. He said, "Well, maybe if you're lucky they'll send you to the Pacific where you won't have nothing but men and you'll be just one of the boys." That was weird. Then I went to a chaplain when I first went overseas. I was a rifleman in the infantry and I was scared. I told a priest that I was a homosexual, and I thought I should get out of the army. He really laid it on me. He told me how much money the government had spent to train me, how human beings had to be expendable in times of need. By the time I left I was practically in tears. If it had been a recruiting office I would have signed up for another hundred years. The third time was when I was in the Phillipines after the war. I laid it on this captain. He said, "Well, the war's over and who really gives a shit!" I said, "But I don't have enough points to go home." He said, "Well, I'll make you a staff sergeant, that'll make up for it." I was promoted to staff sergeant that afternoon. That night the captain and I got drunk and I did him for trade. I thought, "Well, if there's no other way back to the States, I'll do him." And I did. And nothing ever happened.

The pressures in the military were horrendous. You were in a strange situation like in the Solomon Islands, your only outlet was each other—a situational type of homosexuality. They had a little place in the jungle called "vaseline alley." I used to go there and pick up all kinds of trade and tricks. Army, navy, marines, whoever had a hard-on for the night. It was interesting if you like that zipless fuck sort of thing. A lot of these guys would ordinarily never think of doing such a thing in their hometowns, but they would there because it was the only thing to do other than masturbate.

I know a lot of guys in my company suspected me. And I'm sure that entrapments were set hoping that I'd fall into them. I think that they wanted to catch me, yet there was also a degree of respect for me because I was a rifleman. They thought, "Whether he's a homo or gay or a fruit or a fag he's still one of us."

I spent nine years in the army. I had a ball but then my drinking kept getting worse and worse. (I'm a recovered alcoholic.) I got out of the army in 1949, basically for alcoholism. Before I got out they put me in a closed psycho ward because I was an alcoholic and had attempted suicide. One day another queen and I broke out and caught a ride in a snowstorm to downtown Denver. The only bar we knew of was one that a guy on the ward had told us about. It was essentially a straight bar on skid row, but there were gays there and hustlers and whores and everything else. We got busted because we were sitting with queens. They wanted us to meet their friends and had brought all the fairies over. When the law came in, boom, we were arrested with homosexuals "of record" and sent back to the psycho ward.

All they could do at the ward was concentrate on my homosexuality rather than my basic illness which was alcoholism. I was given a discharge for possible homosexual tendencies. I appealed it, though, and got it changed to a general discharge. But they were going to give me a dishonorable discharge after nine years for sitting in this bar with these queens! Sick, huh?

Being gay in the forties and early fifties was a unique experience. You had to be careful; you could get arrested just standing on a corner. They called it "vag-lewd": vagrancy and lewd behavior. It was good for thirty days in California. I can remember one time being taken out of the bus station in Houston for indecent gestures. I was standing at the urinal—I haven't thought of this in years—and looked over to check this guy out. He did have a lovely piece of meat. And he grabbed me. He was a policeman. Boy, was I surprised! He said it was for making gestures and looking at his meat. He thought I was trying to make him. He was probably right, I would have. I didn't say anything, though, nor did I try to touch him. All I did was stand at the urinal and look over.

I can remember we'd be sitting in the park, not cruising or giggling or doing anything obscene, just sitting there talking, and all of a sudden the law would come in on the side of the park and pick us all up and we'd go to jail. This was St. Paul, Minnesota. In a way there was kind of a mystique about being gay when I was young that was kind of interesting. You always had to be one step ahead and that was exciting. You had to be an artist in being subtle. Sometimes the police would swoop down on you if they saw you even walking by a gay bar. There were never bars that were so designated but they were frequented largely by gays. Straights would come just to observe and laugh. Most of the places were just conversation pits because you were afraid to carry on there. If you tried, the managers would throw you out because they were in danger of losing their license for having undesirables.

When I first got involved in gay life we spoke a language all our own. It was very common to use words like "camp," "trade," or "Get her!" So you always felt a little better than the straights because they didn't understand. There were also different categories of queens. There were the "common queens," ones with bleached blond hair and plucked eyebrows. They were the real nellies. Then there were the "belles," the piss-elegant queens. They were the ribbon clerks who would work all day at Woolworth's and go out that evening and have several nickel beers, looking very chic. Then of course there were the drag queens. There was a real mystique about them. Get them out of drag though, and you didn't want a thing to do with them, they looked so tacky. With their plucked eyebrows and all, you wouldn't dare walk down the street with them. But there was a chrisma that would draw you to drag clubs to see these queens and dish with them. Everybody was awed except for the "butch queens," who were the closest thing to being straight. They were kind of sickening.

The idea was to find studs. San Francisco was beautiful for that. You had all the military out there. Sometimes they just wanted a place to eat or to sleep off their drunk. If they got a blow job along with it, well, that was all right with them. I used to make the "milk run" from Seventh and Market to First and Market, over to Howard to Seventh and back. I used to blow out more sets of tires there. I would pick them up just walking down the street or they would need a ride out to Hunter's Point. It was like driving through a flock of whores. You could pick out the ones you wanted to take. Some of them could be dirt, some would want money, and some would rob you. I was almost always lucky. I did get hit in the mouth once by a sailor. I was taking him to Hunter's Point and he asked me for three dollars to suck his dick. I said "Are you kidding? You should pay me." He was furious and I stopped the car. I told him to get his ass out and he swung and hit me in the mouth.

One other time I got in dirt with two sailors. I was taking them to Alameda Naval Base and we got through the tunnel and they had to piss. When I stopped the car they both went to the back to pee. I started the car up because I saw that they were both coming around different sides of the car. One reached through the window and hit me in the side of the head. It was kind of campy, though. I chased them four blocks honking my horn. They lost their caps. Then I saw a squad car come up and I made a U turn and went home. You wouldn't dare turn somebody in if they did a number on you because the cops would arrest *you.* Their attitude was that "queers are open stock." You can rob them, you can beat them, but don't kill them. But a good way to get around a jury in a murder trial was to say that the victim had made a homosexual advance. How ridiculous. The person who killed this gay might be a hustler, too, who does nothing but sell his body to queens.

I can remember in the service that many guys would come back from leave saying they had made eighty or ninety dollars. Some guy had picked them up and wanted to suck their dick. They would let him take them home and then they'd roll him.

You would get your pass for the weekend and on Friday night you would go into town and get enough money rolling queers for Saturday and Sunday. I remember Russ; he used to go into town and get a hotel room. One time I went with him and said, "How are you going to pay for it?" He said, "Don't worry, I'll get that money." And he never failed. Some queen would pick him up and he would roll her and pay the hotel bill. One night I caught him off guard. We did carry on. That child fucked like a mink. I guess he let his hair down, then discovered that "My god, if I get to liking this someone will be rolling me next."

There were two schools of cops. There were the ones on the beat who didn't really dislike you but hated what you did. Or they laughed about it and thought it was kind of cute. They didn't mind as long as you didn't break the law and they didn't catch you. Then there were the snobbish assholes down at headquarters.

After the war I lost a lot with my heavy drinking. Sailors and bar owners would give me money and buy me drinks. They loved to see this big, tall, gangly queen carry on. You know, get her drunk and she'll dance, shimmy or something. Who cares? I was practicing the disease of alcoholism and I didn't care where the money came from. I spent an awful lot of time in San Francisco's Tenderloin. The cops down there were pretty good and quite a number of them could be had.

But I remember Paul, in Chicago. He was picked up for questioning by two cops who took him to the north side, down a dark street, where they made him do them both and then beat the living hell out of him. I never will forget going to Cook County Hospital to visit him. His face, his eyes, just awful! Another time I saw two flaming bitches get on a trolley and ride it to another stop, and five guys followed them off. You could hear the screams blocks away.

Still, what is going on today, some of it I approve of, some of it I don't. Most of it could never have occurred twenty years ago; the police would have cleaned it up. When I was young, very seldom did you see gays with venereal disease—all of the hepatitis and such is bullshit. Homosexuality does not have to be a depraved lifestyle. And I know, because I lived it before I sobered up and my values became clearer. I don't mean to say I wouldn't do a piece of trade if it walked through the door today, I'm not a moralist, but I think people can establish good, lasting relationships. The only reason many of us felt that gay relationships were transient was that the older ones told us, "Well, honey, you know it's not going to last." When I first met Brian he was twenty-four years old and I was forty-eight. He didn't have anything, only a pair of loafers, a green plaid shirt, levis, and a darling smile. I was an administrator of a nursing home and making $650 a month. I lived in a furnished apartment. But the chemistry was there because we have worked hard and been through a lot. We've had fortitude, trust and belief in each other, and made it work. I've got two friends who've just celebrated their fiftieth anniversary. Some would say that is a rarity, but I don't think so. I feel that there are many more like that. But usually you don't see us out there carrying banners.

What is so important about whether or not the guy across the street accepts your homosexuality? You don't know what he does. Maybe he's married with a wife and ten kids and dressing up in women's clothing at night. What the hell difference does it make what you do in the bedroom? Why should I walk down the street and tell everyone that I am a cocksucker? I'll tell them if they want to know, but I'm not going to the theatre and say, "I'm a cocksucker, do you have a particular section I can sit in?"

What I am saying is that you are not going to get the public to accept homosexuality, so why ram it down their throats? Sneak up behind them and ease it in gracefully. Why be so blatant about it? Why demand that they accept us today? Look how many years they have been conditioned not to. I don't think that we should change overnight or that they should change overnight. Perhaps gradually we can be assimilated into society. Not in my lifetime, and thank God, because then the fun of being gay would be gone. The fun is not standing there dancing with your sister, for chrissake. What the hell is the fun of going on the dance floor with some faggot who is just as nelly as you are? Why does everything have to be done right away? It breeds so much hatred and then there is a backlash. Maybe I'm trying to justify points I feel weak on. But I watched a gay parade and wanted to vomit. I saw so many men in sequins and dresses. What are we, caricatures of our mothers? Of course life is not easy. I certainly had to undergo the trauma of coming out in the army. I was scared to death the whole time. This is the type of thing that led to there being so many gay alcoholics. I also think many alcoholics are repressed homosexuals, though there has never been anything latent about me. Brian is an alcoholic, by the way. He has been sober for over thirteen years now. I am very proud of him. Both of our families accept us. I think that maybe they know, but it is nothing we talk about. I feel as welcome around his family as he does around mine. My sisters love him; my nephews and nieces love him.

I'd be lying to you if I said it was always that way. The first year was one of indecision and he didn't know which way he wanted to go. I wasn't completely sold that what I wanted wasn't still out there on the streets—that search for the golden penis. I also didn't know if I wanted responsibility for another person. When Brian went into AA, our lives took a 180-degree turn. It was like the sun coming up over the mountain. We were no longer having the small talk that kept our relationship going the first year. Suddenly we were talking about important things like what it would be like to be alone, to not have each other. We've broken up a couple times though. The longest we were apart was three weeks. But neither one of us liked what we were doing to each other. I met him when he was just twenty-four years old. I gave him the best years of my life.

KV: I would like to return to the chronology of your life and what you did after the army.

I went to Chicago. In Chicago I drank. Then I went home, but I soon left for a geographical drunk, which took me to Houston, Dallas, New York, Miami, San Francisco. I got six months in a Texas jail for being drunk and disorderly. A Texas jail, oh God, but the trade was good. That was the first time I was a prostitute. I turned tricks for cigarettes and candy. I was about thirty-one and didn't have any money.

Then I went to Miami where I met a kid I had been in jail with. He and I sort of buddied up but I never did have him. Then I went to Georgia but my drinking kept on. I was also eating benzedrine like they were lifesavers, and I smoked a lot of pot. Back then you could always go down on the row and somebody would buy you a drink. I guess malnutrition, alcohol, pills and everything caught up with me in Augusta, Georgia. I had a bad back from the army and it really went. Thank God, they had a V.A. hospital there and I had back surgery which started that merry-go-round. I had a cast from my chest down to my waist. I was in the V.A. for six months and all of a sudden they let me out and said we want to see you in three months. There I was, no money, no nothing. There was a gal there who was the activities director and she was absolutely insane about me. But what was I going to do? Where was I going to go? So I lived with her. Why not? I lived with her for about a year and then I got bored. Onward to San Francisco.

I worked in San Francisco as an orderly in Franklin Hospital. Everything went pretty good until my drinking started again. My back went again too. I made the rounds from hospital to hospital as I lost my jobs. I had real peaks and valleys. I'd go for a while and get really straightened out. I had a nice apartment on Potrero Hill and then I drank that up. I ended up with thirteen dollars in my pocket. I don't know if I rolled somebody or how I got it. Probably took it from some drunk in the bar or some prostitute. I got kicked out of a cheap, sleazy hotel for falling over a chair going to the sink to pee. I was drunk. I was on meth. I said, "Jesus what is going to happen to my life?" Finally, I got a call from an aunt in Stockton, God bless her soul, she's dead now. That was the start of my recovery.

She made me promise to get on a Greyhound bus and come to Stockton. I was there two weeks and then I called A.A. and I've been in A.A. ever since. My God, it's a wonder I wasn't killed, the way so many queens on skid row were. Also, in '49, '50, things weren't all that good. I did everything, fried hamburgers, made donuts, worked in hospitals, was kept a couple of times by different women.

I got my first job in Stockton working on an ambulance. I did a couple of runs to the community hospital and impressed one of the doctors. He wanted me to come on staff in the emergency room, so I worked there for a year. Later a bunch of doctors opened a convalescent home and I went to work training nurses' aides. Then in '63 I was having problems with my back again and had a muscle spasm while I was driving. Thank God, I didn't hit anything. To make a long story short, I gained experience and was given the opportunity in '66 to be an administrator of a home in San Jose. That's where I met Brian. And it was also when I realized that there were a lot of people in the nursing home who had a drinking problem, so I started an A.A. group there.

At the home I noticed that there were gay people who had no one. There was Allan—though he did have a lover who would come to visit him. Poor Allan would lie there and one day he groped an orderly. The orderly came running down the hall, screaming, "You know what that old man did to me?" The nurse would say, "Look, he's senile and doesn't realize that you're a man and not a woman." Then the orderly would go back to work. One day I was walking down the hall and I heard this orderly say to Allan, "If you grab my prick one more time I'm going to bust you in the mouth." I stormed into that room, tore that curtain open and said, "You don't know it, but you are on your way out the door, go now!" Poor Allan, God love him, said, "What did I do wrong?" I said, "Honey, you were in the wrong basket." He was thrilled because now he had someone to dish with. I would go down there and tell him about making love to Brian. He'd want to know, "Did you use vaseline or. . . ." I thought, "What the hell, why not tell him?" It was making him comfortable. His friend just loved me for it. Gosh, he took such good care of Allan and he was a much younger man. I guess in a way he was my role model with Brian.

There was a lesbian there who had been with the same woman for thirty-two years. The woman had been killed in an automobile accident in San Jose, and she was left alone and had a stroke. She was only fifty-three years old when we got her as a patient. She was in a very bad way. She had no one, no sisters, no cousins, at least none that she would acknowledge. It hurt me every month to see less and less money in her account.

It would be nice if there was a hotline for older gays. I'm thinking of people going out in pairs who could stop in and say, "Hello, I'm gay too, let's talk."

Julio was another one. He was an artist in Marin County and he had an array of lovers who would love and leave him because he would get very bored supporting them. Anyway, he was eighty-two and dead a week before they found him. Nobody called, nobody bothered. Greg lived about a mile away from Julio and one day he saw the ambulance and the police cars. He went down to Julio's to see what was happening. One of the cops turned to him and said, "Oh, it's just that old cocksucker. He died." So that was his reputation, just old and a cocksucker. The police wouldn't bother him, he was too old; it's the young ones they want to nail. No one cared that he was a brilliant man, a very good artist.

But now I'd like to tell you a funny story. When I was in San Jose I was very friendly with a group of nursing priests and brothers. There was a priest there who was an alcoholic. One night he called me up and asked me to come over. I asked him, "Father, are you all right?" He said, "Could you bring over a case of beer? I'm having a guest tomorrow night." He couldn't get out because he was on crutches. I told him, "Oh sure, Father, I'll bring it right over." But in the back of my mind I always wanted to get him in a corner and begin talking about A.A. His drinking was very bad. I asked Brian if he wanted to come and he said, "Sure." So we went.

When I walked in with Brian, Father said, "Who's this?" Here's Brian, this twenty-four-year-old chicken, and Father was just wowed. Well, he opens a can of beer and one can led to a six pack. I think he was into his second six pack when he said, "I'm going to marry you two." Well, I'm Catholic from the old school and had those years in the monastery behind me. I could just see the heavens coming down around my head and the Holy Ghost striking me dead. Brian was still drinking at this time so he was just as sloshed as Father. I thought, "Oh, I've got to get this kid out of here. This priest is sacreligious, he's horrible, he's going to marry me!" But he started in, "Do you Brian take this lover . . ." I was a nervous wreck – but we were married in the Church!

Brian and I have both lived in furnished apartments and bought homes together. His name has always been on the mortgage, the deed, the cars, and the accounts along with mine. Everything is "us." We've had a taste of affluence, small homes, large tri-levels with swimming pools. The whole bit. Brian has seen me through a serious automobile accident, open heart surgery, then a stroke as a result of the open heart. No one could have taken better care of me. You know, most young people could care less about an old man. I guess neither one of us had anyone. Maybe we deserve each other. But whatever it is, it's good. We still have sex, maybe not with the same frequency, but it's just as exciting. Sometimes I think he has missed a lot, being with me. He missed a lot of the adventure of cruising for one thing. Once in a while he will sneak off to the baths. Not in Arizona because he's already gotten in trouble here.

One night I was at home, still very sick from having had four bypasses; it was early in the morning and I hadn't heard from Brian. At five o'clock in the morning the phone rang. Brian was in jail. What had happened was that he was on his way home when, on the spur of the moment, he made a right turn and went down to this little bookstore. He went in to watch a movie and was beating his meat when some young kid came up and started doing him. Then a guy walked in and stood there and watched the kid suck Brian before he pulled out a badge. They were the only ones in the place. He was arrested for lewd and lascivious behavior, which could have carried five years. At first I was devastated — and aware of what it was like to be alone. I'd just put out about $18,000 in medical expenses, so where does the money come from? How do I get a lawyer? How will I make bond? And if I can't make bond, I'm all alone. The fact that he could be released on his own recognizance never entered my mind.

I called the little queen who lives across the hall from us. I said, "Brian has been arrested," and I told her why and she came right over. Her lover had a fit, but she came. That morning about eight o'clock it was already a hundred degrees downtown, and we went down and walked up about a million steps looking for that jail. They kept saying, "He was here but he was transferred there." We never did find him and had to go back home.

In fact they had let them both out on their own recognizance. Brian had hidden his money in his car so he was able to pay the kid's bus ride home, and he was home by the time I got there. When I arrived he had taken a shower and was getting ready to go to work. I walked in and I really wanted to be mad, to let him know what he had put me through. He said, "Regardless of what you're going to say or what we're going to do, I want you to know

I do love you." And he walked away.

All of a sudden I got to thinking to myself, "Gee, I'm hurt. I feel rejected. I feel all kinds of shit. But you've been arrested before and you've been to jail. You know how he feels, don't you?" I walked back and he was sitting on the bed. I put my arms around him. We just held each other and cried. I said, "Brian, I don't appreciate what you did but you really didn't do it to me, you did it to yourself. Now what we have to do is stick together and show these fuckers that we're going to survive."

Fortunately, he got a good gal lawyer who got him acquitted in favor of diversion and for the past year he has had to go to a counselor. Funny thing, his counselor is some closet queen who hasn't gotten herself out yet. When he gets off diversion we're going to have a party. But the Tucson cops hire University of Arizona kids as special police for entrapment. The cops say you can't carry on like that in a public place. But the lawyer's point was that it is not a public place. No one can go in who is not eighteen and no one would go in unless they were looking for sexually explicit material or sex.

Brian told me a sergeant came in at midnight and said to them, "I don't know why you two guys had to go overboard and ruin it for all the other gays. We have a hands off policy as far as you fruit bars are concerned." The whole experience was really degrading to Brian. He still has not recovered from it. I notice the stress and I'm trying to get him to a regular counselor. He's begun to eat more than ever and gain a lot of weight.

Maybe I am a closet libber. I think that it is horrible the number of police hours they divert to catch a bunch of cocksuckers in a bookstore. There aren't any kids around, what the hell! They have murders, rapes, poor elderly being beaten and robbed and kicked out of their homes. Arson has increased forty-seven percent this last year and what are they doing about it? They're wasting their time on these victimless crimes. What if some broad wants to hustle her ass down on Van Buren, BIG DEAL!

I really think with the permissiveness of today, what they were doing was not that unusual, was not criminal. They were the only two there and were in a private booth. The cop didn't have to come in and watch. It was not a public display. One of the reasons they were concentrating on that particular place was that just two weeks before some of the neighbors had picketed the place. They claimed people sat out in their cars and masturbated while looking at the magazines. Well, if they did it doesn't mean they were gay.

Everytime there's a sex killing where some young man's body has been violated, right away they say it was a gay who did it. It turns out to be a married man with six kids who is the pillar of his peer group. Like this guy in Chicago with thirty-two numbers under the house. He was married, Chamber of Commerce, Santa Claus for the orphans and all that.

I think a lot of hets have missed the boat in relationships. Because they are conditioned to what their relationships should be from birth, they can get stifled. The mother tells the daughter, the father tells the son. With us it's been very fulfilling because it's been an adventure practically every day. We don't have guidelines to go by, we don't have role models. We've had to protect ourselves and each other from society's negative vibes. When we moved in here we had to say that we were uncle and nephew on our application. We've had to protect ourselves that way.

I think we are less demanding on each other than hets would be for the simple reason that a woman, whether she is liberated or not, still has certain stereotyped expectations of the man. Likewise for the man. I think we have a better opportunity to share openly our joys, our sorrows, our love, and not have to worry about who gets the kids or the coffee table if we decide that, "Hey it isn't working." We're not boxed in by those conventions and I think this is good. It's exciting—we're together because we want to be, not because of the kids or whatever.

Only in the beginning have Brian and I ever referred to one another as "my lover." We've never considered ourselves "lovers," but rather partners or companions. Not because we feel that there is a dirty meaning to the word "lover," but when you hear gays talk about "my lover" it's often about a person who is here today and gone tomorrow. "Oh, that was the lover before this one." That type of thing.

KV: Do you have any plans for the future?

I really can't worry about the future. I've got to live for today. I really don't want to live much longer. I don't mean that I'm going to commit suicide, but I think "mid-late sixties" and "leave me alone."

KV: Why so young?

Oh, that isn't early for what I've gone through. Anyway, then Brian could take up his life.

KV: He could do that now if he wanted to.

I guess he could, couldn't he. And I wonder how he could manage without me. The same as I don't know how I could manage without him. I'm sure I would, but God, that would be rough. When he was in the hospital for a month I thought I would go crazy. I think one of the most tender things in my whole life was the day after they did the open heart surgery on me and I had all that shit down inside me. I had a ventilator breathing for me and all those tubes and all that pain. I don't remember a lot of it but I do remember opening my eyes. Brian now tells me I couldn't talk because I had the tubes sticking down my throat, but I do remember looking up and just seeing his face there. There were tears coming out of his eyes. He said later that they were tears of happiness. That, "God, you made it. Because I wasn't ready to let go of you." That was such a good feeling. And, a . . . he has been very good to me. I don't know what I would . . . do. [cries]

Gee, I never really put that much thought into it. What would my life be like without someone like that? So God, and I choose to call it "God," has been pretty good to me. He's given me a hell of a good partner to go through life with and I think that's pretty neat. So I consider myself one of the older faggots but one of the most fortunate. It's nice to know as you grow older – and it's not just because he's younger – that there's someone there.

If I never had any other message to give to a group of gays it would be that homosexual relationships are not transient. You are transient. You make them transient. Because of the search for the golden penis; I looked for it for fifty years, I guess. And honey, if I can't find it, no one ever will.

16
Jordan Lee

Jordan shares a modest studio apartment with two cats in an inner-city neighborhood of San Francisco. His demeanor befits his articulate clarity, a result of having to constantly relearn English as his family travelled extensively during his youth. Jordan is tall, handsome, silver-haired and self-assured.

I WAS BORN IN PROCTOR, VERMONT, BUT MY FAMILY LIVED all over the east coast as well as in Spain and Portugal when I was a child. My grandfather was in the Phillipines during and after the Spanish-American War and helped to set up the school system there. That was where he met my grandmother, who had gone there to teach. There were brilliant people in my family.

I am the eldest of six children, and know now that I am the product of the battered child syndrome. My parents loved their children in infancy but later the child was something to be crushed. They also expected the most of me scholastically. But we never spent more than two years in any one place, and because of my living overseas I did not speak English properly. Then, among other things, I had a touch of polio. It sounds like a hard luck story, but it isn't intended as that. Because of the polio my feet are malformed so that I can't walk properly in normal shoes, and I was a very poor fighter. The consequence of all this was that I became a loner.

There was no one to talk to about the problems in the family. The upshot was that I had a nervous breakdown when I was fifteen. By then things were getting much worse in our home; where before only one of us was getting beaten each week, it developed into at least two or three of us being beaten. My mother was doing these things. I know now that she was mentally ill, but I didn't know it at the time. It would have not done any good if my father had known because I think he willfully ignored it. It is very hard to admit these things in your own home, so he closed his eyes to what he knew. I felt that there was something wrong with me. I had been carefully conditioned to think that I was ugly and unlovable. As a child, that was the only explanation I could think of for not being wanted. I remember one of my uncles told me years later that he had given up knowing our part of the family because he couldn't stand seeing what was happening to the children. I was in therapy a long time before I began to gain confidence in myself.

After my nervous breakdown I couldn't keep on studying. My parents conferred with the principal of the high school who said that I was an ungrateful boy. But he said that if I had a year out of school maybe I would be able to study again. So at sixteen I went to work and they got me a place living by myself in New York City. Therapists have told me it was a wonder I didn't become a hustler. But I didn't know anything about sex. I nearly starved to death because my salary was appallingly low. My parents were impractical people and could not correlate my initiation period at work with having a low salary. But the candid truth is that they never cared for me very much. They wanted a manly youngster who could get high grades in school, get a good job and become self-reliant. They had a great deal of resentment for me. It was suggested that I go into the navy. I did.

This was war time, and I made the mistake of talking to the chaplain stationed there and telling him that my problem was incomplete sexual knowledge. He looked embarrassed and sent me to a psychologist. He couldn't find anything wrong with me but asked me to narrate my concept of the sexual act. As a matter of pure deduction it was pretty good, yet it was clear that I knew nothing about it emotionally or physically. I was put in a closed ward for a while where I met all kinds of hopeless mental cases. Navy policy in those days got me out very quickly. There were many cases where people were caught and irretrievably ruined. They hunted down women as well as men, and they had all sorts of tactics. Most common was, "We won't punish you, but tell us who your friends are."

What we now call gay bars didn't start till World War II. During war time people were living desperately and intensely because they knew they might die. One phenomenon was that a lot of men found out about themselves who wouldn't have otherwise since pressures to get married were awfully strong. They would get into the military in close proximity with a lot of other males and discover that they had feelings about them. That caused a lot of complications. Some of them handled it well and got safely out of the service. Others were quite flagrant yet never crossed that thin line and so got honorable discharges or left at their own rate of speed. Other people, like me, were naive and blundered one way or another and got themselves stigmatized and discharged. It was really a world of darkness. I had a feeling of having to cope with the entire universe.

After I got out of the navy I moved back to New York. I met a man who was a talented artist. He was ten years older then me, but that didn't mean he was wise—he was mixed up, as I was. In the meantime my parents wanted me to show them my bankbook every weekend when I visited them in New Jersey. I was told that unless I did this I would never set foot in the house again. My mother's point of view was that I couldn't take care of myself, I needed someone to give me orders. They did not help me financially, of course. She made me try to get into the marines. But the recruiting sergeant took one look at me—I was skinny, fragile, and had a sensitive face—and said, "Look, anybody who gets into this had better be able to take it. You've got to be tough." Then my mother made me try the merchant marines, which I didn't know was a hotbed of homosexuality—and I doubt that she did either. But they wouldn't take me because of my navy record. I said something like, "If my parents call you, will you please tell them what you told me?" It was at this time that I had my first sexual experience.

KV: Wasn't the artist your first sexual experience?

Yes, but never culminated at that time. I don't think I knew how. I got involved with this other fellow who was rather dominating. We lived together for nearly a year. During that time I had discovered a religious group. Theosophists. A lot of other Jewish people did that too at the time because it helped them to be gentile in a gentile world and yet they could keep on with their Judaism and interpret it in a different way. I wanted an absolute explanation for things. I didn't know at the time that there are no such things as absolute explanations. Anyway, I ended up coming to California and getting a job in the Federal Civil Service Investigations Division.

I felt humiliated about not finishing high school, so I read voraciously. I finally found that I was ahead of most college students and I got into college. I cleaned up my speech. I found out what was wrong with my feet and got proper shoes so I could walk normally. I carried about twelve credits per term and worked about thirty hours a week. It was quite a nervous strain and I began having headaches. If pain goes on long enough you become oblivious to it until it is removed. It relieved my tension to be touched, especially around my shoulders and neck. Half the time the reason I got sexually involved with people was that I needed to be touched. It was very hard going home alone at night. I think I was wretchedly lonely in those days.

At that time I didn't know that there were gay people who had long-term relationships. You will not encounter them in bars or places like that. The consequence is that if you were a beginner in gay life, especially in those days you ran into the self-perpetuating myth that gay people don't have long-term relationships. My life would have been quite different if I had known otherwise.

That period was a very guilty one. There was virtually nothing in print that said anything good about homosexuals; everything I heard about gay people was degrading and vicious. My straight roommate in New York had told me that gays lived only to stab each other in the back. There was nothing in the straight media except scandal. There was one magazine, *Coronet,* which I noticed would periodically come out with articles about the homosexual menace when their circulation was falling. The psychological literature of the period stressed only the most pathological types. I got the impression that most homosexuals couldn't whistle, liked the color green, and were divided into hypermasculine and hyperfeminine types. And in that period gay men did feel they lost their manhood if they were on the receiving end of anal intercourse. I had to send to England for books and yet the ones I got were really no help. They said that homosexuality was a case of infantilism and was caused by a domineering mother and weak father or a domineering father and a weak mother. I envied other minorities because they could at least speak out through their own media. It was a rather isolated life and very hard to get to know other gay people.

The first thing you learned was that you must hide. This is still true in most places. That is why I learned to dress inconspicuously, and to this day I am not quite myself with straight people. There is a slight stiffening up unless I know them very well. Frustrating as gay bars were, at least there was no sexual pretense there. In this town there were about only seven bars. Of course, they only survived because they made payoffs. The police were also willing for gay bars to exist because, as they put it, then they knew where the queers were. If you wanted to indicate decadence in that time you would describe men dancing with men and women dancing with women. It was more the men that shocked them. In one of the periodic "cleanups," the police picked up the son of somebody important. As a result of the public disgrace, this fellow commited suicide. That was not an isolated case. Another stunt the police would pull in the forties was to have the handsomest policeman on the force dress in white satin swim trunks and stand around the men's room on the beach. Of course, passes were made – with the resulting arrests. The only thing worse than being a cardcarrying Communist was to be a homosexual.

At that time "gay" was a secret password. Code words were carefully parceled out. "Chi chi" was another. We used rather derogatory terms for ourselves. The word "fucking" was then called "browning." I had great trouble using these words. There are many others I don't remember. Gays also did a lot of camping. They would do that male-female role – "Oh, she is doing this or that." Some people developed mannerisms for group acceptance. One fellow told me that when he discovered he was gay he went to live in a gay apartment house in Chicago, and ended up carrying a purse to be acceptable in that community.

In my fifth year of college I was hit by a car and was laid up for a year with a broken leg and a fractured skull. I lost my job, and when I was able to work again I had to get a job at the post office.

189

I finally got my college degree and decided to become a teacher. I taught at a private school down south, but I soon discovered that I was not suited to the strain of teaching. You weren't expected to be a teacher but rather a disciplinarian, especially at the grammar school level when children are coping with their puberty and are out to make the world hell for everyone they possibly can.

During that period I had several hobbies. I used to do a lot of Balkan and Israeli folk dancing. I studied singing and they told me that I had the makings of a good lyric baritone. I took public speaking which improved my ability to handle myself with groups. When I was in college I stumbled across a course in Hebrew and was flabbergasted to find that though I had no religious training in Judaism I knew most of the words, or at least had no trouble learning them. Later I learned tai' chi for its meditative and relaxing effects.

When I was planning on teaching I made the mistake of getting involved with a woman. She got me sucked into her problems and somehow made me feel responsible for her. I ended up marrying her. I was in my forties then. I guess I had been maturing rather slowly. I don't make snap judgements about things. I have to wait, give things a clear chance, view things from all sides. Other people who rely more on their instincts wouldn't get involved in my over-conscientious dilemmas. But that is how I am. She was only willing to live as long as she could devour another human being. She needed someone to be her backbone because she was innately afraid of the world. I knew this was true, yet I had given my promise to stick with her and help her.

We had a very long apartment. I was in the back and she was in the front. It was quite an involvement in abnormal psychology because with her I saw hell with the lid blown off. She was quite clever; when she got to the point in therapy where she couldn't kill herself, she tried to get me to do it for her. I don't want to dwell on all the details about it because, really, I have been badly stamped by it. She did say one time, "I don't want to harm anyone, I just want to be out of it all." I flashed out, "That's not true." I knew from my own experiences, when I had felt suicidal, that what you really want is to hurt other people. You want to make them feel guilty and suffer. I don't have many virtues but I prize truth. Well, she backed out that time and I made up my mind that I was going to move out, but shortly thereafter she committed suicide. That was a rough time. Also by then my father and uncle had died under violent circumstances. I immediately got myself into therapy, which was very beneficial.

I never have formed many long-term relationships. Prior to leaving college I got involved with one Latin fellow for about six months. I knew from the onset that it wouldn't last. He regarded himself as heterosexual and then found himself desperately involved with me. More recently I met a man I was involved with for a year. He was ten years younger than me. I guess I'm a prickly sort and not that easy to get close to. I really don't understand these things. I would like either some peace about being alone for the rest of my life or else to be better at enticing people into my diabolical clutches. But I don't want any overnight affairs. I can't take that anymore. I have lots of interests. There is music which is becoming more and more important to me, especially Mozart. I have two very charming cats. The blunt and ugly truth is that virtually no one gets everything they want in this world, and if they do, they are unhappy with it.

Years ago I had been puzzled why so many people wouldn't pay attention to me anymore. I kept thinking that there must be some monstrous defect in me. By then my weight was normal, I didn't have too bad a body though I had gray hair — I'd had it since I was thirty. At the same time, I had joined an all-male encounter group. I was the oldest member, a man in his late forties. The rest ranged from twenty-four to thirty-two.

One evening they spontaneously started discussing their sexual fantasies about one another. There were about twelve men in the group. As they went around the circle happily smiling at one another, getting closer and closer to me, I realized more and more that I was the eternal outsider. Everyone had fantasies about everyone else. No one had the slightest approximation of one about me. I realized that for many younger gays nothing is important about older men but their age. Many people liked me. Most of them valued my knowledge and experience. They didn't mean to make me unhappy. It was that they merely believed that an older gay man is sexually non-existent. They might have wished me to be happy, but always with someone else. My experience with that group drove home to me as perhaps nothing else could have the fact that I was an older man, and what my status was as far as the gay world was concerned.

About eleven years ago, during Gay Pride Week, a seminar was held at Bethany Church. One workshop was about the problems of being older and gay. About six of us attended that workshop, and one woman said, "Pity we can't have a group to talk about these things." That led to a lot of discussions and eventually we got a group together and found a place to meet.

My theory is that because gays didn't have a sense of group identity until recently, only since the late sixties, they didn't wake up to the fact that it was possible for them to grow older. It's part of the general American pattern about youth. In this country the two groups most fixated on being young forever are straight women and gay men. Lesbians are the most emancipated. As one lesbian explained to me, they have had to free themselves from conventional notions about women being women and looking sixteen until they are eighty. There has been a lot of blocking out of the idea of growing older in gay circles. That is partially why there is a good deal of rejection of older men, especially within the city. A lot of people in the gay ghetto honestly believe that they will not live beyond thirty, if that long. And when they hit forty, that is going to be a world disaster. Many younger men won't patronize bars, baths or other places where they think they'll encounter older men. Consequently some places do their best to keep the older ones away. So we are part of a movement to try to rectify that imbalance. Many of the younger ones feel that older gays are slavering after their bodies. In reality, I, like most older men I know, prefer men near my own age. The basic life experiences are incommunicable, you have to have been through love and death and loss before you truly comprehend what they're like. I also agree with one man in his sixties who says, "I like sex, but I like it with someone who's read a book."

So far as I can see, older gay men have substantially the same problems as straight older ones, but with the added dimension of being gay. There's the worry of finances, a fixed income in inflationary times. Employment—how do you prove they don't hire you because you're older, if they don't say that's the reason, even if you know it is? Or that you are gay—an older man living with another and never married? Older people are not usually looked upon as a needed part of the community, gay or straight. Hopefully this will change. In G40+ we have changed our attitudes about becoming older. Being among our peers and seeing how many of us are leading full, successful lives is stimulating. We are enjoying our lives with gusto and are more at ease with ourselves than in adolescence. Most of the members lead fulfilling sex lives. And if you take care of yourself, your health can be good too.

However, it's terrifying to think what it might be like to be in your eighties, incapacitated and in a straight convalescent home. You're possibly bedridden, more or less helpless. What will it be like to be looked after by persons perhaps kind enough but who don't understand? There are already older lesbians and gay men in such circumstances. We know they're there, but for the most part we have no way of contacting them. And how many doctors are generally aware of the problems of gay people? There are still many, many parts of this country where it's dangerous to reveal yourself, even to doctors. And if they don't know your special problems, what would be the good of it? Fear, too, is more deeply implanted in us than in younger persons. How do you possibly come out after forty years of hiding or leading a double life? It's gone on for so long you've forgotten any other mode of existence. There are few groups for older gays in this country, only a handful. In many places there are no gay organizations whatsoever.

There are special problems, too, about the loss of your partner of twenty or forty years. Unless the deceased partner has taken special legal steps, his family may possibly seize all his property, even though you and he have pooled your expenses all those years. Where do you go if you're bereaved? If you have a strong friendship network they'll rally to you, but otherwise, who or what is there?

Despite the possible grimness of all this, I would never again want to be even ten years younger. I'm now experiencing a degree of inner peace and self-acceptance and confidence I never knew before. I'm not altogether sure I'd like to be younger in the world in which younger people find themselves. Too, I'd say that most older gay men I know are happier than the younger ones. They seem more relaxed about who and what they are. They are worth knowing because they are survivors. And my experience of them, particularly the older ones in their seventies and eighties, is that they're pretty tough customers.

My advice is to become still, don't run around in circles. Just learn to relax. When your life alters, it seems to start inside of you. I have noticed how much better life is after I have done some form of meditation such as practicing tai 'chi. It forces you to develop a fresh direction. But I don't have all the answers. People are going to do what they want anyway. They want advice that echoes what they intend to do to begin with. They want sanction, not recommendation. That is something I do *not* anticipate will change with time.

17

Tony Isaac

Tony was the only child of a farming family who lived outside of Grand Rapids, Michigan, during the Depression. He remembers having his first gay feelings at the age of seven when he saw Dick Powell dancing with Ruby Keeler on the silver screen. His lover of nineteen years, with whom he formed a "Holy Union" in the Metropolitan Community Church, died not too many years previous to our discussion.

I WAS BORN IN 1925 IN A LITTLE RURAL AREA OUTSIDE OF Grand Rapids, Michigan. My father worked in town but we were just small farmers. I went to a one-room school until it burned down and they had to send us into the city. Summers, I spent on the farm, a real farm, either my mother's father's or my dad's stepfather's. We always had to work in the summers. I lived sort of a normal childhood. I now know that I realized I was gay when I was very young though I didn't think of it that way then. My first big crush was Dick Powell dancing with Ruby Keeler in the movies. I didn't identify with her at all. I must have been six or seven. My part in all the kids' games was pointedly toward the boys, never the girls. Like what they used to call "dirty play," doctor and all that stuff. When I was fourteen I got a job in a hospital scrubbing pots and pans in a kitchen and I slowly graduated to twenty cents an hour. I was lucky to have a job.

I had what I thought was a happy childhood. I didn't find out until recently that maybe I wasn't so happy. We all worked hard because we weren't very rich and the Depression was on. My father was the richest in the family because he made $18 a week. So we had lots of aunts and uncles and other people living with us because they didn't have work and were starving to death. I was an only child and grew up with a boy cousin and a girl cousin who I consider my brother and sister.

When I was fourteen I also developed a crush on a priest. My family wasn't very religious and I was searching for some kind of spirituality. I went to instruction and started going to Mass. Father Dino raised me. We had been carrying on orally for five or six months when one night, right in the church, he raped me. It just blew my mind away from anything like that for a long long time. Of course, I never did become Catholic.

I realized that I was sort of a sissy in my class. Even though I'm big now, I was the littlest guy then, which was kind of tough. There were a lot of bullies, even one bully girl who used to beat up on me once in a while. I studied music, was in the band and orchestra and I played four instruments, none of them very well, but good enough to be second or third chair. I got beat up so much coming home, got so much teasing that my father once told me that if I came home beat up once more he was going to beat me himself. I said "I don't know what to do!" He said "Well, if they're too big for you then get a club or use anything. It's fair—you're littler than they are." So a week later I clubbed the biggest bully in school with a clarinet case and never was bothered again.

During the period I worked in the hospital, I graduated to being an orderly. At this time the richest kid in our school, who was a severe epileptic, became my best friend and his mother grew to love me very much. She was always sending him on trips to New York or Chicago for theatre and symphonies and operas, and she would hire me to go with him. Through him I began to develop a little culture that I would have never gotten through my own family.

During all those years I had never considered myself a fruit or gay. I'd heard some people at school call me a fruit but I didn't know what it meant and was afraid to ask. Well, we were pretty wild in those days. We'd hold beer parties in the cemeteries where no one would bother us. We'd get really wiped out, and I would walk home. One night about halfway home one of the guys from the party who I did not know came along in his car and offered me a ride. He started playing around, and I got very excited. It was the first time I had done anything since the Catholic priest. He went down on me and it was great! But then he forced me to do the same to him and it was not great. It made me sick. Most of my experience as a kid on the farm with my cousins was anal. I was the active one, not the passive one, which is kind of a surprising role for this little sissy. So this experience bothered me, I had a lot of guilt. I decided I had to talk to somebody so I talked to my pal, the epileptic. He said "Well, I've been wanting to talk to you for quite a long time. I think it's time you realized that you're gay." I didn't even know what "gay" meant. So he brought me out, so to speak, not physically but in my head.

My friend was gay, too, and I had never known that. This was near graduation and I began to go *crazy* with the idea that I was a gay fruit, a homosexual. It was a terrible thing to be in those days! Just awful! They think it's bad now. . . . So I cried myself to sleep several nights.

I was walking to the post office one day and there was a big sign out front which said, "Men Make the Navy and the Navy Makes Men." I went in and enlisted. I thought, *that* will do it!

I had exactly one month between graduation and leaving for the navy. My father was a defense worker in Buffalo, New York. For graduation my parents gave me a choice of either a watch or a trip to New York. By this time I was all hung up on the stage and my favorite girl cousin was in New York, so I chose that. Mom and I drove to Buffalo to be with my father and then later I took a train to New York. It's ironic that I had my first really successful homosexual experience that very first day in Buffalo. My dad got two rooms in the hotel we met at and mine was on a different floor from theirs. The bellhop first took my mother and me up to Dad's room and then he took me down to my room and put the make on me. That was really good.

Within two weeks of being in the navy I realized that I had made a big mistake. All of a sudden I was being called names. I found out that I was still a sissy and a fruit and I didn't know what to do about it. Finally, I picked the roughest, toughest guy in my boot camp and started copying everything he did. I even held my cigarette the same way. When he spit, I spit. I learned how to say "fuck" like a trooper – I had never sworn before. I went out and got a tattoo as soon as I got out of boot camp. I did everything I could to try to hide it. Strangely, I had almost no homosexual contact during the navy even though there was a lot of it offered. I lived in terror of what could happen to me.

I remember going through the Panama Canal on the way to combat duty. One morning they held a roll call and the chief corpsman was in a real nasty mood. He paraded up and down in front of us and said "I have word that there's a damn queer in my outfit and I'm going to find out who it is!" I almost fainted. I thought he meant me because I still figured I was probably one of the only ones in the world. A few days later one of the corpsmen disappeared. There was a lot of talk about what could have happened to him. Well, whenever we pulled into a port everybody that wasn't on duty would always crowd along the rail and watch what was going on on the dock. Suddenly they took this kid named O'Reilly off in chains. Word was out that O'Reilly had sucked off a patient. That's what they did to queers then. They didn't just get dishonorable discharges, they got sentences. I never saw such a sad looking boy in my whole life when he went down that gangplank with his chains on. So that definitely strengthened my resistance to playing around in the navy.

When the war was over, they shipped us all back here to Treasure Island but I had to go into the hospital because I had gotten hurt during the war. When I was there I had two operations and in between I'd get liberty and come into San Francisco. Even then it was a pretty wild scene compared to Grand Rapids. I had several passes made at me but I was still scared to death of them. I just wouldn't play at all. But I started going to a bar called "Mona's" – a dyke bar. There was a male singer there called Jimmy and I fell in love with him. Every liberty I'd be in that damn bar. Finally one day Jimmy told me she was a dyke. That's how dumb I was in those days.

When I finally got back to Grand Rapids I didn't have a long time being single before I fell in love, really very deeply in love. Our love affair, however, was doomed from the beginning, because my lover had been a priest and couldn't handle sex. I had a hard time with it, too, when I found out that he had been a priest – because of my previous experience, you know. We'd go along for about three months without sex then have wild sex after which he'd go into a severe depression and it would be just miserable for another three months. I was young and horny and I'd just found my gayness. I stuck it out with him for seven years. There was really very little sexual outlet in that city. There was a public john at the zoo and one gay bar which was segregated. It was straight in the front and gay in the back. The gay people had to come in by the back door. Even though the people in the front knew we were back there we weren't allowed up front. It was a benign place because everyone was so scared. They would have a raid every once in awhile so you went there totally afraid. They would raid by coming in the back and front of the bar at once. I never got caught – I was just very lucky.

As for my lover – I was going to junior college at the time and living at home when my mother and father caught us together. They came home from vacation two days early and we were on the couch. We didn't hear them come in. All hell broke loose. He was a leading disc jockey in Michigan at that time. My parents blamed everything on him, of course, even though I was his first and only. So we ran from the house!

My father's best friend was the sheriff and they found us in a straight bar and started a big scene. My father was going to kill my lover and told me that the sheriff was looking for me. They said that I was sick and they were going to put me in an institution. I don't know how we got away because it was such an awful scene. We poured out onto the sidewalk and my lover and my father were fighting. My mother was trying to grab me and scratch me and I was trying to get away. We somehow escaped them. We only had $35 between us and a beat-up old car and we took everything I owned – while my parents were out hunting for us downtown we went back to their house and got all my things, jammed them in that car, and I took off for Chicago. This was then about one o'clock in the morning and I drove all night.

My lover had to stay because he was taking care of an elderly mother and he was the only breadwinner. Fortunately, my parents didn't pursue him. I laid low in Chicago and used a general delivery address, and didn't contact my parents at all. I had some really awful experiences in Chicago just getting started. Except for the navy I had never been away from home. Everything happened at once.

Somebody broke into my car and stole all my possessions that first morning in Chicago. Fortunately, my epileptic friend lived there and I was able to go to him for help. We both knew that his place would be the first place my parents would look, so I got a little room just a short distance from him. Job hunting was terrible. Finally I got a job jogging books for *Popular Mechanics* as an apprentice printer. I was paid sixty cents an hour and worked like hell.

I didn't know it but my father was coming to Chicago repeatedly looking for me. He centered on the neighborhood where my buddy lived and he proved to be right. One day he parked the car right in front of the building I was working in and there I was in the window. Can you imagine that? Finding me in that big city?!

He came right in and gave my boss some lie about my mother being ill. He's a big, gruff, seemingly non-emoting man—but I learned that he does emote and does care. The individual who I thought cared, my mother, really didn't care. His first words to me were, "Let's go have a beer." We went and had a beer and I was scared to death of him. He hemmed and hawed for about two beers and then he just blurted it out, which is the only way he knows how to talk. He said "Hey, I don't know what this is all about. I don't like it. It sort of makes me sick to my stomach. But you're my son and it will be OK by me as long as you're happy. However, your mother will never understand it. All I want to ask is that you'll come home once in a while and we'll lie to her, we'll do everything in our power." I told him I wasn't sure but he talked until he was blue in the face and I finally agreed to go home for a weekend. Little by little I grew to feel that she had accepted me. It was never discussed but I felt more comfortable and the anger was gone, at least on the surface.

I was keeping a long-distance romance going with my lover in Grand Rapids. Believe it or not, I was monogamous during the time I was in Chicago. We had a total of about seven years before we really broke up. He came and lived with me for about nine months but he couldn't stand not working for a radio station. He couldn't get radio work in Chicago so he went back home. Incidentally he's still one of my very finest friends. He's more like a brother now.

I decided to go back to school. I went to the county hospital and began x-ray school. Finally I got a job in the field and it was the first time in my life I made any decent money. I had a nice little apartment and I started living. I went to New York for a vacation and just went berserk. I remember suffering guilt on the plane on the way back home because I had been really terrible, had done everything two or three times! I met an ice skater in Chicago from the Sonja Henie revue and had a big romance. He turned out to be a pathological liar plus he tried to kill me a couple of times, so that didn't last long. I didn't get any meaningful relationships going but I sure did get wild.

I took a job in industrial x-ray at the Ford Motor Company in the aircraft engine division. The wages were more than twice what I was making at the hospital though the work was more boring. But I got rid of that old sissy image that I'd always had because here I was dressing like a factory worker and acting like one, so to speak. That's when I got my nickname from a dyke friend. She called me "Titty Tony, boy dyke." My first camp name. That drove me wild because I didn't camp even though I had come out. She said, "I know you're a dyke because you wear steel-toed shoes, you work in a factory, and you've got hair on your chest!" She was probably the best thing ever in my whole progress because she used to give me the shock treatment. I would walk into the bar where we all hung out and if she was in there she would just yell it out real loud and I'd almost shit. But I got used to it and it was one time I was really enjoying my life and getting rid of those old fears. I was getting to the point that I didn't care if they *did* raid the place.

I worked in what was then the world's biggest plant. You had to walk half a mile to get out of the plant and then the parking lot was half a mile across. Then I also had a horrible commute home because there were no freeways. I decided to rent a room near the plant and found a place with a man named Ben. I didn't realize he was gay when he interviewed me and he didn't realize I was. Of course, you didn't have anything like that known at work — you would have been fired immediately. He turned out to be the most promiscuous person I have ever known. He had a technique that wouldn't quit.

He would take a bus and go up by the airport which was a couple of miles away. The highway there was one of the busiest in Illinois. He would hitchhike back to the house with truck drivers. And he was very brazen, he'd use obscene gestures and everything. Instead of using his thumb he would hike up his crotch. He'd leave the house and be back within twenty-five minutes with a truck driver. He also introduced me to a bar out in the industrial section which was composed of mostly hillbillies. You found out that hillbillies first wanted a woman and if they couldn't get a woman they'd take anything. I think they'd rather have a cow than a man but they'd take a man. So I did a lot of trade in those days.

The year that Sputnik went up, Eisenhower cancelled all the orders for jet engines which we were working on and started concentrating on space. Within two weeks eighteen thousand people at Ford had lost their jobs. I was used to making some pretty fancy money because I had also become foreman of the department. I had a new car every year and was living high on the hog. I remember going into total shock when I lost my job. I couldn't eat for several days and couldn't find a job either in industrial x-ray or in hospitals in Chicago. Well, one of my buddies from school was a chief technician at a hospital in Wisconsin. He got me a job working with him and I also lived with him and his lover. They charged me only ten bucks a week but I still couldn't make ends meet. I was used to $900 a month and now had to manage with $300. I had car payments of $110 and so on. So, believe it or not, I moved back home to Michigan.

Grand Rapids was still very uptight; it had only one gay bar and that was still half straight. I didn't like living with my folks again but was making so little money I had no choice. Then my old roommate from Ford starting writing me from California. He wrote, "What are you doing in that pagan part of the world?"

I was almost thirty when I moved to San Francisco. I had a very hard time finding a job. But I did stay with my former roommate. By this time my lifestyle had changed quite a bit and I didn't like all the "nellyness" going on in his home even though I still loved the guy as my friend. Anyway, one of the first places he took me to was "Jack's on the Waterfront." Well, I almost shit when I saw those bikes and all those guys in leather. Back in Chicago I had been a motorcyclist and thought that I was the only gay one in the world. They used to look down on me in bars. They would move and not even sit next to me. I enjoyed that. I was a big sissy yet I kind of liked the *macho* image. I immediately called my cousin in Grand Rapids and asked him to send my motorcycle out to me.

Before I even got my bike I met a fellow.

I still had some sexual hangups: it couldn't be done without the lights out. I think that's why I used to like the glory holes because I didn't have to look at them. Anyway, I met this guy who is a rather famous poet, an Englishman. He treated me like a king. Well, when he got me home and started to take his clothes off, I said, "I want the light out." He said, "Oh, come on. What do you think I'll do, laugh or something?" I said, "I hope not."

We both laugh about it now. He's still one of my sweetest friends and was loyal to me all through my illness. So I said, "All right." I closed my eyes and he took my pants down and let out this big laugh. "Ha, it looks just like mine." I opened my eyes and sure enough, we were just like twins. We started in on the wildest romance two people could ever have, it was incredible. This went on for three months until he won a literary award to be spent in Europe travelling. I had just got notice from the V.A. hospital in Oakland that I had a job so I didn't take up his offer to go along with him. Looking back on it, I wish I had gone. But I stayed on in his apartment to take care of it and he would send me German francs for rent. It was the first time I had ever been kept. He also had a lover back East whom he had split up with because the guy wanted a marriage and he was not that type. Well, he decided to visit the guy on his way back from Europe. His old lover resented the fact that he was living with someone, so when he returned he moved out and I kept his apartment. We still saw each other three or four nights a week.

This is when I met Doug in a leather bar. He and I were both from rural areas and our backgrounds were similar. He had been very promiscuous but grew up under the same oppression I had. He came from central Florida. He was nearly eleven years younger than I but our experiences were very much alike. Old Doug and I started courting for about six months. I wasn't about to get married, but I couldn't resist him. When we finally decided to get together it was because he had gotten into a motorcycle accident on Golden Gate Bridge. We were both riding doubles with guys on the back of our bikes when he flew up in the air and missed going over the railing by about a foot. For an instant I thought I'd lost him. His buddy rider was OK and it turned out Doug had no broken bones, just skins and bruises and a wrecked bike. That night when we got into bed he announced he was in love.

His previous lover had just died when he met me and he'd said he didn't want to get married. In fact, the reason we started dating was that we both said we didn't want a lover. That night he said, "I'm going to say something I promised I wouldn't say." Well, I knew what he was going to say and I was about to berate him for it. But I guess it was just the experience of thinking I'd almost lost him that made me change my mind. I said, "OK, except for one thing, you're too young for me." He said, "Is that the only thing holding you back? I thought you were too young for me!" His previous two lovers had been in their forties. So we started in and had two very stormy years together. I've got crooked fingers to prove it. We'd fight! But we got past those first years and stayed together for nineteen years until I lost him just a few years ago. He died of cancer and I still miss him.

Yeah, he was a lovely guy. Only recently, since my illness, have I been able to think in terms of having another relationship because getting so close to death myself made me realize his leaving wasn't all that bad. I got so close to death it was like a new beginning. I think I'm ready now but I've been too sick to do too much about it.

I have a touch of the flu which wouldn't be so bad if I hadn't had recent surgery which makes the flu more dangerous. I was coughing so hard I was hurting stuff inside. I had to go to the hospital Monday and go through a battery of tests to make sure I hadn't gotten my infection back. I had endocarditis. Oh lord, I had a tooth infection that went down into my heart. I had a healthy heart but that damn infection shot up two valves. I didn't know it could do that until it happened. I had a heart murmur ever since I was a little kid and was told by my doctor "not to worry about it."

Well, Doug was an ambulance driver and very butch. We ended up selling two motorcycles and a sports car for the down payment on a house in Marin. I found out as soon as I got over there that the reason he wanted me out of the city is that he thought I was out fucking around while he was at work. We were on different shifts then. I could not convince that man that I wasn't screwing around! I wouldn't fool with anybody. Nobody even looked good to me. Some of our biggest fights were about that. I'd say, "I didn't move to California to be stuck up on this fuckin' hill in the woods!" Little by little we calmed down and settled into a pretty good relationship. We went through a bad scene there for five years, though, when he was alcoholic. But I joined Al-anon.

The first thing you learn in Al-anon is that whether you leave or stay, you can be happy doing either. Once I found out that I could be happy with him I decided I'd rather stay with him than leave. He got dry and unfortunately two years after that he got cancer. So I lost him anyway. Well, I'm glad I had the other two years. He was a remarkable guy. His biggest fear when he was dying was what was going to happen to me. Isn't that something?

We were daring in those early days. Even in San Francisco it was so bad that we almost got arrested one night for having a beer in a gay bar. The cops came in and grabbed us for lewd and lascivious behavior. A lot of guys got arrested but somehow we didn't. They grabbed us because I was leaning on him. Imagine! My own roommate and just leaning! This is a picture of him and me in the early sixties up at Glacier Point in Yosemite. We'd go up there at least two times a year on our bikes. Our friend took this picture and we had to look around to make sure that nobody was looking so we could touch. Isn't he handsome?

And this picture was taken just before he died. He had four wishes. One was that he wanted to get married and have what we call in the MCC Church a "Holy Union." Another was that he wanted to go home and see his family. The third was that he wanted to leave the Baptist Church and officially join MCC. The last one is that he wanted to die at home. He got all four.

The picture was taken at our holy union. You can see he was dying — his collar is too big on him and he was wearing a wig because he lost all of his hair in chemotherapy. We had the ceremony at the house because he was too sick to come into town. I got him the wig for that but he hated it and it was the only time he ever wore it. I told him I liked his bald head just as well, that bald men turned me on.

The Marin Hospice helped Doug and me. In fact the lady that helped us later told me that we were her first gay clients and she almost refused our case when she found out we were gay. She ended up loving us. During the time he was in the hospital, I had full run of it. Doug got so he wouldn't let anyone touch him but me. The nurses would call me at home, "Doug's fussing again." I'd get dressed and go down there. They treated us just like we were a married couple and they were rather overwhelmed by the support he got from his gay community, his church, and from me, his other half. Both ladies, the one from the hospice and the other from the cancer institute, told me after Doug died, "If it's any consolation, your and Doug's ordeal opened an awful lot of eyes to gay love."

It took him six months and two days to die. It was beautiful that he had the chance to die at home. I wouldn't have had it any other way. The night he died was very special to me. He was six-two and weighed eighty-two pounds. He looked like a little wrinkled-up old man. He went from this big tall handsome guy to that in six months. The doctor had told me that afternoon that his vital signs were strong and that he probably had another month. So I never dreamed he was going to go that night.

I had a hospital bed in the living room and I was able to take care of him because of my hospital background. My doctor let me give him shots and everything. Between my neighbors and me and friends, I never had to hire a nurse. I lived in a gay community that was very supportive—despite what most of us think. Anyway, he was tossing a little bit that night. I slept on the couch next to the bed. He wanted a backrub so I got up. All he had on was a pair of boxer shorts and I was giving him a backrub and he looked up and said, "Babe, how can you stand me when I'm so awful?" I said, "Doug, look!" I had a hard-on while I was giving him his rubdown. He still turned me on after all those fucking years. He gave me the biggest smile. That was the last time he ever smiled that way.

Gay people go through the same thing as straight people when they lose their other half. In Marin County most people are couples. Over the years you get into a circle of exchanging dinners and parties and things. So then when you lose your partner they're all very good to you for a little while. Gradually at first, but then more rapidly, you discover that you're not being invited to dinner, to parties. Back home it's called the "widow syndrome." So I call it the "gay widower syndrome." It's a normal thing. You become a threat to them or you're just a fifth wheel—plus the fact that you're still down emotionally and they don't want to hear about it. Most of the people are still good friends of mine but they just couldn't handle it after a while, that's all. This guy here, Perry, the one I'm living with, is the only one who could. He along with my neighbor across the street never abandoned me. Perry

206

used to come over and say, "Tony, we're going out tonight." I'd think of a thousand excuses why I couldn't leave the house but he wouldn't take no for an answer. He'd go lay out my clothes, turn on the shower and order me in there. When I went out I was still down, but it was good that he forced me out of that house.

During Doug's illness I didn't fuck up at work or anything. I had been an exemplary employee. I had three meritorious service awards and I was never late for work in all the years I worked at the post office. Yes, I had changed occupations because the commute to Oakland from Marin had become too much. Anyway, I had four hundred hours of sick leave on the books when Doug died. I took off a week for the funeral and they suspended me because I wasn't a blood relative. Well, it was really because the boss didn't like gays. We had a quiet hatred going between us ever since the time I came out at work. At that time he waited until we were out of earshot of the other employees and said, "I hear you're a faggot." I said, "I'm a homosexual but not a faggot." He said he didn't know what the difference was and I told him there was a difference. He said, "Well, all I know is that you better never make a pass at me." I said, "Ted, out of the ninety-three people and two bosses in this department you're one of the two who is too ugly for me ever to make a pass at." So he was the same one who suspended me and one of the two, out of all those employees, who turned on me when I told them I was gay. I fought the suspension and won. The day I won I told him to stick the job up his ass and walked out the door.

Things reached a head with my parents after Doug's death. It started with my cousin, who wrote to say that maybe I should invite my elderly parents to come live with me. Since I was an only child, he suggested, they were my responsibility. They used to come out and visit Doug and me for two months every winter, and we'd had good times. I mulled it over and thought since I was so lonely it might be good for them to come. It would also relieve me of a lot of the chores. I hadn't realized that Doug had run that whole fucking household until he died. I thought my parents might relieve part of the stress of finances and upkeep. I knew I would probably have to sell the house otherwise because it was too big and expensive for just me.

I called my parents. They must have been sitting there waiting because they were out within two weeks. They went whole hog and sold almost everything they had. The second day they were at the house they said they thought we all should have a talk since we were going to live together. My mother said, "Doug's dead now and we're here so you don't have to be gay anymore." I was fucking speechless! I wasn't even through mourning yet. I knew I was in trouble from that moment on. I decided to visit a friend in Australia for a short while and when I got back my life was absolute hell. I had to put out of my mind any thought of Doug or mourning him or trying to get over it. It was so bad that on the way home from work I would stop at some woods below our house and just cry. I didn't want to go home and I didn't know what to do.

It degenerated into constant arguments with my mother. My father couldn't stand it. I told him, "You've got to get her out of here. I don't know how you could have taken it all these years." He said, "I've lived with her for fifty-seven years, what am I going to do now?" I told him that he must be a saint. She'd do bizarre things. I had a lot of straight friends who'd come by the house and she'd tell them, "What do you want to visit him for, he's just a cocksucker!" One by one my friends just disappeared. My gay friends couldn't stand her either. It was a hell I can't describe. I told my dad to get her out of there. She started in on me, "We sold all of our things to come here." I said, "Take anything you want." And do you know she took me literally. She took all my good furniture, all my crystal, the pictures off the walls—all the stuff that Doug and I had scrimped and saved and sacrificed for over the years. She completely denuded me, all my good silver, the couch and chair I had restored . . . everything, even my own television set. My own family ripped me off. My old man was a tool freak and they took over $4,000 worth of tools and didn't even leave me with a screwdriver. But I'll tell ya, I didn't care. I was so elated that they were gone, I wouldn't have given a shit if they had taken the house.

When I got into counseling the therapist got out of me that I was a battered child. I can now remember the time she caught me playing with the boy next door's pee-pee and broke three of my ribs. I lied to the doctor and said I fell off the porch. Well, she was still trying to batter me. When I was in the hospital with an infection I didn't tell my parents. But my father's a smart old bird and called the hospitals until they found me. My mother started in on me and asked why I didn't let them know. I told her it was because I didn't want her to know or to come out to be with me. She was speechless but I felt so damn proud of myself standing up to that tyrant. They love me but hate homosexuals, that's all it is. I would give anything if I could see my parents with "Parents of Gays" marching down the street.

My philosophy is basic. I'm not very materialistic. That's another reason I was able to let my stuff go with my folks. It just didn't mean that much to me. It meant a lot to have a nice home with Doug because that was for the two of us and something to be proud of. But it ended right there. My philosophy is to try to be happy and not hurt anybody—basically the Golden Rule. I believe God comes out of the heart, I don't think he's up there in the mind. I don't care if he's a Christian god or a Jewish god or what. It's all the same God. The only real sin is separation from God, and when you're deliberately hurting someone you are separating yourself from God.

My first priority is to get back to work and get completely well. Then I want to get married again. When I was in my thirties, a man in his fifties seemed ancient. For a while I applied this shallow attitude: that all the men in my age bracket were either married or went after chickens. But not now! God, I've got more than I can handle. I had a little romance with a bus driver which might have developed into something but he couldn't handle my illness. He turned out to be a very shallow man. I'm glad I learned that. I'm still friendly with him and he'd like to get it going again but I told him, "No, that's over now. But I'll tell you one thing you did for me—you let me know that I am capable of a relationship again." I'm a rough one to live with but I'm loyal—though not sexually anymore.

You know, I was monogamous for the first year with Doug until I came home and caught him with someone. I almost left him that night. He had a trick and had fallen asleep, so the shit hit the fan when I got home. He literally came to the garage and lay in front of my motorcycle so I couldn't get out. After that we came to an agreement that if there was something real special or things had built up to that point, then go ahead. But it had to be with a lot of discretion. You never bring anyone home. I had affairs once in a while because as you stay together your sex life gets less and less. But your affection gets better. The thing I missed most after

209

Doug died was getting into bed with him at night – that was hard. Even if we hadn't been getting along that well, that old foot of his would start about here and go all the way to my ankle and say "Goodnight, Tony." The affection was so much better than the sex.

Our rules were that you never dated. I lived up to that, but Doug fell in love twice during our time together. Those were kind of rough times but I just played it by instinct; both times I threw him out of the house and changed the locks. He was happy as hell that I was brazen enough to lock him out of his own house, and he accepted it. And both times he came back with his tail between his legs begging to come home. He'd go to a friend's house and sleep on the couch. That seemed to kill the love affairs.

I'd love to get it on with somebody else again and grow old with him. I don't consider myself old yet, I consider myself middle-aged. At first I didn't think I'd want to take the chance on losing someone again, but now, if I only had him six months it would be worth it. I am fairly spiritual and I don't feel that Doug is really gone. He's around. I feel his presence every now and then. I have to find somebody who will accept that fact, that there will be a little part of my heart just for Doug.

I hear people in my age group saying, "Oh, I wish I was twenty again." I say, "Not me." It was the worst time in my life. I did not start to live until my thirties, and I didn't know how to handle living until I got into my forties. I slipped for three years after Doug died but I'm getting it back again now. So I'm very happy. Age and nature and God have a marvelous way, if you allow them, of helping you get used to getting older. It's very gradual. Maybe you're not as attractive so you don't get as many offers as you used to, but then you don't need as many either. So you can't swim across the lake anymore; well, you really don't feel like it. When I'm ten years older I assume life will have taught me how to handle that as I handle my life now.

I go to a bar down the street because there seems to be less age discrimination there. Younger people who come in usually like older men or feel comfortable with them, or you meet a guy your own age.

I'd be in better shape today if I didn't have this flu. But I've been really going. Most of my friends can't believe how I go. I got home from the hospital and could hardly walk because everything hurt. But I've got to tell you my favorite story from the hospital.

Well, I had a needle in here and here and here and a thermometer hung on a belt and an IV stand. And they make you walk every night. It kills you to walk, you know. You're all hunched over and you kind of stagger down the hall. You have to walk to the end of the hall and back. And your monitor shows on a TV screen at the nurse's station. It shows all your heart movements and blood pressure and everything. So the first night that I went out on the walk there was a guy from the kitchen. Instantly, just my type—tall, dark and he smiled at me. He's the guy who comes up and gets the dinner carts and takes them back down to the kitchen.

I got back into bed and started thinking, "Hmm, that guy smiled at me pretty heavy. Oh no, it's just the drugs, I'm hallucinating." They didn't sew me, it was just staples so it looks like a zipper. And it looks like hell. You can't believe what a mess you are. Next night I went out on my walk, and the same thing happened, only a lot warmer this time. I know a cruise when I see it. This fucker must like sickies! The third night he overtly approached me. Can you imagine? I mean I was no pretty sight. I was totally shaved from the chest down to the toes. No hair whatsoever. I've got pictures of myself—my complexion was as white as a sheet. I said to myself, "That son of a bitch is cruising me." Well, I told him, "I don't think I could do much." He said, "Well, couldn't you give me head?" And I said, "I'll try but there isn't any place to go!" He told me, "Yeah there is, right around the corner there's a john that locks from the inside." A friend pointed out later that it also unlocks from the outside.

It was a great effort but I got my IV stand in there, sat down on the john, and gave him head. But I got so excited that when I came out into the hall there were three nurses running up and down the hallway hunting for me. My monitor was going crazy. I told my friends about it and they said, "Shit, we don't have to worry about you anymore. You're going to live."

Summary

The research and writing of *Quiet Fire* turned out to be an adventure that surpassed my most hopeful expectations. No camera was required on this trip but the eye of the mind, no ticket needed but the desire to listen and understand. The journey led me into the lush undergrowth of the jungles of the Solomon Islands, backstage behind the hot lights in the Golden Age of Hollywood, up the crumbling steps of the Great Pyramid at Giza with an Egyptian guide, and into the hearts of lovers who have compromised their differences for over forty years. It was an inner journey of finding friends and family where I only vaguely suspected there were any to be found. It was learning, though not in the way one learns the icy facts of a text—my learning came through hours spent witnessing and sharing experiences with older gay men. My initial objectives were: 1) to gain insight into the history of gay persons in the 20th century from a highly personal perspective; 2) to unearth a "sense" of role models from among those I would meet; and 3) to break down the stereotype of the sad and lonely older gay in America. I accomplished all three goals.

The subjects of these interviews were born near the beginning of the twentieth century, a period that still subscribed to notions of Victorian sentimentality laid on top of a puritan ethic. Regardless of the lack of sexual information available at that time most of these men knew that they were "different" from an early age. The luckier ones were able to find others like themselves. Raymond Friedman cruised the public toilets in the New York of

212

the 1910s. Don the Longshoreman attended private parties in New York's elite gay underground of the 20s. Overall, it was a world of great danger and secret liasons. The short-lived flamboyance and testing of restrictive norms in the 20s was followed by the great stock market crash and Depression. Although Radcliffe Hall's *The Well of Loneliness* was published in 1928, and remained for many gays the only clue that there might be others of their kind, the years leading up to World War II were, for most, a time of charade and secrecy. Gay bars developed primarily during wartime and the first political organizations which were to precede the present day liberation movement came shortly thereafter.

Most of the participants of this book have taken a backseat to the youth oriented gay culture that has emerged to become America's visible prototype of what gays are all about. But the aging of the younger liberationists, recent trends in the study of aging, and the maturing of the liberation movement have coalesced to reverse this trend. Gay elders are slowly stepping forward to add a sense of heritage and vitality to one of the most diverse minority groups.

Still the stereotype of the sad, lonely older gay man who is forced to seek out young children is a prevalent notion. One might even go further and say that the stereotype is that older gay men don't exist, they burn out like a candle at both ends, they die, they vanish, kaput! When I explained the purpose of this book to people, a few honestly commented that they did not know that there *were* older gays. Unfortunately, a few older gay men buy part of this package themselves, viewing themselves as the fortunate exception to what older gay men are like.

Through stereotyping we are led to believe that the bulk of our lives beyond the few years of youth are characterized by loneliness, degeneracy, inactivity or general ennui. The vast majority of gays who could disprove these beliefs are not given media coverage. Instead, as with all minorities, the media flourishes by finding and focusing on the sensational rather than the usual. Gay events are most often symbolized by the "Amos and Andy" image of the gay man in drag. The gay media itself, often reinforces youth-orientation in an effort to sell their products or promote patronage.

A small but growing body of gerontological research has been especially helpful in exploding the stereotypes surrounding the older homosexual. Contrary to prevalent mythology, most older gays are found to have a wide range of interests, including lovers, ex-lovers, friends of all ages, and occasionally children who compose the self-selected "family network." Researcher Deborah Wolf notes that most gay people learn early in life that they must be able to fend for themselves, whereas many heterosexuals are not faced with a massive dose of independence from the support of blood family and society until old age. Then their spouse and same-aged friends may have died, their children moved away, and they are left without the skills needed to live by themselves. Often the widow is unaccustomed to the ascribed "masculine" chores of providing upkeep on the home while the widower may be unaccustomed to cooking, cleaning, or shopping within a fixed budget.

Wolf also notes that gays tend to live the "single" life longer than heterosexuals. "When they do enter a couple relationship," she says, "there's less of the romantic fantasy that they can find total happiness just in each other." Gay people tend to preserve more friendships outside of the lover relationship and more autonomy. Also because they have been discriminated against for their sexual/affectional preference all their lives, they are better able to handle the stigmitization of old age. Curent social trends among the heterosexual population for later marriages, fewer marriages, increased mobility, smaller families, both partners working and sharing in a more egalitarian relationship suggest that older gays, who have already lived a life characterized by these factors, may be considered pioneers in these provinces. Wolf purports that gay people, overall, tend to adjust to older age more easily than heterosexuals, "In fact, the ways gay people deal with aging might be a good model for the rest of us."

Sociological research places a heavy emphasis on physical and psychological well-being, life satisfaction, and morale in studying the overall profile of population groups. Current research by Minnegerode, Adleman, and Fox (1979) concludes, "Homosexual and heterosexual respondents did not differ on measures of physical or psychological well-being. Results provided little empirical support for the stereotyped beliefs concerning homosexual men and women in old age." An even more positive finding is reported in Raymond Berger's *Gay and Gray* that states, "Older homosexual men report levels of life satisfaction as high as or higher than those of older men and women in the general population." There is also evidence that older gay men are cumulatively more satisfied with themselves and their lives than are younger gay men.

This book of life stories is meant to complement statistical research by presenting a personal, easily readable approach to the subject. One intent is to show the vast diversity among older gay men. There is, of course, no such thing as a "representative sampling" of older gay men. To seek one would be as ridiculous an ambition as it would be to try to locate a representative sampling of older heterosexual men in America. At best, after examining all research results we may come away with a better *insight* into who these older men are. Adding to this impossible task is the fact that persons grow more individual with age and more unlike one another as a result of their differing experiences.

The subjects for this book were solicited by way of advertisement (newspapers, fliers), organizational contacts, and, most successfully, word of mouth. Only a handful responded directly to the cry for subjects. I met a few at parties and even met one sitting at a busstop. In otherwords, the occasion of the "professional respondent" was minimized. As a result, I feel that the participants portray a high multiformity not often attained by other methods of research. Unfortunately, much older men (80s +) and men other than Caucasians were especially hard to locate. Many of both groups understand themselves as same-sex oriented in practice and desire, but do not define themselves as "gay," a prerequisite for inclusion. Non-Caucasians often feel greater alignment with their race, and/or given the double indemnity of both racial and sexual discrimination (as well as racism within the gay community), have entrenched themselves into a comfortable lifestyle best characterized by its obscurity.

I refrained from interviewing the leaders of the first gay organizations because I wanted to keep away from a political orientation. I abstained from speaking with those with a heavy sociological schema because I sought to curtail possible dogmatic discourse. Finally, I chose not to search out the famous because their stories are too often well-rehearsed and guarded. The focus was on those unaccustomed to the limelight, the unsung heroes of daily life, in short, that part of each of us that speaks to the rest.

I found that many men discussed their sex and sexuality. For after all, wasn't I interviewing them as older *gay* persons? Society defines us by our same SEX orientation. I felt that no matter what the respondents discussed they were speaking as gay persons. It did not necessarily have to be about being gay itself since I believe one's sexuality is an innate part of personhood. The obvious result is that the interviews might sometimes reflect sex and sexuality in a way that is not ordinary to the participants' every day lives.

I interviewed mainly in California and Arizona, in cities and suburbs. Also included were men newly transplanted from other geographical locations which added more dimension to the scope of the book. I chose the arbitrary age of 55 as the base age for subjects. Approximately one fifth instructed me to use their actual names but I did not feel it was necessary to designate which names were actual and which were nom de plumes. Interviews ranged in length from two to ten hours. Although I talked with over 100 gay men and lesbians, only 17 men are included in this text. It was the publisher's belief that the subject could be better addressed if this book included only men. I did not use a standard list of questions but rather a more free-associative method of asking the men to speak of their past lives, future expectations, plans and goals. When I did question, it was mostly for further clarification or exposition. Interviews were collected over the six year period from 1978 to 1984.

In the course of working on this book I've often been asked, "Why do a book on gay people? Aren't you just intensifying the differences between people, making things worse than they already are?" Or, "Aren't there enough books on gay people?" In answer to the latter question, I don't feel the 10% of the population that is gay is adequately represented in books. In answer to the first question, I only wish that society as a whole found it unnecessary to precategorize gays as a minority in usually the most derogatory terms. Until such a time as this precategorization ceases to exist, it is important for every minority to first take stock of itself and then to move out to educate all of society.

In my experiences as a social service administrator to the elderly I know that older gay people are often overlooked in planning services, social activities, etc. They are discriminated against in many subtle ways including the withholding of financial favors given to the heterosexual couple, social denial in the grieving process (a lover of many years will often have to play second fiddle to long-absent blood relatives during the death and dying of a partner or lose possessions to these relatives after the partner's death because of lack of legal rights), lack of respectful treatment in medical facilities, lack of government housing for indigent couples, and so on. In short, there are special considerations that surround the older gay person in his/her lifestyle because the discrimination that comes with aging is compounded by the discrimination that comes with being homosexual.

My findings confirm the findings of current research. Very few older men come close to rounding out the stereotype of the older male homosexual in America. Many of the men who lived alone expressed a desire for a lover yet admitted that this conflicted with their greater need for independence. They rarely expressed a sense of loneliness or dissatisfaction; for many living alone was an affirmative choice. Most respondents kept in close touch with other gay persons, had established at least short-term love relationships at some time in their lives, related well to younger gay persons, and overall, attested to that elusive state termed "happiness." Moreover, most described themselves as having a greater sense of self-confidence and contentment in their later years than in their youth. All in all, I uncovered only a few insights I had not expected.

One was the high prevalency of lovers who had been together for a number of years. Nearly all of the single men professed to knowing a great many others who were in lover relationships though, they themselves were not. They believed that the stereotype of the "transience" of gay relationships was incorrect and over-played. Most had younger friends and only found difficulty with the "flamboyance" and openness of younger men. There also seemed to be a high degree of inter-generational relationships among the men I met. I attribute that not so much to preference as to their lack of hesitancy in entering into such age-segregated relationships. The stigma against these types of relationships does not appear to be as strong in the gay community as it is in society in general. Furthermore, the stereotype of the older man exchanging status, security and financial favor for the younger man's physical beauty did not hold up. Often the older man did not have those worldly possessions to offer, suggesting that the relationship was less trade and barter in the presupposed sense. Current research by Richard Steinman supports this finding.

I was also impressed by the importance that attitude toward career had on the participants' overall well-being. Even those highly successful by conventional standards appeared more at ease with themselves if they considered their careers secondary to the rest of their lives. In other words, those with a fixation on career as an end in itself rather than as a means to an end, appeared less satisfied with their lives.

Finally, many of those men who seemed to have aged well were men with a somewhat metaphysical or religious attitude toward life. They sought something beyond the immediate demands of their bodies. They were at times disappointed, angry and unresolved with the diminished capacity of their physical selves, but their spirits soared.

The science of gerontology informs us that people age very much in the same manner they've lived the earlier portions of their lives. Of course there are changes and realizations brought about by experience, fate and choice, but overall, if they were crazy kids they're likely to be crazy old folks; if they were serious children, they're likely to be serious elderly. This suggests that in order to improve the quality of one's later life, one has to improve the quality of one's life today — too bad for the young who fear age with dread and loathing, who live in age-segregated communities and associate only with others similar to themselves.

The experience of meeting these men is behind me now but only in the way a moment seems lost to time, for the joy in the discovery and the experience of these men continues with me. At times when I have felt discouraged, I remembered the right phrase or word of reassurance from these brothers, uncles, fathers and grandfathers. Perhaps the most important thing these men taught me is that there is no one way to live. There is no such thing as the perfect relationship. These men did not compare themselves against the psychobabble of popular thought or the "well-adjusted" prime time t.v. family member, but rather found their own roads to their own goals. Despite their great differences there was one message that emerged from all as if spoken in one voice, "Watch your health, enjoy yourself and by all means LIVE!"

— *Keith Vacha*

Summary Notes

1. Wolf, Deborah, in "Growing Older Homosexual," by Michael Castleman in *Medical Self-Care*, winter 1981, #15, p. 20.

2. Minnegerode, Adleman, and Fox. "Aging and Homosexuality" (1979) (monograph).

3. Berger, Raymond M. *Gay and Gray*, Chicago; University of Illinois Press, c1982, p. 145.

4. Steinman, Richard, "Social Exchanges Between Older and Younger Partners: Lesbians, Gay Men, and Nongays." Paper delivered June 25th, 1983 at the Second National Conference on Lesbian and Gay Aging, San Francisco; sponsored by the National Association for Lesbian and Gay Gerontology, San Francisco.